Psychological Testing
in Child Custody Evaluations

Psychological Testing in Child Custody Evaluations has been co-published simultaneously as *Journal of Child Custody*, Volume 2, Numbers 1/2 2005.

Psychological Testing in Child Custody Evaluations

James R. Flens
Leslie Drozd
Editors

Psychological Testing in Child Custody Evaluations has been co-published simultaneously as *Journal of Child Custody*, Volume 2, Numbers 1/2 2005.

Routledge
Taylor & Francis Group
New York   London

First published by

The Haworth Press, Inc., 10 Alice Street, Binghamton, NY 13904-1580

This edition published 2012 by Routledge

Routledge
Taylor & Francis Group
711 Third Avenue
New York, NY 10017

Routledge
Taylor & Francis Group
27 Church Road, Hove
East Sussex BN3 2FA

Psychological Testing in Child Custody Evaluations has been co-published simultaneously as *Journal of Child Custody*, Volume 2, Numbers 1/2 2005.

Cover design by Lora Wiggins

Library of Congress Cataloging-in-Publication Data

Psychological testing in child custody evaluations / James R. Flens and Leslie Drozd, editors.
    p. cm.
    "Co-published simultaneously as Journal of child custody, volume 2, numbers 1/2 2005."
    Includes bibliographical references and index.
    ISBN-13: 978-0-7890-2971-3 (hard cover : alk. paper)
    ISBN-10: 0-7890-2971-5 (hard cover : alk. paper)
    ISBN-13: 978-0-7890-2972-0 (soft cover : alk. paper)
    ISBN-10: 0-7890-2972-3 (soft cover : alk. paper)
1. Parents–Psychological testing–United States. 2. Divorced parents–Psychological testing–United States. 3. Custody of children–United States–Psychological aspects. 4. Psychological tests–United States. 5. Expert testimony–United States. I. Flens, James R. II. Drozd, Leslie. III. Journal of child custody.

HQ755.83.P79 2005
346.7301'73–dc22

2005006429

Psychological Testing in Child Custody Evaluations

CONTENTS

INTRODUCTION

THEORETICAL AND TEST USAGE ISSUES

THE USE OF THE MMPI-2 AND THE RORSCHACH
IN THE CHILD CUSTODY CONTEXT

ABOUT THE EDITORS

James R. Flens, PsyD, is in private practice in Brandon, Florida. His practice centers around family law-related evaluations, work product review and consultation with both the legal community and custody evaluation professionals. He is also an instrument-rated pilot and factory-trained Schwinn bicycle mechanic.

Leslie Drozd, PhD, is a clinical and forensic psychologist. She has an independent practice in Newport Beach, California. She has conducted child custody evaluations for over 15 years and spoken nationally and internationally on issues related to custody, including substance abuse and domestic violence. She is one of the leading experts in the country on domestic violence in child custody cases. Dr. Drozd is author or co-author of many important articles, book chapters, and books including *Domestic Violence: True or False?; Is It Domestic Violence, Alienation and/or Estrangement?; Safety First: Understanding the Impact of Domestic Violence on Children in Child Custody Disputes; What to Do and When to Do It When Children Are Exposed to Domestic Violence; Problems with Attachment in Divorcing Families; Child Placement and Custody Decision-Making in Domestic Violence Families;* and *Hearing the Child's Voice, Supporting the Child's Needs in Child Custody Evaluations.* She is co-author of *The Missing Piece: Solving the Puzzle of Self,* with Claudia Black.

INTRODUCTION

Introduction to the Volume
on Psychological Testing
in Child Custody Evaluations

James R. Flens

This volume addresses the subject of testing. The articles can be divided into three sections. The first section concerns theoretical and test usage issues. The first article, by Flens, is devoted to test selection from both legal and psychological perspectives. An article by Martindale explores the possibility of bias that may interfere with the evaluator's ability to obtain data objectively. He is followed by Gould, who describes

James R. Flens, PsyD, has a private practice in Brandon, Florida. His practice is centered around family law-related evaluations, including evaluations regarding custody, modification and relocation, work product review, and consultation with both the legal community and custodial evaluation professionals. He is also an instrument-rated pilot and factory-trained bicycle mechanic.

Address correspondence to: James R. Flens, PsyD, 1463 Oakfield Drive, Suite 111, Brandon, FL 33511 (E-mail: jayflens@aol.com).

[Haworth co-indexing entry note]: "Introduction to the Volume on Psychological Testing in Child Custody Evaluations" Flens, James R. Co-published simultaneously in *Journal of Child Custody* (The Haworth Press, Inc.) Vol. 2, No. 1/2, 2005, pp. 1-2; and: *Psychological Testing in Child Custody Evaluations* (ed: James R. Flens, and Leslie Drozd) The Haworth Press, Inc., 2005, pp. 1-2. Single or multiple copies of this article are available for a fee from The Haworth Document Delivery Service [1-800-HAWORTH, 9:00 a.m. - 5:00 p.m. (EST). E-mail address: docdelivery@haworthpress.com].

Digital Object Identifier: 10.1300/J190v02n01_01

an approach for using psychological tests in the child custody evaluation. In this section's final article, Gould-Saltman describes psychological testing from an attorney's point of view.

The articles in the second section of this volume focus on the use of the MMPI-2 and the Rorschach Inkblot Test in the child custody context. Caldwell shares in his knowledge of the MMPI-2 in the child custody context. The articles by Erard and Calloway address the use of the Rorschach in child custody evaluations, and authors Johnston, Walters, and Olesen report the findings from their study using the Rorschach to address specific parenting variables.

The third section presents a point-counterpoint discussion of The Ackerman-Schoendorf Scales for Parent Evaluation of Custody (ASPECT). In the first article, Ackerman provides the reader with an up-to-date discussion on the ASPECT. Connell then offers the reader with an up-to-date review and critique of the ASPECT. Ackerman then responds to Connell's review and critique.

This volume is not exhaustive or representative of the use of psychological testing in child custody evaluations which would involve dozens of authors writing hundreds, if not thousands, of pages of text to address the myriad issues associated with psychological testing in a child custody evaluation. Future special issues of the *Journal of Child Custody* may address not only these issues, but other complex issues associated with the methods and procedures used in child custody evaluations.

THEORETICAL AND TEST USAGE ISSUES

The Responsible Use of Psychological Testing in Child Custody Evaluations: Selection of Tests

James R. Flens

SUMMARY. The responsible use of psychological tests in child custody evaluations requires an advanced understanding of both psychological issues of test selection and legal criteria regarding admissibility of

James R. Flens, PsyD, has a private practice in Brandon, FL. His practice is centered around family law-related evaluations, including evaluations regarding custody, modification and relocation, work product review, and consultation with both the legal community and custodial evaluation professionals. He is also an instrument-rated pilot and factory-trained bicycle mechanic.

Address correspondence to: James R. Flens, PsyD, 1463 Oakfield Drive, Suite 111, Brandon, FL 33511 (E-mail: jayflens@aol.com).

The author wishes to thank Jon Gould, PhD, and Leslie Drozd, PhD, for assistance in preparing this paper.

[Haworth co-indexing entry note]: "The Responsible Use of Psychological Testing in Child Custody Evaluations: Selection of Tests." Flens, James R. Co-published simultaneously in *Journal of Child Custody* (The Haworth Press, Inc.) Vol. 2, No. 1/2, 2005, pp. 3-29; and: *Psychological Testing in Child Custody Evaluations* (ed: James R. Flens, and Leslie Drozd) The Haworth Press, Inc., 2005, pp. 3-29. Single or multiple copies of this article are available for a fee from The Haworth Document Delivery Service [1-800-HAWORTH, 9:00 a.m. - 5:00 p.m. (EST). E-mail address: docdelivery@haworthpress.com].

expert testimony. This paper discusses the psychological and legal issues associated with test selection and with admissibility of expert testimony pertaining to psychological test data. It is argued that the legal standards of relevance and helpfulness require the methodology underlying an expert's testimony to be both reliable and valid. Therefore, it is essential to select psychological tests with demonstrated reliability and validity. Case law regarding expert testimony and the integration of professional practice guidelines pertaining to the use of psychological tests with ethical standards will be discussed. *[Article copies available for a fee from The Haworth Document Delivery Service: 1-800-HAWORTH. E-mail address: <docdelivery@haworthpress.com> Website: <http://www.HaworthPress.com> © 2005 by The Haworth Press, Inc. All rights reserved.]*

KEYWORDS. Assessment, child custody, ethics, evaluation, Daubert, Kumho, test selection

PART 1. SELECTION OF TESTS

Then the king said, "Bring me a sword." So they brought a sword before the king. And the king said, "Divide the living child in two, and give half to one, and half to the other." (1 Kings 3:24-25)

As the first recorded child custody dispute reveals, historical resolution of child custody disputes was a little bit different than it is today. Unlike King Solomon–who had only his sword and his wits–today's custody evaluators operate in two worlds. They operate in the legal world, which encompasses state statutes, case law precedents, and rules of evidence. They also operate in the mental health world, which encompasses the application of forensic methods and procedures (Martindale & Gould, 2004) and an arsenal of tests and measures used in conducting child custody evaluations (Kirkpatrick, 2003; see, e.g., Ackerman, 2001; Condie, 2003; Gould, 1998, 1999; Heilbrun, 2001; Schutz, Dixon, Lindenberger, Child, & Ruther, 1989; Stahl, 1994; Woody, 2000). In this article, I describe the interdependence between legal standards and psychological ethics applied to the selection of psychological tests in child custody evaluations. I argue that evaluators' responsible use of psychological tests begins with an understanding of rules of evidence governing expert testimony and an understanding of legal and psychological concepts of reliability, relevance, and helpfulness.

A BRIEF REVIEW OF PSYCHOMETRIC CONCEPTS

The use of psychological testing in child custody evaluations requires evaluators to possess (or develop) an advanced understanding of psychometric issues (i.e., reliability, validity), the effects of context on the test data, the use of context-specific normative data, and the legal criteria and admissibility standards for psychological data that are found in statutes and case law. It also requires evaluators to consider sources of bias that may affect interpretation of test results, including evaluator biases such as confirmatory bias (Borum, Otto, & Golding, 1993), confirmatory distortion (Martindale, in press) or "psychotic certainty" (Martindale, 2004), and test-taker bias (e.g., response styles including impression management and self-deceptive enhancement; see e.g., Friedman, Lewak, Nichols, & Webb, 2001; Greene, 2000; Paulhus, 1998). A quick review of three common psychometric[1] terms might be appropriate at this time for those who are not familiar with testing terminology (see, e.g., American Educational Research Association, American Psychological Association, & National Council on Measurement in Education, 1999; Anastasi & Urbina, 1997). *Reliability* refers to the consistency of results, including but not limited to consistency across time, situation, and evaluator; it asks the question, "Does the test consistently measure what it is purported to measure?" *Validity* refers to the accuracy of the test; it answers the question, "Does the test accurately measure what it is purported to measure?" The *Standard Error of Measurement* refers to the margin of error surrounding a test score; it answers the question, "What are the likely upper and lower boundaries of a person's true score on a test?"

There are important relationships between the reliability and validity of a test. First, a test's validity cannot be more than its reliability because the reliability coefficient is part of the denominator of the validity equation. Second, a test may be reliable and invalid. That is, a test may measure something consistently, but does not measure the factor accurately. The converse is not true. If a test is valid, it must be reliable. Third, if a test has low reliability, it also has low validity. As Otto, Edens, and Barcus (2000) stated, "[T]he reliability of a measure limits its validity, tests with poor reliability are tests with poor validity, and tests with unknown reliability are tests with unknown validity" (p. 33).

It is important to understand that the term "reliability" has different meanings when used in the psychological or legal communities. From a psychological perspective, the term reliability means "consistency," as noted above. From a legal perspective, however, the term reliability refers to accuracy, which is "validity" from the psychological perspective. The different uses of this term may cause confusion when discussing psychological and legal issues.

AREAS OF THE LAW

Custody evaluators should be familiar their state's rules of evidence, with particular attention paid to rules governing expert testimony and the admissibility of expert testimony. For the purposes of this article, I draw attention primarily to these important areas of the law. However, evaluators also need to be familiar with two other areas of the law. It is important to have knowledge of case law decisions relevant to child custody determinations. Case law decisions are how the Court interprets and clarifies the legal standards (statute, rule). For example, many states may have case law decisions that specifically identify factors to be examined in a relocation case or factors that define a reliability analysis. Florida, for example, codified the relocation criteria espoused by the Court in *Mize v. Mize* (1993) and *Russenberger v. Russenberger* (1996). Various states have used case law to define and clarify the admissibility of expert opinion testimony. California, for example, modified the Frye test with *People v. Kelly* (1976). Tennessee, on the other hand, rejected the use of the Frye test in its opinion of *McDaniel v. CSX Transportation, Inc.* (1997). In that case, the Court expanded the Daubert criteria to make that state's rule more stringent than the federal standard.

The third area is knowledge of state statutes defining the best interest of the child standard and other concepts relevant to child custody determinations. These standards and concepts inform the evaluator about what specifically can and should be addressed in the evaluation itself. The Michigan Standard, for example, is often considered as the model set of guidelines or criteria the Court uses to determine the best interests of the child (see, e.g., Otto, Buffington-Vollum, & Edens, 2003) (see Table 1).

Rules of Evidence

Rules of Evidence define what can and cannot be admitted into evidence. There are Federal Rules of Evidence (FRE) that apply to federal courts and there are state rules of evidence that apply to state courts. Most state courts have adopted rules that closely resemble the FRE. It is

TABLE 1. Michigan's Child Custody Statute for Determining "Best Interests of the Child"

The "Michigan Standard"[4]

- The love, affection, and other emotional ties existing between the parties involved and the child;

- The capacity and disposition of the parties involved to give the child love, affection, and guidance and continuation of educating and raising the child in his or her religion or creed, if any;

- The capacity and disposition of the parties involved to provide the child with food, clothing, medical care, or other remedial care recognized and permitted under the laws of this state in lieu of medical care, and other material needs;

- The length of time the child has lived in a stable, satisfactory environment and the desirability of maintaining continuity;

- The permanence, as a family unit, of the existing or proposed custodial home;

- The moral fitness of the parties involved;

- The mental and physical health of the parties involved;

- The home, school, and community record of the child;

- The reasonable preferences of the child, if the court deems the child to be of sufficient age to express a preference;

- The willingness and ability of each of the parents to facilitate and encourage a close and continuing parent-child relationship between the child and the other parent;

- Any other factor considered by the court to be relevant to particular child custody dispute.

strongly recommended that custody evaluators become aware of relevant statutes, codes, rules of court, and case law. Although most states have evidence codes that are quite similar in structure and intent to the FRE, not all states follow the FRE. It is important, therefore, that evaluators know their state's evidence code in relevant areas. For the purposes of this article, the FRE will form the basis of our discussion.

Two of the most important sections of the evidence code that are used to determine the admissibility of expert testimony address the relevance of the evidence and the helpfulness to the judge of the evidence. State Evidence Codes will have at least one definition of relevance. The examples described below are from the FRE (see Table 2). The first rule (FRE 401) defines "relevant evidence" as any information that may make the existence of a fact more or less likely. The assumption is that the testimony provided to the court will help in determining a fact, and that without the testimony the determination of the fact would be less probable. All testimony is admissible unless the testimony does not help make a fact more or less likely. Then, the testimony is deemed as not relevant and, therefore, inadmissible (Rule 402). However, some evidence may be ruled as inadmissible if it is harmful, confusing, misleading, a waste of time, or a repetition of facts already in evidence (Rule 403).

Another important part of any evidence code (FRE 702; see Table 2) addresses opinions and testimony provided by experts. State codes, following the structure of the FRE, will often provide both a definition of

TABLE 2. Federal Rules of Evidence: Relevance and Helpfulness

Relevance (FRE 401, 402, 403) and Helpfulness (FRE 702)

Rule 401 Definition of "Relevant Evidence": "Relevant evidence" means evidence having any tendency to make the existence of any fact that is of consequence to the determination of the action more probable or less probable than it would be without the evidence.

Rule 402 Relevant Evidence Generally Admissible; Irrelevant Evidence Inadmissible: All relevant evidence is admissible, except as otherwise provided by the Constitution of the United States, by Act of Congress, by these rules, or by other rules prescribed by the Supreme Court pursuant to statutory authority. Evidence which is not relevant is not admissible.

Rule 403 Exclusion of Relevant Evidence on Grounds of Prejudice, Confusion, or Waste of Time: Although relevant, evidence may be excluded if its probative value is substantially outweighed by the danger of unfair prejudice, confusion of the issues, or misleading the jury, or by considerations of undue delay, waste of time, or needless presentation of cumulative evidence.

Rule 702 Testimony by Experts: If scientific, technical, or other specialized knowledge will assist the trier of fact to understand the evidence or to determine a fact in issue, a witness qualified as an expert by knowledge, skill, experience, training, or education, may testify thereto in the form of an opinion or otherwise, if (1) the testimony is based upon sufficient facts or data, (2) the testimony is the product of reliable principles and methods, and (3) the witness has applied the principles and methods reliably to the facts of the case.

expert testimony and a description of the court might identify expert from no-expert testimony. As discussed below, the evidence rules governing expert testimony are drawn both from Rules of Evidence (see Table 2) and from case law.

Prior to 1923, admissibility of expert testimony was governed by the court's review of an expert's credentials and a review of the potential testimony to determine if this testimony would be helpful. If it was determined that the testimony would be helpful, the expert was then allowed to testify (see, e.g., *Congress & Empire Spring Co. v. Edgar*, 1878; *Winans v. New York & Erie Railroad Co.*, 1858). Beginning in 1923, however, the standard for admissibility of expert testimony was governed by the "General Acceptance Test" articulated in *Frye v. U.S.* (1923). In that case, a federal appellate court opined:

> Just when a scientific principle or discovery crosses the line between the experimental and demonstrable stages is difficult to define. Somewhere in this twilight zone the evidential force of the principle must be recognized, and while courts will go a long way in admitting expert testimony deduced from a well-recognized scientific principle or discovery, the thing from which the deduction is made must be sufficiently established to have gained general acceptance in the particular field in which it belongs. (p. 1014)

Echoing the court's focus on helpfulness, the Federal Court held in *Jenkins v. U.S.* (1962) that, "The test, then, is whether the opinion offered will be likely to aid the trier in the search for the truth" (p. 643).

Scholarly debate and diverging decisions in the Federal Court addressing whether the General Acceptance Test or an analysis of the reliability of the proffered testimony were the relevant admissibility standards led the Supreme Court of the United State to reexamine the criteria for admissibility of expert testimony (Goodman-Delahunty, 1997; Krauss & Sales, 1999; Shuman & Sales, 1999). In 1993, the U.S. Supreme Court ruled in *Daubert v. Merrell Dow Pharmaceuticals, Inc.* (1993) that the FRE focus on reliability was the proper standard for examining admissibility of expert testimony. This ruling has become known as the "Daubert standard" or "Daubert criteria." The *Daubert* Court defined "scientific knowledge" as follows:

> "The adjective 'scientific' implies a grounding in the methods and procedures of science. Similarly, the word 'knowledge' connotes more than subjective belief or unsupported speculation" (p. 590).

But in order to qualify as scientific knowledge, an inference or assertion must be derived by the scientific method. Proposed testimony must be supported by appropriate validation (i.e., "good grounds") based on what is known. In short, the requirement that an expert's testimony pertain to scientific knowledge establishes a standard of evidentiary reliability. (p. 590)

The *Daubert* Court identified the judge as a gatekeeper for admissibility of expert testimony. Judges now had the responsibility of examining the underlying scientific methodology for its reliability. If the methodology was judged reliable, then information that flowed from that methodology and the opinions upon which expert testimony was based were allowed. The standard envisioned was to be a flexible set of guidelines the trial Court *could* use (as opposed to "should") in determining the admissibility of expert testimony. More specifically, the Court noted:

Faced with a proffer of expert scientific testimony, then, the trial judge must determine at the outset, pursuant to Rule 104(a), whether the expert is proposing to testify to (1) scientific knowledge that (2) will assist the trier of fact to understand or determine a fact in issue. This entails a preliminary assessment of whether the reasoning or methodology underlying the testimony is scientifically valid and of whether that reasoning or methodology properly can be applied to the facts in issue. We are confident that federal judges possess the capacity to undertake this review. Many factors will bear on the inquiry, and we do not presume to set out a definitive checklist or test. But some general observations are appropriate. (*Daubert v. Merrell Dow Pharmaceuticals, Inc.*, 1993, pp. 592-593)

The following (flexible) guidelines were offered by the Court and became known as the *Daubert Standard*:

[Testability or Falsifiability] Ordinarily, a key question to be answered in determining whether a theory or technique is scientific knowledge that will assist the trier of fact will be whether it can be (and has been) tested. "*Scientific methodology today is based on generating hypotheses and testing them* (emphasis added) to see if they can be falsified; indeed, this methodology is what distinguishes science from other fields of human inquiry." (p. 593)

[Peer Review] Another pertinent consideration is whether the theory or technique has been subjected to peer review and publication. Publication (which is but one element of peer review) is not a sine qua non of admissibility; it does not necessarily correlate with reliability, and in some instances well-grounded but innovative theories will not have been published. Some propositions, moreover, are too particular, too new, or of too limited interest to be published. But submission to the scrutiny of the scientific community is a component of "good science," in part because it increases the likelihood that substantive flaws in methodology will be detected. . . . The fact of publication (or lack thereof) in a peer reviewed journal thus will be a relevant, though not dispositive, consideration in assessing the scientific validity of a particular technique or methodology on which an opinion is premised. (pp. 593-594)

[Error Rate and Standards of Control] Additionally, in the case of a particular scientific technique, the court ordinarily should consider the known or potential rate of error, and the existence and maintenance of standards controlling the technique's operation. (p. 594)

[General Acceptance] Finally, "general acceptance" can yet have a bearing on the inquiry. A "reliability assessment does not require, although it does permit, explicit identification of a relevant scientific community and an express determination of a particular degree of acceptance within that community." Widespread acceptance can be an important factor in ruling particular evidence admissible, and "a known technique which has been able to attract only minimal support within the community," may properly be viewed with skepticism. (p. 594)

The inquiry envisioned by Rule 702 is, we emphasize, a flexible one. Its overarching subject is the scientific validity and thus the evidentiary relevance and reliability–of the principles that underlie a proposed submission. The focus, of course, must be solely on principles and methodology, not on the conclusions that they generate. (pp. 594-595)

The Court went on to state:

To summarize: "General acceptance" is not a necessary precondition to the admissibility of scientific evidence under the Federal Rules of Evidence, but the Rules of Evidence–especially Rule 702–do assign to the trial judge the task of ensuring that an expert's testimony both rests on a reliable foundation and is relevant to the task at hand. Pertinent evidence based on scientifically valid principles will satisfy those demands. (p. 597)

In 1997, the U.S. Supreme Court further extended their thinking on *Daubert* in *General Electric Co. v Joiner* (1997). The *Joiner* decision focused attention on the need for the expert to show how opinions expressed were connected to the data upon which the opinions are based. No longer was an expert's say-so appropriate. An expert had to show a relationship between reliable data and expressed opinion:

But conclusions and methodology are not entirely distinct from one another. Trained experts commonly extrapolate from existing data. But nothing in either *Daubert* or the Federal Rules of Evidence requires a district court to admit opinion evidence that is connected to existing data only by the ipse dixit[2] of the expert. A court may conclude that there is simply too great an analytical gap between the data and the opinion proffered. (p. 146)

In other words, the Court may not allow an expert to opine something simply because the expert "says it's so." There must be something more than just the expert's word tying the data and the opinion. The focus of the *Daubert* Court, noted in Footnote 8 from the Court's decision, was on scientific knowledge because that was the nature of the testimony offered into evidence in that case: "Rule 702 also applies to 'technical, or other specialized knowledge.' Our discussion is limited to the scientific context because that is the nature of the expertise offered here" (p. 590).

The third prong in what has come to be called the Daubert trilogy was a 1999 U.S. Supreme Court case that expanded the Daubert standard beyond scientific knowledge to include all expert testimony. In the case *Kumho Tire Co. v. Carmichael* (1999), the Court noted the following:

The *Daubert* "gatekeeping" obligation applies not only to "scientific" testimony, but to all expert testimony. Rule 702 does not distinguish between "scientific" knowledge and "technical" or "other specialized" knowledge, but makes clear that any such knowledge might become the subject of expert testimony. It is the Rule's word "knowledge," not the words (like "scientific") that modify that word, that establishes a standard of evidentiary reliability. *Daubert* referred only to "scientific" knowledge because that was the nature of the expertise there at issue. (p. 138)

We conclude that *Daubert*'s general holding–setting forth the trial judge's general "gatekeeping" obligation–applies not only to testimony based on "scientific" knowledge, but also to testimony based on "technical" and "other specialized" knowledge. We also conclude that a trial court may consider one or more of the more specific factors that *Daubert* mentioned when doing so will help determine that testimony's reliability. But, as the Court stated in *Daubert*, the test of reliability is "flexible," and *Daubert*'s list of specific factors neither necessarily nor exclusively applies to all experts or in every case. Rather, the law grants a district court the same broad latitude when it decides how to determine reliability as it enjoys in respect to its ultimate reliability determination. (p. 141)

The Court clarified that the focus of attention on FRE 702 should be on the term "knowledge" rather than on "scientific" (see Table 2). The Court made clear that it was concerned about underlying reliable methodology as the foundation for expert testimony that is sound, reliable, and generally accepted and concerned about the opinion itself, whether such testimony came from a medical doctor or from a tire specialist. To borrow from the Clinton Presidential Campaign, "It's the methodology, stupid."

The *Daubert*, *Joiner*, and *Kumho* cases were clarifications of the FREs, and therefore did not apply directly to the states. Many states, however, have adopted the Daubert standard. Several states have continued their reliance on the Frye test, or an expanded version of the Frye test. California, for example, has the Kelly-Frye test (*People v. Kelly*, 1976) and Florida has the Ramirez-Frye test (*Ramirez v. State*, 1995). Both of these states have expanded the Frye test to determine if the methodology underlying the expert's opinion is reliable, valid, and helpful to the Court.

The relevance of these case law precedents to child custody evaluations is that the methodology underlying the evaluator's opinion must be reliable, relevant, and helpful to the court. Therefore, the prudent custody evaluator should select assessment tools that are both reliable and valid.

Test Selection and Relevance

In 1971, a case came before the U.S. Supreme Court that had nothing whatsoever to do with custody work, but the reverberations of which have been dramatically felt by evaluators. *Griggs et al. v. Duke Power Company* (1971) was a case involving procedures employed in the selection, placement, and promotion of personnel in an industrial setting. In deciding the case, the court ruled that any testing procedures must be demonstrably reasonable measures of (or predictors of) job performance. The lesson to be taken from the *Griggs* decision is that the selection of psychological tests must be reasonably linked to assessment of factors identified as the focus of the evaluation.

ETHICS, EXPERT TESTIMONY, AND THE SELECTION OF PSYCHOLOGICAL TESTS AND MEASURES

Rules of Evidence place a burden on psychologists–and other professions–to provide expert testimony that is reliable, relevant, and helpful. Expert testimony must reveal both a reliable methodology used in an evaluation and how the opinions drawn from the data derived from the use of the reliable methodology are connected to the data. Psychological ethics also place emphasis on reliability and relevance. For example, Section 2.04 of the American Psychological Association's (APA) *Ethical Principles of Psychologists and Code of Conduct* (APA, 2002; see also APA, 1992) describes that basis for scientific and professional judgments: "Psychologists' work is based upon established scientific and professional knowledge of the discipline." Psychologists also have a responsibility to keep up with changes in the field as noted in Section 2.03 (Maintaining Competence): "Psychologists undertake ongoing efforts to develop and maintain their competence" (p. 1064).

The APA Ethics Code section addressing use of psychological assessment techniques reveals a focus on reliability and relevance similar to the focus expressed in the evidence code standards discussed above. Similar to the *Joiner* concern about insuring that opinions are connected to reliable data, Standard 9.01(a) of the Ethics Code describes the need for psychologists to base their opinions on information and techniques sufficient to substantiate their findings: "(a) Psychologists base the opinions contained in their recommendations, reports, and diagnostic or evaluative statements, including forensic testimony, on information and techniques sufficient to substantiate their findings" (p. 1071; see also

Standard 2.04, Bases for Scientific and Professional Judgments). Parallel to the Supreme Court decision in *Griggs* cited above, the APA Ethics Code further admonishes psychologists to uses tests that are relevant for the purpose for which it is intended to be used. Section 9.02 (Use of Assessments) states, "(a) Psychologists administer, adapt, score, interpret, or use assessment techniques, interviews, tests, or instruments in a manner and for purposes that are appropriate in light of the research on or evidence of the usefulness and proper application of the techniques" (p. 1071).

Remember that the lesson to be taken from the *Griggs* decision when applied to child custody work is that evaluators should focus their attention and their assessment efforts on functional abilities that bear directly upon the attributes, behaviors, attitudes, and skills that published research suggests are reliably associated with effective parenting and co-parenting. Examining an attribute in the absence of evidence of its connection to parenting effectiveness and related factors leaves a psychologist open to criticism on several fronts. For the custody evaluator, test selection and the data derived from the use of those tests must always be directly or indirectly addressing questions about parenting effectiveness, child development, or parent-child fit and co-parenting issues (Gould, this volume).

Admissibility of expert testimony is often dependent upon a showing that the methodology is reliable and that the opinions expressed by the expert are reasonably connected to the data. When psychologists select tests whose reliability and validity have not been established for use with members of the population tested, it is possible that legal standards of reliability and relevance would not permit testimony drawn from those tests to be admitted. The use of a test that has no demonstrated reliability and validity in the population for which it is being used may be viewed as an unreliable methodology. Opinions based upon unreliable methodology are, by definition, inadmissible. The requirement stated in Standard 9.02(b) to "describe the strengths and limitations of test results and interpretation" when "validity or reliability (of a test) has not been established" (APA, 2002, p. 1071) may be a critical component of any custody evaluation. The evaluator may need to explain how information drawn from a test of unknown reliability provides any probative value or how the presentation of information that appears to be scientifically derived yet is based upon an unreliable methodology is not "substantially outweighed by the danger of unfair prejudice, confusion of the issues, or misleading (the court or a) . . . waste of time" (FRE 403, see Table 2).

Standard 9.06 might be viewed as parallel to concerns expressed in *Daubert* about scientific knowledge. *Daubert* was concerned, in part, about expert testimony based upon the notion that "an inference or assertion must be derived by the scientific method. Proposed testimony must be supported by appropriate validation–i.e., 'good grounds,' based on what is known. In short, the requirement that an expert's testimony pertain to 'scientific knowledge' establishes a standard of evidentiary reliability" (*Daubert* at 590).

I believe that the proper interpretation of psychological test data includes understanding test factors, test-taking abilities, and situational factors such as personal, linguistic, and cultural differences that might affect the accuracy of interpretations. There is a significant literature on test factors that may affect individual test responses in a forensic context. It is incumbent upon the evaluator to consider test factors and test-taking abilities when interpreting test results. It is also important to explain in the body of a report how each of these test factors may have affected the confidence in the meaning of the test data and the certainty of conclusions drawn from those data. Framed within the *Daubert* language, evaluators must apply the field's scientific knowledge when interpreting psychological test data in order to increase the probative value of expert testimony. As noted in the *Daubert* (1993) decision, "Scientific methodology today is based on generating hypotheses and testing them . . ." (p. 593). Conveniently for custody evaluators, the appropriate use of psychological testing in child custody evaluations (or any situation, for that matter) specifically involves generating and testing hypotheses. Consistent with this position is Section 9.06 (Interpreting Assessment Results) of the Ethics Code (APA, 2002):

> When interpreting assessment results, including automated interpretations, psychologists take into account the purpose of the assessment as well as the various test factors, test-taking abilities, and other characteristics of the person being assessed, such as situational, personal, linguistic, and cultural differences, that might affect psychologists' judgments or reduce the accuracy of their interpretations. They indicate any significant limitations of their interpretations. (See also Standards 2.01b and c, Boundaries of Competence, and 3.01, Unfair Discrimination) (p. 1072)

Another Ethical Standard tied to expert testimony is Section 9.09 (Test Scoring and Interpretation Services):

(a) Psychologists who offer assessment or scoring services to other professionals accurately describe the purpose, norms, validity, reliability, and applications of the procedures and any special qualifications applicable to their use.

(b) Psychologists select scoring and interpretation services (including automated services) on the basis of evidence of the validity of the program and procedures as well as on other appropriate considerations. (See also Standard 2.01b and c, Boundaries of Competence.)

(c) Psychologists retain responsibility for the appropriate application, interpretation, and use of assessment instruments, whether they score and interpret such tests themselves or use automated or other services. (p. 1072)

Standard 9.09(a) appears to parallel concerns about the reliability and relevance of testimony (see above). Courts may need to be informed about the purpose for selecting a particular test and how the interpretation of data from that test may be reasonably tied to the concerns before the court. A problem in the use of interpretive scoring programs provided by testing services is that the ethical criteria of 9.09(b) may be impossible to meet. Presently, the algorithms (i.e., program logic and decision rules) used to generate the statements in the computer generated test interpretations (CGTI) are proprietary secrets and not available for review by the evaluator. Therefore, it is not possible for evaluators to know how to answer important questions about how the program generates the statements found in CGTIs. This issue created enough concern that a letter, co-authored by three psychologists, was sent to the APA Ethics Committee for clarification. The response from the APA Ethics Committee Chairperson suggested two questions that psychologists should consider regarding the use of any CGTI program (Behnke, 2004): Given the purpose for which the service is utilized, what evidence of the program's validity do I require so that I may benefit, and not harm, my client? and What information about a program need I have in order to take responsibility for what my assessment contains? In addition to these two questions, I submit that evaluators might want to consider the following additional questions before using the interpretive statements offered on CGTI:

• Is the program an actuarial interpretation program or an automated interpretation program?
• What is the level of significance regarding the test scores?

- Are there different levels of significance for different scales?
- At what point does the program actually generate a statement for a particular scale?
- Are there different statements depending on the level of elevation for any given scale?
- Does the program take into consideration profile configurations or combinations of elevated scales, or are the statements based on single-scale elevation?
- Does the program take into consideration the response style when offering the CGTI statements?
- Does the program use context-specific normative data to facilitate interpretive statements?

These questions raise additional issues about what (and how much) "research" and/or "evidence of the usefulness" of a test is necessary and/or sufficient for use in a forensic evaluation in general, and more specifically, a child custody evaluation. This discussion is beyond the scope of the present article. Suffice it to say that the custodial evaluator should be prepared to address a variety of questions about the use of a CGTI report in the event the custody evaluation is challenged on legal or psychological grounds.

DEVELOPMENT OF CRITERIA FOR SELECTION AND USE OF PSYCHOLOGICAL TESTS IN CHILD CUSTODY CONTEXT

As mental health professionals have considered how best to assist courts in determinations of psychological and psychiatric issues, several authors have proposed criteria for the selection of psychological tests and measures used in court-related activities. Heilbrun (1992) developed a list of eight criteria that can be used by the evaluator in determining a test's appropriateness for use in forensic evaluation. More recently, Otto and colleagues (2000) have taken Heilbrun's eight-step model and adapted it specifically for the child custody context. The Heilbrun and Otto et al. models are quite similar, as can be seen in Table 3.

Depending on which model you choose, the answers to these questions can typically be found in the test manual and the relevant literature regarding the specific methodology. In addition, the literature is likely to include criticisms of a particular test or methodology. It is strongly recommended that copies of the relevant literature regarding specific assessment methodologies be readily available to the evaluator

TABLE 3. Model Criteria for Selection of Psychological Tests

Heilbrun (1992)	Otto et al. (2000)
Test must be commercially available	Is the test commercially published
Test must have published manual describing development, psychometric properties, and procedures for administration	Is a comprehensive test manual available
Test-retest reliability is at least 0.80	Are adequate levels of reliability demonstrated
There is ongoing research exploring its usefulness (validity)	Have adequate levels of validity been demonstrated
The test must be relevant to the legal issue or to a psychological construct underlying a legal issue	Is the test valid for the purposes in which it will be used
There is standard administration	What are the qualifications necessary to use this instrument
Test is reviewed in peer-reviewed journals	Has the instrument been peer reviewed
Test must have measures of response style	[The Otto et al. model does not address this issue][5]

for future reference, and also for defense of the evaluator's selection decisions. Critiques of the various methodologies used by the evaluator should also be included in this collection of literature. As can be imagined, the witness stand is the least desirable place to learn about a body of (substantial) literature that is highly critical of the chosen methodology.

It is important to remember that child custody evaluations take place in an adversarial legal system. It is not uncommon for the custody evaluator's report, opinions, and recommendations to be reviewed by another expert hired by the side dissatisfied with the report. This "battle of experts" can be unpleasant, and is not the appropriate forum to learn that the psychological tests employed by the evaluator have been bitterly attacked or criticized in the literature. It is therefore important for the prudent custody evaluator to have a balanced understanding of the literature on a particular assessment methodology that includes both supportive and critical reviews.

There are resources available regarding critical reviews of most published psychological tests. For example, the *Mental Measurements Yearbook* and *Tests in Print* (both published by the Buros Institute of Mental Measurement; for more information, go to www.unl. edu/ buros/) are two excellent sources for critical reviews. The literature also includes analyses of several psychological tests regarding their admissibility under different legal criteria (i.e., Frye test, Daubert's four-prong standard) and psychological issues of test selection. This includes Human Figure Drawings (Lally, 2001), the MCMI-III (McCann, 2002; see Rogers, Salekin, & Sewell, 2000, for an opposing view; and Dyer & McCann, 2000, for a reply), the MMPI-2 (see, e.g., Otto, 2002; Otto & Collins, 1995), the Rorschach (Gacono, Evans, & Viglione, 2002; McCann, 1998; for an opposing view, see, e.g., Grove & Barden, 1999; Grove, Barden, Garb, & Lilienfeld, 2002; Wood, Nezworski, Lilienfeld, & Garb, 2003; and for a reply see, e.g., Ritzler, Erard, & Pettigrew, 2002a, 2002b), and child custody-specific tests (e.g., the Bricklin scales, ASPECT, Parent-Child Relationship Inventory; see Ackerman, this volume; Connell, this volume; Otto et al., 2000; Yañez & Fremouw, 2004) and other parenting assessment instruments (i.e., Child Abuse Potential Inventory, Parenting Stress Index; Yañez & Fremouw, 2004).

Psychological test usage in the child custody context has not gone without criticism (Brodzinsky, 1993; Grisso, 1986, 2003; Melton, Petrilla, Poythress, & Slobogin, 1997). Early criticism involved inappropriate use of tests and diagnostic impressions that were misleading and pejorative (Grisso, 1986, 2003). Other criticisms involved over-utilization of psychological tests without psycho-legal relevance (Brodzinsky, 1993; Melton et al., 1997). It would be appropriate for the responsible and competent evaluator to have an awareness of the literature regarding the pros and cons of test usage. Recent research, however, has found that current child custody evaluation practices do not support these concerns (Ackerman & Ackerman, 1997; Bow & Quinnell, 2001, 2002; Horvath, Logan, & Walker, 2002; Quinnell & Bow, 2001).

Several studies have looked at assessment methodology within the child custody context. These studies can be divided into two types:

those that utilized survey methodology (Ackerman & Ackerman, 1997; Bow & Quinnell, 2001; Karras & Berry, 1985; Keilin & Bloom, 1986; Quinnell & Bow, 2001) and those that reviewed the methodology contained within child custody reports (Bow & Quinnell, 2002; Horvath et al., 2002). The first study was conducted by Keilen and Bloom almost 20 years ago. The results of their survey showed that approximately 75% of respondents used testing with parents and children. The MMPI-2 was the most common test utilized with parents, used by approximately two-thirds of the respondents. This study serves as the jumping off point for all subsequent studies investigating psychological test usage in child custody evaluations.

In a follow-up to the Keilen and Bloom (1986) study, Ackerman and Ackerman (1997) found that custody evaluators spent an average of 5.2 hours doing psychological testing. Tables 2 and 3 [pp. 139-140] of their study show the frequency of test usage with children and adults. The Hagen and Castagna (2001) study raised an issue about the concept of "standard of practice" based on the Ackerman and Ackerman data. In a reanalysis of the Ackerman data, the authors found that none of the tests–except the MMPI-2–reached a level of usage consistent with a "standard of practice." LaFortune and Carpenter (1998) made several conclusions from their data, the most concerning of which is the following:

> Even with this large number of diverse findings, a number of general conclusions emerge from the data. . . . Eighth, although tests play a smaller role than interviews and observation, many experts employ procedures with little or no know [sic] valid basis for informing custody decisions. (p. 221)

Quinnell and Bow (2001) compared the results of their survey study to the Ackerman and Ackerman and the Keilen and Bloom studies, and noted the following:

> First, participants in the study only ranked psychological testing as moderately important (fourth and sixth) among ten main custody evaluation procedures. . . . These findings suggest that psychological testing is no longer the primary procedure in custody evaluations; but instead is used to supplement other procedures or to create "working hypotheses," as defined by Heilbrun (1995). (p. 498)

Otto et al. (2000) noted the following regarding child custody-specific tests (e.g., Bricklin Scales, ASPECT) after reviewing the above noted studies:

> Although these tests have good face validity (i.e., their item content makes senses and appears to assess factors relevant to child custody decision making), significant questions remain regarding their utility, and their appropriateness for use in custody evaluations at the present time. (p. 317)

After reviewing these child custody-specific tests (e.g., Bricklin Scales, ASPECT), Otto et al. noted:

> In essentially every published review of these custody assessment instruments, concerns about their reliability and validity have been identified, and the need for research has been made clear. Unfortunately, child custody evaluators continue to wait for that research. (p. 336)

In the first of two content analysis studies, Horvath et al. (2002) noted a somewhat surprising finding that custody evaluators may actually not use enough psychological testing in child custody evaluation cases. Specifically, they noted:

> On the basis of this review of custody evaluations and others (Logan, Walker, Jordan, & Horvath, in press), we found that there are clearly a few areas frequently neglected by evaluators, including assessment of domestic violence and child abuse, adequate assessment of parenting skills, assessment of health status, formal psychological testing, and using multiple methods of information gathering. (p. 563)

In addition to the need for standardized interviews, it also appears that evaluators need to be encouraged to include psychological testing or behavioral assessment instruments in their evaluations. There is a substantial risk to the intended objectivity of child custody recommendations when there are no independent anchors for opinions such as those that can be obtained through the use of validated instruments (p. 563). In the second content analysis study, Bow and Quinnell (2002) found similar results to those of the Quinnell and Bow (2001) study, and noted, "In general, psychological test find-

ings were not given undue weight and reviewed as one data source"
(p. 174).

Suggested Models of Test Selection

There are essentially two different models for the selection of psychological tests in a child custody evaluation. The descriptions of these
two models are intentionally somewhat exaggerated and polarized for the
sake of discussion. In the Scientist-Practitioner Model,[3] the evaluator selects testing methodologies based on the psycho-legal issues involved in
the specific case and the psychometric qualities of the particular tests.
Using the Scientist-Practitioner Model permits the evaluator to answer
questions regarding a test's appropriateness for use in evaluation from
both legal (i.e., relevance and helpfulness) and psychological perspectives (i.e., reliability and validity). Alternatively, in the Lemming Syndrome Model the evaluator selects testing methodologies based on the
frequency of test usage described in the literature. The Lemming Syndrome Model allows the evaluator to answer questions regarding a
test's appropriateness with the statement, "The research says that lots of
people use it." This statement is offered by the evaluator to suggest that
the reliability and validity of a test is both measured and increased by
popular vote.

It is important to remember that a psychological test has little value if
it does not measure something consistently or accurately. As noted
above, both the Heilbrun (1992) and Otto et al. (2000) models recommend that a test should be commercially available/published and have
an accompanying test manual. These two criteria, however, do not guarantee that the test is reliable, valid in general, or valid for specific use in
a child custody evaluation. Publishers of psychological tests are in the
business of making money. Colorful brochures and catchy phrases are
marketing tools that should have no bearing on an evaluator's decision
to use a test. As noted by Martindale (2001), "The frequency with which
certain instruments are utilized may be attributable more to marketing
and related phenomena than the psychometric integrity" (p. 500).

CONCLUSION

The decision to use psychological testing in the child custody context
is a complex matter that involves both an understanding of and integration with legal and psychological concepts. The issues of relevance and

helpfulness are two essential concepts regarding the admissibility of evidence in the legal arena. This is true with all expert testimony and not just that of the child custody evaluator. The child custody evaluation report, underlying methodology, and ultimate testimony are all considered evidence. Therefore, the report, the methodology underlying the evaluation, and the custody evaluator's testimony are all subject to the evidence code of a particular jurisdiction. As such, we can only provide information to the Court if the evidence is relevant to the issue at hand and helpful to the Court. Although this is not something we get to decide, our decisions about the selection of psychological testing can make it easier–or less likely–for the Court to accept our work product. Ensuring our methods and procedures comport with the essential elements of the law allows our work products and testimony to aid the Court in resolving these challenging child custody matters. Relevant and helpful evaluations do not, however, guarantee the expert's work product and testimony will go unchallenged on other legal (and psychological) grounds.

Equally as important to the legal issues of relevance and helpfulness are the psychological issues associated with test selection. Although these issues were discussed following the discussion of legal issues, the psychological issues involved in test selection I believe are of even more importance. Undoubtedly, the use of unreliable or invalid data collection methods cannot only undermine or compromise the evaluator's findings, but also raise legal challenges to the admissibility of the work product and resulting expert testimony. The use of reliable and valid psychological testing is one of multiple procedures underlying the evaluator's methodology. A review of the findings from the Daubert trilogy made it clear that the focus of the Court's inquiry into helpfulness will be the methodology underlying the expert's opinion. Using reliable and valid psychological testing is unarguably important to ensure the methodology underlying the work product passes muster with legal issues of relevance and helpfulness and psychological issues of reliability and validity.

The psychometric issues of reliability and validity are essential ingredients in the value of any psychological test. Value, here, can be measured by both how consistent (i.e., reliable) and accurate (i.e., valid) the specific assessment methodologies are as data collection methods. The APA (2002) Ethics Code speak to the issues of reliable and valid test instruments, as do writers addressing the use of psychological testing in a forensic context. The attention to the selection of reliable and valid assessment instruments transcends philosophical arguments about the (alleged) differences in models used by child custody evaluators. This appears to be a more simplistic argument: opinions and recommendations based on inconsistent and inaccurate data are of little or no value to anyone, let alone the Court. The statement by Otto et al. (2000) noted above deserves repeating at this point: "[T]he reliability of a measure limits its validity, tests with poor reliability are tests with poor validity, and tests with unknown reliability are tests with unknown validity" (p. 33).

The use of an unreliable assessment method provides inaccurate data and erroneous opinions and recommendations that form the basis of the evaluator's work product. Testimony resulting from this data, opinions, and recommendations will be misleading and unhelpful to the Court, the parents in dispute, and the child at issue. Therefore, the selection of both reliable and valid assessment instruments is crucial to developing a solid foundation from which the opinions and recommendation of the evaluator are based, and presented in the form of the work product or testimony.

NOTES

1. Psychometric qualities refer to the statistical properties of a test.

2. ipse dixit: "he himself said it; an assertion by one whose sole authority for it is the fact that he himself said it." Gifis, S. H. (1991). *Law Dictionary* (3rd ed., p. 252). Hauppauge, NY: Barron's Educational Series, Inc.

3. The term "Scientist Practitioner" is used with permission from Katherine Kuehnle, PhD. See, e.g., Kuehnle (1996, 1998).

4. *Michigan Child Custody Act of 1970*, MCL § 722.23 (1993 amended)

5. Apparently, this was an oversight, as the authors consider the need for response style measures essential in forensic assessment methodology (R. Otto, personal communication, October 6, 2004).

REFERENCES

Ackerman, M. J. (2001). *Clinician's guide to child custody evaluations* (2nd ed.). New York: John Wiley & Sons, Inc.

Ackerman, M. J. (2005). The Ackerman-Schoendorf Scales for Parent Evaluation of Custody (ASPECT): A review of research and update. *Journal of Child Custody*, 2(1/2), 179-193.

Ackerman, M. J., & Ackerman, M. C. (1997). Custody evaluation practices: A survey of experienced professionals (revised). *Professional Psychology: Research and Practice*, 28(2), 137-145.

American Educational Research Association, American Psychological Association, & National Council on Measurement in Education. (1999). *Standards for educational and psychological testing* (3rd ed.). Washington, DC: American Educational Research Association.

American Psychological Association. (1992). Ethical principles of psychologists and code of conduct. *American Psychologist, 47*(12), 1597-1611.

American Psychological Association. (2002). Ethical principles of psychologists and code of conduct. *American Psychologist, 57*(12), 1060-1073.

Anastasi, A., & Urbina, S. (1997). *Psychological testing* (7th ed.). Upper Saddle River, NJ: Prentice Hall.

Behnke, S. (2004). Test-scoring and interpretation services. *APA Monitor, 35*(3), 58-59.

Borum, R., Otto, R., & Golding, S. (1993). Improving clinical judgment and decision making in forensic evaluation. *The Journal of Psychiatry & Law, 21*, 35-76.

Bow, J. N., & Quinnell, F. A. (2001). Psychologists current practices and procedures in child custody evaluation: Five years after American Psychological Association guidelines. *Professional Psychology: Research and Practice, 32*(3), 261-268.

Bow, J. N., & Quinnell, F. A. (2002). A critical review of child custody evaluation reports. *Family Court Review, 40*(2), 164-176.

Brodzinsky, D. M. (1993). On the use and misuse of psychological testing in child custody evaluations. *Professional Psychology: Research and Practice, 24*(2), 213-219.

Condie, L. O. (2003). *Parenting evaluations for the court. Care and protection matters.* New York: Kluwer Academic/Plenum Publishers.

Congress & Empire Spring Co. v. Edgar, 99 U.S. 645 (1878).

Connell, M. (2005). Review of "The Ackerman-Schoendorf Scales for Parent Evaluation of Custody" (ASPECT). *Journal of Child Custody, 2*(1/2), 195-209.

Daubert v. Merrell Dow Pharmaceuticals, Inc., 509 U.S. 579 (1993).

Dyer, F. J., & McCann, J. T. (2000). The Millon clinical inventories, research critical of their forensic application and Daubert criteria. *Law & Human Behavior, 24*(4), 487-497.

Friedman, A. F., Lewak, R., Nichols, D. S., & Webb, J. T. (2001). *Psychological assessment with the MMPI-2.* Mahwah, NJ: Lawrence Erlbaum Associates.

Frye v. U.S., 293 F. 1013 (D.C. Cir. 1923).

Gacono, C. B., Evans, F. B., & Viglione, D. J. (2002). The Rorschach in forensic practice. *Journal of Forensic Psychology Practice, 2*(3), 33-53.

General Electric Co. v. Joiner, 522 U.S. 136 (1997).

Goodman-Delahunty, J. (1997). Forensic psychological expertise in the wake of *Daubert. Law and Human Behavior, 21*(2), 121-140.

Gould, J. W. (1998). *Conducting scientifically crafted child custody evaluations.* Thousand Oaks, CA: Sage Publication.

Gould, J. W. (1999). Scientifically crafted child custody evaluations. Part two: A paradigm for forensic evaluation of child custody determination. *Family and Conciliation Courts Review, 37*(2), 159-178.

Gould, J. W. (2005). Use of psychological tests in child custody assessment. *Journal of Child Custody, 2*(1/2), 49-69.

Greene, R. L. (2000). *MMPI-2/MMPI: An interpretive manual* (2nd ed.). Boston: Allyn & Bacon.

Griggs et al. v. Duke Power Company, 401 U.S. 424 (1971).

Grisso, T. (1986). *Assessing competencies: Forensic assessment and instruments*. New York: Plenum Press.

Grisso, T. (2003). *Assessing competencies: Forensic assessment and instruments* (2nd Ed.). New York: Plenum Press.

Grove, W. M., & Barden, R. C. (1999). Protecting the integrity of the legal system: The admissibility of testimony from mental health experts under Daubert/Kumho analyses. *Psychology, Public Policy, and Law, 5*(1), 224-242.

Grove, W. M., Barden, R. C., Garb, H. N., & Lilienfeld, S. O. (2002). Failure of Rorschach-comprehensive-system-based testimony to be admissible under the Daubert-Joiner-Kumho standard. *Psychology, Public Policy, and Law, 8*(2), 216-234.

Hagen, M. A., & Castagna, N. (2001). The real numbers: Psychological testing in child custody evaluations. *Professional Psychology: Research and Practice, 32*(3), 269-271.

Heilbrun, K. (1992). The role of psychological testing in forensic assessment. *Law and Human Behavior, 16*(3), 257-272.

Heilbrun, K. (1995). Child custody evaluation: Critically assessing mental health experts and psychological tests. *Family Law Quarterly, 29*, 63-78.

Heilbrun, K. (2001). *Principles of forensic mental health assessment*. New York: Kluwer Academic/Plenum Publishers.

Horvath, L. S., Logan, T. K., & Walker, R. (2002). Child custody cases: A content analysis of evaluations and practice. *Professional Psychology: Research and Practice, 33*(6), 557-565.

Karras, D., & Berry, K. K. (1985). Thus evaluations: A critical review. *Professional Psychology: Research and Practice, 16*(1), 76-85.

Keilin, W. G., & Bloom, L. J. (1986). Child custody evaluation practices: A survey of experienced professionals. *Professional Psychology: Research and Practice, 17*, 338-346.

Kirkpatrick, H. D. (2003). A floor, not a ceiling: Beyond guidelines–an argument for minimum standards of practice in conducting child custody and visitation evaluations. *Journal of Child Custody, 1*(1), 61-75.

Krauss, D. A., & Sales, B. D. (1999). The problem of "helpfulness" in applying *Daubert* to expert testimony: Child custody determinations in family law as an exemplar. *Psychology, Public Policy, and Law, 5*(1), 78-99.

Kuehnle, K. (1998). Child sexual abuse evaluations: The scientist-practitioner model. *Behavioral Sciences and the Law, 16*(1), 5-20.

Kuehnle, K. (1996). *Assessing allegations of child sexual abuse*. Sarasota, FL: Professional Resource Press.

Kumho Tire Co. v. Carmichael, 526 U.S. 137 (1999).

LaFortune, K. A., & Carpenter, B. N. (1998). Custody evaluations: A survey of mental health professionals. *Behavioral Sciences and the Law, 16*, 207-224.

Lally, S. J. (2001). Should human figure drawings be admitted into court? *Journal of Personality Assessment, 76*(1), 135-149.

Martindale, D. A. (2001). Cross-examining mental health experts in child custody litigation. *The Journal of Psychiatry & Law, 29*, 483-511.

Martindale, D. A. (2004, October 6). *Child custody evaluations: Legal, clinical, & ethical issues*. Department of Mental Health Law & Policy, Louis de la Parte Florida Mental Health Institute, University of South Florida.

Martindale, D. A. (2005). Confirmatory bias and confirmatory distortion. *Journal of Child Custody*, 2(1/2), 31-48.

Martindale, D. M., & Gould, J. W. (2004). The forensic model: Ethics and scientific methodology applied to custody evaluations. *Journal of Child Custody*, 1(2), 1-22.

McCann, J. T. (1998). Defending the Rorschach in court: An analysis of admissibility using legal and professional standards. *Journal of Personality Assessment*, 70(1), 125-144.

McCann, J. T. (2002). Guidelines for forensic application of the MCMI-III. *Journal of Forensic Psychology Practice*, 2(3), 55-69.

McDaniel v. CSX Transportation, Inc., 955 S.W.2d 257 (1997).

Melton, G. B., Petrilla, J., Poythress, N. G., & Slobogin, C. (1997). *Psychological evaluations for the courts* (2nd ed.). New York: Guildford Press.

Mize v. Mize, 621 So.2d 417 (Fla. 1993).

Otto, R. K. (2002). Use of the MMPI-2 in forensic settings. *Journal of Forensic Psychology Practice*, 2(3), 71-91.

Otto, R. K., Buffington-Vollum, J. K., & Edens, J. F. (2003). Child custody evaluation. In I. B. Weiner (Series Ed.) & A. M. Goldstein (Vol. Ed.), *Handbook of psychology: Vol. 11 Forensic psychology* (pp. 179-208). New York: John Wiley & Sons, Inc.

Otto, R. K., & Collins, R. P. (1995). Use of the MMPI-2/MMPI-A in child custody evaluations. In S. E. Hobfoll (Series Ed.) & Y. S. Ben-Porath, J. R. Graham, G. C. N. Hall, R. D. Hirschman, & M. S. Zaragoza (Vol. Eds.), *Applied psychology: Individual, social, and community issues: Vol. 2. Forensic applications of the MMPI-2* (pp. 222-252). New York: John Wiley & Sons, Inc.

Otto, R. K., Edens, J. F., & Barcus, E. H. (2000). The use of psychological testing in child custody evaluations. *Family and Conciliation Courts Review*, 38(3), 312-340.

Paulhus, D. L. (1998). *Paulhus Deception Scales (PDS): The Balanced Inventory of Desirable Responding-7*. North Tonawanda, NY: MHS.

People v. Kelly, 549 P.2d 1240 (1976).

Quinnell, F. A., & Bow, J. N. (2001). Psychological tests used in child custody evaluations. *Behavioral Sciences in the Law*, 19, 491-501.

Ramirez v. State, 651 So. 2d 1164, 1995.

Ritzler, B., Erard, R., & Pettigrew, G. (2002a). Protecting the integrity of Rorschach expert witnesses: A reply to Grove and Barden (1999) re: The admissibility of testimony under Daubert/Kumho analyses. *Psychology, Public Policy, and Law*, 8(2), 201-215.

Ritzler, B., Erard, R., & Pettigrew, G. (2002b). A final reply to Grove and Barden: The relevance of the Rorschach comprehensive system for expert testimony. *Psychology, Public Policy, and Law*, 8(2), 235-246.

Rogers, R., Salekin, R. T., & Sewell, K. W. (2000). The MCMI-III and the Daubert standard: Separating rhetoric from reality. *Law & Human Behavior*, 24(4), 501-506.

Russenberger v. Russenberger, 669 So.2d 1044 (Fla. 1996).

Schutz, B. M., Dixon, E. B., Lindenberger, J., & Ruther, N. J. (1989). *Solomon's sword. A practical guide to conducting child custody evaluations*. San Francisco: Jossey-Bass Publications.

Shuman, D. W., & Sales, B. D. (1999). The impact of *Daubert* and its progeny on the admissibility of behavioral and social science evidence. *Psychology, Public Policy and Law*, 5(1), 3-15.

Stahl, P. M. (1994). *Conducting child custody evaluations. A comprehensive guide.* Thousand Oaks, CA: Sage Publication.

Winans v. New York & Erie Railroad Co., 62 U.S. 88, (1858).

Wood, J. M., Nezworski, M. T., Lilienfeld, S. O., & Garb, H. N. (2003). *What's wrong with the Rorschach?* San Francisco, CA: Jossey-Bass.

Woody, R. H. (2000). *Child custody. Practice standards, ethical issues & legal safe-guards for mental health professionals.* Sarasota, FL: Professional Resource Press.

Yañez, Y. T., & Fremouw, W. (2004). The application of the Daubert standard to parental capacity measures. *American Journal of Forensic Psychology, 22*(3), 5-28.

Confirmatory Bias
and Confirmatory Distortion

David A. Martindale

SUMMARY. The author reviews research on confirmatory bias, discusses its role in evaluations of comparative custodial fitness, and creates a distinction between confirmatory bias and confirmatory distortion, in which there is an indisputably conscious endeavor to find and report information that is supportive of one's favored hypothesis. Information is provided concerning the dynamics of confirmatory bias and distortion, the ways in which these phenomena manifest themselves, and

David A. Martindale, PhD, ABPP, author of *Cross-Examining Mental Health Experts in Child Custody Litigation*, is a diplomate in Forensic Psychology, American Board of Professional Psychology. For 16 years, he performed court-appointed evaluations of comparative custodial fitness in New York. He now is in private practice in New Jersey as a forensic psychological consultant to attorneys and psychologists. His work is concentrated in the areas of child custody, professional ethics, and malpractice. He regularly lectures on custody-related topics. Dr. Martindale is Adjunct Clinical Supervisor, Graduate Program in Psychology, John Jay College of Criminal Justice, City University of New York, and has taught graduate courses in ethical issues in forensic psychology there. He is also Adjunct Clinical Professor of psychiatry, State University of New York-Stony Brook.

Address correspondence to: David A. Martindale, PhD, ABPP, 1 Jenni Lane, Morristown, NJ 07960 (E-mail: david@damartindale.com).

The author would like to express his deep appreciation to Dr. James R. Flens for his invaluable assistance in the preparation of this article.

[Haworth co-indexing entry note]: "Confirmatory Bias and Confirmatory Distortion." Martindale, David A. Co-published simultaneously in *Journal of Child Custody* (The Haworth Press, Inc.) Vol. 2, No. 1/2, 2005, pp. 31-48; and: *Psychological Testing in Child Custody Evaluations* (ed: James R. Flens, and Leslie Drozd) The Haworth Press, Inc., 2005, pp. 31-48. Single or multiple copies of this article are available for a fee from The Haworth Document Delivery Service [1-800-HAWORTH, 9:00 a.m. - 5:00 p.m. (EST). E-mail address: docdelivery@haworthpress.com].

the ways in which they can be addressed by reviewers and by cross-examining attorneys. *[Article copies available for a fee from The Haworth Document Delivery Service: 1-800-HAWORTH. E-mail address: <docdelivery@ haworthpress.com> Website: <http://www.HaworthPress.com> © 2005 by The Haworth Press, Inc. All rights reserved.]*

KEYWORDS. Confirmatory bias, confirmatory distortion, anchoring, selective attention

An exhaustive literature search has failed to identify any published articles addressing the role of confirmatory bias in evaluations of comparative custodial suitability. It seems reasonable to infer that custody evaluators as a group do not perceive confirmatory bias as a significant threat to the quality of their work. Evaluators would be wise to conceptualize confirmatory bias as a stealthy enemy with numerous allies. Research suggests that the phenomenon is more prevalent than might be expected. There is little variation in definitions of confirmatory bias, and, to date, writers have not elected to distinguish between bias of which one is aware; bias of which one is unaware; and an indisputably conscious endeavor to find and report information that is supportive of one's favored hypothesis (see Arkes, 1981; Borum, Otto, & Golding, 1993; Dailey, 1952; Davies, 2003; Garb, 1994; Greenwald & Pratkanis, 1988; Greenwald, Pratkanis, Leippe, & Baumgardner, 1986; Haverkamp, 1993; Hogarth, 1981; Klayman & Ha, 1987; Mahoney, 1977; Otto, 1989; Strohmer, Shivy, & Chiodo, 1990; Tversky & Kahneman, 1974).

Though not described by Rosenhan (1973) as a study of confirmatory bias, his classic study, *On Being Sane in Insane Places*, cogently demonstrates how a diagnosis, once having been made, affected the manner in which experienced mental health professionals perceived and processed additional information. Rosenhan's subjects presented themselves at 12 different hospital admissions offices in five different states on the East and West coasts. The subjects described atypical auditory hallucinations; specifically, voices that uttered the words "empty," "hollow," and "thud." In 11 cases, a diagnosis of schizophrenia was made, and in one case a diagnosis of manic-depressive disorder was made. After having been admitted, the subjects (referred to by Rosenhan as "pseudopatients") behaved normally. An examination of their files revealed that ordinary behaviors were perceived as being related to their presumed psychiatric disorders and that unremarkable histories and family dynamics were also interpreted as being related (in some cases, causally) to the presumed disorders. Information taken and behaviors observed were construed as being supportive of the intake diagnosis.

Social psychologists and policy makers believe it is important that we distinguish between prejudice (an attitude) and discrimination (a pattern of behaviors presumably motivated by prejudice). Whether conscious or unconscious, confirmatory bias, like prejudice, can be difficult to identify and, as a result, difficult to address. I propose that we endeavor to distinguish between the internal processes that we have referred to as confirmatory bias and a more readily detectable pattern of professional behavior that can effectively be addressed in the cross-examination of an expert. *Confirmatory distortion* is the term that I herewith offer to describe the process by which an evaluator, motivated by the desire to bolster a favored hypothesis, intentionally engages in selective reporting or skewed interpretation of data, thereby producing a distorted picture of the family whose custody dispute is before the court. Some might presume that such premeditated misrepresentation of data is rare. Golding (1995) would disagree. In commenting on the involvement of mental health professionals in custodial suitability evaluations, he has opined that "biased advocacy is . . . rampant" (p. 422).

The inclination to seek information that will confirm an initially-generated hypothesis and the disinclination to seek information that will disconfirm that hypothesis has been repeatedly documented (Beattie & Baron, 1988; Skov & Sherman, 1986; Snyder & Swann, 1978). This should come as no surprise to us since several well documented psychological dynamics function either to elicit or to support confirmatory bias.

DYNAMICS

Cognitive Dissonance

Uncovering information that supports one's initial impressions is inherently gratifying. Uncovering information that calls into question one's initial impressions generates discomfort. In describing this dynamic, I am merely reminding readers of a phenomenon originally described by Leon Festinger and his colleagues more than four decades ago (Aronson, 1968; Aronson, 1992; Brehm & Cohen, 1962; Cooper &

Fazio, 1984; Elliot & Devine, 1994; Festinger, 1957; Festinger & Carlsmith, 1959; Festinger, Riecken, & Schachter, 1956; Gerard, 1967; Steele, Spencer, & Lynch, 1993; Wicklund & Brehm, 1976).

Suggestibility

Though much has been written about the effect of suggestion on children (e.g., Bruck & Ceci, 1995; Bruck, Ceci, & Hembrooke, 1998; Ceci & Hembrooke, 1998), Strohmer, Shivy, and Chiodo (1990) have demonstrated that mental health professionals are also susceptible to the power of suggestion. In the Strohmer et al. (1990) study, counselors were asked to consider a particular clinical hypothesis and, in doing so, reflect upon a narrative report read by them one week earlier. The counselors recalled more confirmatory information than disconfirmatory information even though the report contained more disconfirmatory information. In a second study, also by Strohmer et al. (1990), counselors were asked to consider a particular clinical hypothesis and, using a narrative report available to them as they contemplated the hypothesis, to list "confirmatory and disconfirmatory pieces of information" (p. 469). More confirmatory pieces of information than disconfirmatory pieces of information were listed even though the narrative report contained more pieces of disconfirmatory information. Perhaps it should be emphasized that the hypothesis suggested to the counselors was offered by those conducting the research (not a peer; not a supervisor; not a more experienced colleague).

In their discussion of confirmatory bias, Klayman and Ha (1987) have hypothesized the operation of what they refer to as a *positive test strategy*–a tendency to pose questions the answers to which are more likely to yield confirmatory information than non-supportive information. An example: Parent A alleges that Parent B is an "angry person." The custody evaluator, meeting with Parent B after having heard this allegation, poses questions to Parent B concerning situations in which experiencing anger would be more likely than not. The evaluator, both in posing her questions and in reporting Parent B's responses, makes no distinction between the internal emotional experience of anger and the overt expression of anger. Further, in formulating her hypothetical questions, the evaluator selects situations whose connection to matters of parenting is tenuous.

The notion that adults are susceptible to suggestion is often met with skepticism. The decision-making power that we give to others can best be understood by examining the dynamic in its extreme form–in the form of obedience. Those who were studying psychology in the mid-1960s may recall with relative ease the details of Stanley Milgram's (1963) classic study of obedience. When Milgram moved his study from the prestigious setting provided by the campus of Yale University to a dilapidated warehouse in the industrial section of Bridgeport, Connecticut, and when the authority figure firmly reciting "verbal prods" was an assistant whose only symbol of authority was his white lab coat, levels of obedience remained high.

The suggestion to which an evaluator perceptually and cognitively responds does not need to be presented by an authority figure. It may be presented by a highly likeable litigant or by a litigant that is perceived as credible. An example: The mother is the first to be seen by the evaluator, and during the initial session she expresses concern that her husband, with his greater financial resources, "may have been coached for this." Early in the initial session with the father, the evaluator poses several hypothetical questions to which the father provides well-reasoned responses. A notation appears in the margin of the evaluator's contemporaneously-taken notes. It reads: "Coached!!!" For all intents and purposes, the evaluator has made his call. Allegations registered by the father and denials by him of allegations registered by the mother will not be deemed credible; test data that cast him in a favorable light will be viewed with suspicion; and healthy interactions between him and the children will be seen as further evidence of coaching. If the evaluator follows the American Psychological Association's *Guidelines for Child Custody Evaluations in Divorce Proceedings* (American Psychological Association, 1994) and employs "multiple methods of data gathering" (p. 679), if those methods include gathering information from collaterals, and if the collaterals provide information that is in accord with the statements made by the father, his test data, and observational data, perhaps the evaluator will conclude that the father is as he presents himself. As a side note, readers may wish to contemplate how their reactions to the example above might have been different if the sexes of the parents had been reversed.

Anchoring

Anchoring refers to a perceptual and cognitive dynamic in which information that may not be pertinent and may be false is presented in a manner that gives it salience. Information that is perceptually and cognitively prominent functions as a reference point (an anchor) and is used in the processing of other information. Operating by means of an attentional mechanism that Arkes (1991) refers to as "priming," the anchor leads us to selectively attend. In a study conducted by Chapman and Johnson (1999), subjects considering the features of various apartments were more attentive to positive features when they had first been told that the rental fee was high and were more attentive to negative features when they had been informed that the rental fee was low. As cognitive dissonance theory suggests, we like things to make sense. It makes sense if an expensive apartment has many positive features and few negative features. It makes sense if an inexpensive apartment has many negative features and few positive features. If two pieces of a puzzle fail to fit but one of those pieces is malleable, it is that piece that we will endeavor to manipulate. The price of each apartment is presented as a given. Perceptions of the positive and negative features of each apartment, however, can be shaped to fit that which is given. Through the operation of selective attention, perceptions of the apartments are constrained by the anchor–the rental fee. Northcraft and Neale (1987) conducted a similar study, included real estate appraisers among their subjects, and asked that a house with a pre-determined listing price (the anchor) be appraised. Even the professional appraisers were affected in their judgments by the stated listing price.

Expectancy, Selective Attention, and Selective Recall

Some would suggest that the presentation of a hypothesis creates an expectation that, in turn, fosters selective recall and selective attending (Strohmer et al., 1990). Haverkamp (1993) found in her research that when hypotheses are "self-generated," a significant risk is created that "information relevant to alternative hypotheses will not be elicited" (p. 313). It is noteworthy that Haverkamp reports a "lack of significant differences for experience and training levels" (p. 313). Haverkamp's findings differed from those of Strohmer et al. (1990) in one important respect: Haverkamp did not find evidence of confirmatory bias when hypotheses were "client-initiated."

What we see depends upon the direction in which we look (Kuhn, 1962). Within the context of custody work, theory testing does not proceed as promoters of the scientific method would wish it to. Notwithstanding Haverkamp's findings with respect to client-initiated hypotheses, there is reason for concern that the presentation of a hypothesis by a persuasive litigant can create an expectation (Rosenthal, 1966). That expectation can lead to selective attending as the evaluation progresses and to selective recall as the evaluator begins to mentally assemble the information that will appear in his or her report. Though survey data are unavailable, anecdotal evidence suggests that custody evaluators are not always successful at remaining disinterested parties and that ego-involvement is a factor to be considered. Greenwald et al. (1986) have reported that confirmatory bias is pervasive in research endeavors. Greenwald and Pratkanis (1988) have concluded that when people become ego-involved, they "persevere with data-collection variations until support for the theory is obtained" (p. 575).

Confidence Levels and Credibility

Evaluators whose work has been contaminated by confirmatory bias may express high levels of confidence in the opinions that they express and may, as a result, be quite persuasive. Ironically, confirmatory bias contributes to overconfidence. Bumper sticker humor often provides sagacious observations about the human condition. "My mind's made up; Don't confuse me with facts." When new information calls a hypothesis into question, uncertainty follows. Section VI.C. of the *Specialty Guidelines for Forensic Psychologists* (Committee on Specialty Guidelines for Forensic Psychologists, 1991) admonishes us to examine "the issue at hand from all reasonable perspectives, actively seeking information that will differentially test rival hypotheses" (p. 661). When faced with competing hypotheses, each of which is supported to some extent by the data that have been collected, the critical thinker is unable to achieve complete certainty (Koriat, Lichtenstein, & Fischhoff, 1980). The foolish are often more certain than the wise. When called upon to support an opinion that has been offered, the expert who has never seriously contemplated more than one hypothesis engages in a confirmatory mental search process. Data supportive of the focal hypothesis readily come to mind; non-supportive data are not encountered.

Primacy and Information Integration

Research suggests that where conflicting information must be contemplated in order to formulate an opinion, information received earlier in the deliberative process has greater impact than information received subsequently (Crano, 1977; Belsky & Gilovich, 1999). As applied to custody evaluations, the research suggests that unless something in a litigant's initial presentation immediately arouses suspicion, there is a natural (albeit unintentional) tendency to accept the essential accuracy of the fact pattern as it is related by the individual from whom background information is initially obtained.

A computer can accept input and neither store it nor integrate it with previously stored information until an appropriate command is given. Humans operate differently (Heider, 1946; Leeper, 1935). Humans are not passive recipients of sensory input. Whether the sensory stimulation is visual, auditory, tactile, gustatory, or olfactory, humans cannot avoid endeavoring to make sense of that which they perceive. A computer can hold information in a not-yet-assigned space until further instructions are provided. In humans, the integration of new information with information already stored occurs as stimuli are perceived. No human evaluator can take information from Parent A and avoid processing that information until Parent B has been heard from.

In their survey of psychologists' practices and procedures in child custody evaluations, Bow and Quinnell (2001) found that, among respondents, 31% conducted the initial evaluative session with both parents. In my opinion, with only rare exceptions, the methodological advantages of an initial joint session are significant. If, instead of conducting the initial evaluative session with both parents, an evaluator meets with one parent before meeting with the other, it is on the basis of statements made by the first parent that the evaluator begins to construct a mental framework within which information is placed. Even if the framework is a temporarily-constructed mechanism for sorting information, it is during the initial session that an evaluator develops an understanding of the pre-marital relationship, the marital relationship, the sources of marital conflict, the obstacles to voluntary and cooperative dispute resolution, and the strengths and deficiencies in each party's parenting ability. Though first impressions are not cast in cement, the research evidence suggests that they are strong. Belsky and Gilovich (1999) have found that if potential stock buyers are provided with a mix of information about a company, the decision to purchase or not to purchase the company's stock is significantly influenced by the sequence in which information is presented. When positive information precedes negative information, a "buy" decision is more likely. A decision not to buy is more likely when negative information precedes positive information.

MANIFESTATION

Premature Hypothesis Generation

At what point in the evaluative process do evaluators formulate their initial hypotheses? There are no current survey data that might shed light on this important issue. Three decades ago, Sandifer, Hordern, and Green (1970) reported that psychiatrists formulated their initial diagnostic hypotheses only minutes into their intake interviews. Reviews of custody evaluators' contemporaneously taken notes suggest that evaluators occasionally record hypotheses in the early pages of their first session notes and, at times, record what can only be described as premature conclusions. An example: In examining contemporaneously taken notes, a reviewer notices the notation "LLPF" in the margin next to some statements made by the mother during the initial–and joint–interview. At trial, the evaluator explains, with some embarrassment, that "LLPF" is an abbreviation for "Liar, liar, pants on fire." Further explanation is not needed. Early in her first session, the evaluator appears to have concluded that the mother is a liar. The evaluator's notation is particularly interesting in light of the fact that the first session was attended by both parents and the father neither refuted nor modified the information provided by the mother. Though test data were not suggestive of deception, in response to vigorous cross-examination, the evaluator asserts and reasserts his confidence in his "clinical judgment."

Early conclusions by evaluators that they can discern the forthright from the deceitful is particularly interesting in light of published research suggesting that mental health professionals are no better at it than anyone else and that, in general, "[h]umans lack the ability to detect deceptive communication. . . . Twenty years of research in deception has shown that there is not a reliable set of nonverbal or verbal indicators of deceptive communication" (Feeley & Young, 1998, p. 109). It is also noteworthy that confidence is unrelated to accuracy (DePaulo, Charlton, Cooper, Lindsay, & Muhlenbruck, 1997). Ekman and O'Sullivan (1991) have reported that experience does not necessarily heighten one's ability to detect deception. Finally, even where some studies have shown that individuals with specialized deception detection training (e.g., members of the Secret Service) can perform at a level significantly above chance, none of the studies has measured the "generalizability of training effects over situation and time" (Frank & Feeley, 2003, p. 72).

The Investigative Component

The utilization of information provided by third parties (collateral sources) and obtained through the review of pertinent records, as recommended by Gould (1998), has, indisputably, become an integral component of the custody evaluation process. Data collected by Ackerman and Ackerman (1997) suggest that approximately 28% of the evaluative time expended by those responding to a survey was devoted to information verification (obtaining information from documents, from disinterested collateral sources, and from other non-parties). Despite the fact that the investigative component of custody evaluations is receiving much attention, Kirkland and Kirkland (2001) have opined that little is known concerning standards and practices in this important area (p. 185).

Indiscriminate investigations (those that might euphemistically be referred to as "fishing expeditions") are ill-advised and possibly unethical (creating undue risk of harm, with little likelihood that pertinent information will be unearthed). An evaluator cannot, for practical reasons, assure litigants that every document described by them as being of potential importance will be reviewed and that every collateral source identified by them as having useful information will be interviewed. Though lists of documents to be reviewed and lists of collaterals to be interviewed must sometimes be trimmed, the evaluator must take great care to avoid conducting a focused search for data supportive of a favored hypothesis.

The Interpretation of Assessment Data

Stephen Behnke, the Ethics Director for the American Psychological Association, has observed that "Principle A [of the APA Ethics Code] recognizes the influence that psychologists have over others and exhorts psychologists to use that influence responsibly and with care. In few places of our profession is this influence felt more than in psychological assessment . . ." (Behnke, 2004, p. 58). The portion of an advisory report in which evaluators outline assessment data and offer interpretations of those data is fertile ground for the operation of confirmatory bias and confirmatory distortion. It is not uncommon to encounter discussions of assessment data under a heading such as "Test Results." Readers of reports may mistakenly presume that there is no room for deliberate distortion in the reporting of "test results" and only minimal room for subjectivity.

Referring to an instrument as a "test" creates in the minds of readers a certain aura of precision. Evaluators may describe as "tests" assessment devices that are far from precise. The generally agreed upon definition of "test" is to be found in the Introduction to the most recent edition of the *Standards for Educational and Psychological Testing* (American Educational Research Association, American Psychological Association, & National Council on Measurement in Education, 1999): "A test is an evaluative device or procedure in which a sample of an examinee's behavior in a specified domain is obtained and subsequently evaluated and scored using a standardized process" (p. 3). The importance of standardization is emphasized: "In all cases . . . tests standardize the process by which test taker responses to test materials are evaluated and scored" (p. 3). Further, those who utilize various assessment devices are reminded that "[t]he applicability of the *Standards* to an evaluation device or method is not altered by the label applied to it . . ." (p. 3). Presumably, this reminder is intended to exhort mental health professionals to choose assessment instruments based upon "written documentation on the validity and reliability of [those instruments] for the specific use intended" (American Educational Research Association, American Psychological Association, & National Council on Measurement in Education, 1985, p. 41). In the 1999 edition of the *Standards for Educational and Psychological Testing* (American Education Research Association et al., 1999), we are reminded that "[t]he greater the potential impact on test takers, for good or ill, the greater the need to identify and satisfy the relevant standards" (p. 112).

Some of the instruments utilized by evaluators are not accompanied by any documentation relating to validity or reliability. In commenting on projective devices, Anastasi (1988) has opined that "the final interpretation of projective test responses may reveal more about the theoretical orientation, favorite hypotheses, and personality idiosyncrasies of the examiner than it does about the examinee's personality dynamics" (p. 614). Even those who feel that Anastasi has overstated the case against projective assessment devices would presumably agree that, in the interpretation of a test taker's responses, there is ample room for confirmatory bias or confirmatory distortion to operate.

The use of self-report inventories (often referred to as objective tests) and the use of computer-generated interpretive reports has been the subject of considerable discussion (Butcher, 2003; Eyde, Kowal, & Fishburne, 1991; Fowler, 1969; Moreland, 1985; Otto & Butcher, 1995; Otto & Collins, 1995; Otto, Edens, & Barcus, 2000). Theodore Millon (1997), commenting on self-report inventories, has opined that "there are distinct boundaries to the accuracy of the self-report format; by no means is it a perfect data source. Inherent psychometric limits, the tendency of similar patients to interpret questions differently, the effect of current affective states on trait measures, and the effort of patients to affect certain false appearances and impressions all lower the upper boundaries of this method's potential accuracy" (p. 7). Rarely do evaluators include in their advisory reports all the data that are generated when such instruments have been administered to litigants. Rarely do evaluators exclude any mention of the data. As might be expected, evaluators tend to cite those data that are deemed pertinent by the evaluators. As evaluators decide what is pertinent, confirmatory bias can influence the decision-making process. When confirmatory distortion is involved, we find that all the pertinent data (those that appear in the report) are supportive and all the non-supportive data (identified in a review of the file) have been excluded from the report.

Evaluators who utilize computerized scoring services but who interpret the data independently can (if they are so inclined) be selectively attentive to supportive data. The problem is not resolved by the use of computer-generated interpretive reports. For many reasons, not the least of which is "the effect of current affective states on trait measures" (referred to by Millon, above), evaluators must review interpretive reports with great care. Standard 9.09 (c) of the psychologists' Ethics Code reminds psychologists that they "retain responsibility for the appropriate application, interpretation, and use of assessment instruments, whether they score and interpret such tests themselves or use automated or other services" (American Psychological Association, 2002, p. 1072). The responsibility alluded to presents an opportunity for confirmatory bias or confirmatory distortion to play its pernicious role. The evaluator can select from a lengthy narrative report those passages that are in accord with the evaluator's impressions, omit passages that would call into question the evaluator's impressions, and explain both of these editorial actions by referring to the expert's ultimate responsibility for the interpretation of test data.

ADDRESSING THE ISSUE

Contemporaneously Taken Notes

Elsewhere, I have opined that "[t]he search for indications of bias is most efficiently begun by comparing the contents of an evaluator's contemporaneously taken notes with the evaluator's description of factors supporting the opinion(s) offered" (Martindale, 2001, p. 488). The operation of confirmatory bias or confirmatory distortion is most easily demonstrated where there is a discernible pattern of discrepancies between the information that appears in contemporaneously taken notes and the information that appears in the advisory report. Where parenting strengths in the non-favored parent are described in the contemporaneously taken notes but the favorable descriptors are nowhere to be seen in the advisory report, either bias or outright distortion is at work. Bias or distortion is also operating when parenting deficiencies in the favored parent are noted in the contemporaneously taken notes but not alluded to in the advisory report.

Document Inspection

It is likely that most evaluators retain for inspection documents that they have relied upon in formulating their opinions. Some evaluators, however, feel no obligation to retain items that have been considered but *not* relied upon. In law, *considering* something involves examining it and deliberating about it (Nolan & Nolan-Haley, 1990, p. 306). Attorneys or mental health professionals reviewing an evaluator's work should be afforded the opportunity to explore the possibility that documents, the contents of which should have been utilized were, instead, ignored. On occasion, evaluators will decline to review documents that have been brought to their attention and that are reasonably viewed as pertinent. In a recently-decided custody matter, the judge, in her Decision, observed that the evaluator had "refused to review and consider a submission . . . [that] included an affidavit . . . containing information about [the] mental health and stability" of one of the participants in the evaluation[1] (*Frankel v. Frankel,* Index No. 350141/01, unpublished decision of 1/6/04, Honorable Jacqueline W. Silbermann, New York State Supreme Court,[2] New York County).

Assessment Data Review

Evaluators whose neutrality has not been contaminated by bias "describe the strengths and limitations of test results and interpretations," even if their profession is not psychology (American Psychological Association, 2002, p. 1071). Similarly, when factors come into play that might affect their "judgments or reduce the accuracy of their interpretations . . . [t]hey indicate any significant limitations of their interpretations" (p. 1072). It is difficult to imagine a situation in which there would not be limitations worthy of mention. When no statement of limitations appears, it is prudent to explore the possibility that the evaluator is endeavoring to persuade rather than to educate.

CONCLUSION

Life's decisions must be made by humans. Where decisions are made by computers, as is done when computers interpret test data, the algorithms that create the interpretive statements have been developed by humans. Our mental capacity to make decisions, however, is affected by various emotional needs. Even when we have undertaken a task that demands objectivity, our efforts are often undermined by a variety of biases. Confirmatory bias (the desire to identify data that support an initially developed hypothesis) and confirmatory distortion (in which overconfidence in the accuracy of one's initial hypothesis leads evaluators to intentionally select the data to be considered and to be reported) present a threat to evaluator objectivity, the severity of which appears to have been underestimated. As is the case with all biases, neither now nor in the future is there likely to be a convenient and efficient method by which evaluators can prevent confirmatory bias from distorting their judgment. The best answer lies in heeding the guidance contained in the American Psychological Association's *Guidelines for Child Custody Evaluations in Divorce Proceedings* (American Psychological Association, 1994), to employ "multiple methods of data gathering" (p. 679) and to be skeptical concerning information from one source that is not congruent with information from other sources.

NOTES

1. In New York, information about the "mental health and stability" of parents and potential parent figures is deemed relevant, and participants in a custody evaluation may be viewed as having placed their "mental and emotional well-being into issue" (*Baecher v. Baecher*, 396 N.Y.S.2d. 447, at 448 [N.Y.A.D. 2 Dept. 1977]).

2. In New York, the Supreme Court is a trial court. The highest court is the Court of Appeals.

REFERENCES

Ackerman, M. J., & Ackerman, M. C. (1997). Custody evaluation practices: A survey of experienced professionals (revisited). *Professional Psychology: Research and Practice, 28,* 137-145.

American Educational Research Association, American Psychological Association, & National Council on Measurement in Education. (1985). *Standards for educational and psychological testing.* Washington, DC: American Psychological Association.

American Educational Research Association, American Psychological Association, & National Council on Measurement in Education. (1999). *Standards for educational and psychological testing.* Washington, DC: American Psychological Association.

American Psychological Association. (1994). Guidelines for child custody evaluations in divorce proceedings. *American Psychologist, 49,* 677-680.

American Psychological Association. (2002). Ethical principles of psychologists and code of conduct. *American Psychologist, 57,* 1060-1073.

Anastasi, A. (1988). *Psychological testing* (6th ed.). New York: Macmillan.

Arkes, H. R. (1981). Impediments to accurate clinical judgment and possible ways to minimize their impact. *Journal of Consulting and Clinical Psychology, 49,* 323-330.

Arkes, H. R. (1991). Costs and benefits of judgment errors: Implications for debiasing. *Psychological Bulletin, 110,* 486-498.

Aronson, E. (1968). Dissonance theory: Progress and problems. In R. P. Abelson, E. Aronson, W. J. McGuire, T. M. Newcomb, M. J. Rosenberg, & P. H. Tannenbaum (Eds.), *Theories of cognitive consistency: A sourcebook* (pp. 5-27). Chicago: Rand McNally.

Aronson, E. (1992). The return of the repressed: Dissonance theory makes a comeback. *Psychological Inquiry, 3,* 303-311.

Beattie, J., & Baron, J. (1988). Confirmation and matching biases in hypothesis testing. *Quarterly Journal of Experimental Psychology, 40A,* 269-297.

Behnke, S. (2004). Ethics rounds: Test scoring and interpretation services. *Monitor on Psychology, 35,* 58-59.

Belsky, G., & Gilovich, T. (1999). *Why smart people make big money mistakes and how to correct them.* New York, NY: Simon & Schuster.

Borum, R., Otto, R. K., & Golding, S. (1993). Improving clinical judgment and decision making in forensic evaluation. *Journal of Psychiatry and Law, 21,* 35-76.

Bow, J. N., & Quinnell, F. A. (2001). Psychologists' current practices and procedures in child custody evaluations: Five years after American Psychological Association Guidelines. *Professional Psychology: Research and Practice, 32,* 261-268.

Brehm, J. W., & Cohen, A. R. (1962). *Explorations in cognitive dissonance.* New York: Wiley.

Bruck, M., & Ceci, S. J. (1995). Amicus brief for the case of *State of New Jersey v. Michaels* presented by committee of concerned social scientists. *Psychology, Public Policy, and Law, 1,* 242-322.

Bruck, M., Ceci, S. J., & Hembrooke, H. (1998). Reliability and credibility of young children's reports: From research to policy and practice. *American Psychologist, 53*(2), 136-151.

Butcher, J. N. (2003). Computer-based psychological assessment. In J. R. Graham & J. Naglieri (Eds.), *Comprehensive handbook of psychology, Volume 10: Assessment psychology* (pp. 141-164). New York: Wiley.

Ceci, S. J., & Hembrooke, H. (1998). *Expert witnesses in child abuse cases: What can and should be said in court.* Washington, DC: American Psychological Association.

Chapman, G. B., & Johnson, E. J. (1999). Incorporating the irrelevant: Anchors in judgments of belief and value. In T. Gilovich, D. Griffin, & D. Kahneman (Eds.), *Heuristics and biases: The psychology of intuitive judgment* (pp. 120-138). Cambridge, UK: Cambridge University Press.

Committee on Specialty Guidelines for Forensic Psychologists. (1991). Specialty guidelines for forensic psychologists. *Law and Human Behavior, 15*(6), 655-665.

Cooper, J., & Fazio, R. H. (1984). A new look at dissonance theory. In L. Berkowitz (Ed.), *Advances in experimental social psychology* (Vol. 17, pp. 229-264). Orlando, FL: Academic Press.

Crano, W. D. (1977). Primacy vs. recency in retention of information and opinion change. *Journal of Social Psychology, 101*, 87-96.

Dailey, C. A. (1952). The effects of premature conclusions upon the acquisition of understanding of a person. *Journal of Psychology, 33*, 133-152.

Davies, M. F. (2003). Confirmatory bias in the evaluation of personality descriptions: Positive test strategies and output interference. *Journal of Personality and Social Psychology, 85*(4), 746-744.

DePaulo, B. M., Charlton, K., Cooper, H., Lindsay, J. J., & Muhlenbruck, L. (1997). The accuracy-confidence correlation in the detection of deception. *Personality and Social Psychology Review, 1*, 346-357.

Ekman, P., & O'Sullivan, M. (1991). Who can catch a liar? *American Psychologist, 46*, 913-920.

Elliot, A. J., & Devine, P. G. (1994). On the motivational nature of cognitive dissonance: Dissonance as psychological discomfort. *Journal of Personality and Social Psychology, 67*, 382-394.

Eyde, L., Kowal, D. M., & Fishburne, F. J. (1991). The validity of computer-based test interpretations of the MMPI. In T. B. Gutkin & S. L. Wise (Eds.), *The computer and the decision-making process* (pp. 75-123). Hillsdale, NJ: Lawrence Erlbaum.

Feeley, T. H., & Young, M. J. (1998). Humans as lie detectors: Some more second thoughts. *Communication Quarterly, 46*(2), 109-126.

Festinger, L. (1957). *A theory of cognitive dissonance.* Stanford, CA: Stanford University Press.

Festinger, L., & Carlsmith, J. M. (1959). Cognitive consequences of forced compliance. *Journal of Abnormal and Social Psychology, 58*, 203-210.

Festinger, L., Riecken, H. W., & Schachter, S. (1956). *When prophecy fails.* Minneapolis: University of Minnesota Press.

Fowler, R. D. (1969). Automated interpretation of personality test data. In J. N. Butcher (Ed.), *MMPI: Research developments and clinical applications.* New York: McGraw-Hill.

Frank, M. G., & Feeley, T. H. (2003). To catch a liar: Challenges for research in lie detection training. *Journal of Applied Communication Research, 21*(3), 58-75.

Garb, H. N. (1994). Cognitive heuristics and biases in personality assessment. In L. Heath, R. S. Tindale, J. Edwards, E. Posavac, F. Bryant, E. Henderson et al. (Eds.), *Applications of heuristics and biases to social issues* (pp. 73-90). New York: Plenum.

Gerard, H. B. (1967). Choice difficulty, dissonance, and the decision sequence. *Journal of Personality, 35,* 91-108.

Golding, S. L. (1995). Mental health professionals and the courts. In D. N. Bersoff (Ed.), *Ethical conflicts in psychology* (pp. 421-422). Washington, DC: American Psychological Association.

Gould, J. W. (1998). *Conducting scientifically crafted child custody evaluations.* Thousand Oaks, CA: Sage Publications.

Greenwald, A. G., & Pratkanis, A. R. (1988). On the use of "theory" and the usefulness of theory. *Psychological Review, 95*(4), 575-579.

Greenwald, A. G., Pratkanis, A. R., Leippe, M. R., & Baumgardner, M. H. (1986). Under what circumstances does theory obstruct research progress? *Psychological Review, 93,* 216-229.

Haverkamp, B. E. (1993). Confirmatory bias in hypothesis testing for client-identified and counselor self-generated hypotheses. *Journal of Counseling Psychology, 40*(3), 303-315.

Heider, F. (1946). Attitudes and cognitive organization. *Journal of Psychology, 21,* 107-112.

Hogarth, R. M. (1981). Beyond discrete biases: Functional and dysfunctional aspects of judgmental heuristics. *Psychological Bulletin, 90,* 197-217.

Kirkland, K., & Kirkland, K. L. (2001). Frequency of child custody evaluation complaints and related disciplinary action: A survey of the Association of State and Provincial Psychology Boards. *Professional Psychology: Research and Practice, 32*(2), 171-174.

Klayman, J., & Ha, Y-W. (1987). Confirmation, disconfirmation, and information in hypothesis testing. *Psychological Review, 94,* 211-228.

Koriat, A., Lichtenstein, S., & Fischhoff, B. (1980). Reasons for confidence. *Journal of Experimental Psychology: Human Learning and Memory, 6,* 107-118.

Kuhn, T. S. (1962). The structure of scientific revolutions. Chicago: University of Chicago Press.

Leeper, R. W. (1935). A study of a neglected portion of the field of learning: The development of sensory organization. *Journal of Genetic Psychology, 46,* 41-75.

Mahoney, M. J. (1977). Publication prejudices: An experimental study of confirmatory bias in the peer review system. *Cognitive Therapy and Research, 1,* 161-175.

Martindale, D. A. (2001). Cross-examining mental health experts in child custody litigation. *Journal of Psychiatry and Law, 29,* 483-511.

Milgram, S. (1963). Behavioral study of obedience. *Journal of Abnormal and Social Psychology, 67,* 371-378.

Millon, T. (1997). *MCMI-III manual* (2nd ed.). Minneapolis, MN: NCS Pearson.

Moreland, K. L. (1985). Validation of computer-based interpretations: Problems and prospects. *Journal of Consulting and Clinical Psychology, 53,* 816-825.

Nolan, J. R., & Nolan-Haley, J. M. (1990). *Black's law dictionary* (6th ed.). St. Paul, MN: West.

Northcraft, G. B., & Neale, M. A. (1987). Experts, amateurs, and real estate: An anchoring-and-adjustment perspective on property pricing decisions. *Organizational Behavior and Human Decision Processes, 39,* 84-97.

Otto, R. K. (1989). Bias and expert testimony of mental health professionals in adversarial proceedings: A preliminary investigation. *Behavioral Sciences and the Law, 7*(2), 267-274.

Otto, R. K., & Butcher, J. N. (1995). Computer-assisted psychological assessment in child custody evaluations. *Family Law Quarterly, 29*(1), 79-96.

Otto, R. K., & Collins, R. P. (1995). Use of the MMPI-2/MMPI-A in child custody evaluations. In Y. S. Ben-Porath, J. R. Graham, G. C. N. Hall, R. D. Hirschman, & M. S. Zaragoza (Eds.), *Forensic applications of the MMPI-2.* New York: Sage.

Otto, R. K., Edens, J. F., & Barcus, E. H. (2000). The use of psychological testing in child custody evaluations. *Family and Conciliation Courts Review, 38*(3), 312-340.

Rosenhan, D. L. (1973). On being sane in insane places. *Science, 179,* 250-258.

Rosenthal, R. (1966). *Experimenter effects on behavioral research.* New York: Appleton-Century-Crofts.

Sandifer, M., Hordern, A., & Green, L. (1970). The psychiatric interview: The impact of the first three minutes. *American Journal of Psychiatry, 126,* 968-973.

Skov, R. B., & Sherman, S. J. (1986). Information-gathering processes: Diagnosticity, hypothesis-confirmatory strategies, and perceived hypothesis confirmation. *Journal of Experimental Social Psychology, 22,* 93-121.

Snyder, M., & Swann, W. B., Jr. (1978). Behavioral confirmation in social interaction: From social perception to social reality. *Journal of Experimental Social Psychology, 14,* 148-162.

Steele, C. M., Spencer, S. J., & Lynch, M. (1993). Self-image resilience and dissonance: The role of affirmational resources. *Journal of Personality and Social Psychology, 64,* 885-896.

Strohmer, D. C., Shivy, V. A., & Chiodo, A. L. (1990). Information processing strategies in counselor hypothesis testing: The role of selective memory and expectancy. *Journal of Counseling Psychology, 37,* 465-472.

Tversky, A., & Kahneman, D. (1974). Judgment under uncertainty: Heuristics and biases. *Science, 185,* 1124-1131.

Wicklund, R. A., & Brehm, J. W. (1976). *Perspectives on cognitive dissonance.* Hillsdale, NJ: Erlbaum.

Use of Psychological Tests
in Child Custody Assessment

Jonathan Gould

SUMMARY. This article describes a functional, comprehensive approach to the use of psychological tests and measures in a child custody evaluation. I describe a conceptual framework to be used in choosing assessment techniques that are used to assess functional aspects of parenting competencies and other related variables helpful in creating a reliable foundation from which to generate opinions about custodial placement and visitation access. Finally, I provide a practical example of how psychological test data might be presented in an advisory report to the court. *[Article copies available for a fee from The Haworth Document Delivery Service: 1-800-HAWORTH. E-mail address: <docdelivery@haworthpress.com> Website: <http://www.HaworthPress.com> © 2005 by The Haworth Press, Inc. All rights reserved.]*

KEYWORDS. Child custody assessment, psychological testing, reliability, relevance in court

---

Jonathan Gould is engaged in the practice of forensic psychology and is a partner in the national consulting firm, Child Custody Consultants. He has written extensively about forensic methods and procedures applied to CCEs, including the use of psychological tests in CCEs. He has recently co-authored an article describing how to review and critique a colleague's work product and several articles about conducting clinical treatment within a forensic context. He is author of several books on child custody evaluations, the most recent book written with David A. Martindale, PhD, ABPP.

Address correspondence to Dr. Gould at <jwgould@aol.com>.

[Haworth co-indexing entry note]: "Use of Psychological Tests in Child Custody Assessment." Gould, Jonathan. Co-published simultaneously in *Journal of Child Custody* (The Haworth Press, Inc.) Vol. 2, No. 1/2, 2005, pp. 49-69; and: *Psychological Testing in Child Custody Evaluations* (ed: James R. Flens, and Leslie Drozd) The Haworth Press, Inc., 2005, pp. 49-69. Single or multiple copies of this article are available for a fee from The Haworth Document Delivery Service [1-800-HAWORTH, 9:00 a.m. - 5:00 p.m. (EST). E-mail address: docdelivery@haworthpress.com].

Digital Object Identifier: 10.1300/J190v02n01_04

INTRODUCTION

Formal psychological assessment is a distinctive and unique aspect of psychological practice. It is comprised of two areas: psychological testing and psychological assessment (Meyer, Finn, Eyde, Kay, Moreland, Dies et al., 2001). *Psychological testing* is a relatively straightforward process. A particular scale is administered to obtain a specific score. A descriptive meaning can be applied to the score based on data obtained from a normative group (Meyer et al., 2001). This has been called *nomothetic* evaluation because the normative meaning associated with a particular test score describes only the meaning of the score. It does not examine the individual's score within the context of the person's life. The sole purpose is to provide a description of the data relative to a normative group.

In *psychological assessment*, the evaluator "takes a variety of scores generally obtained from multiple test methods, and considers the data in the context of history, referral information, and observed behavior to understand the person being evaluated, to answer referral questions, and then to communicate findings . . ." (Meyer et al., 2001, p. 131). *Psychological assessment* has been called *idiographic* evaluation because the assessment task is to understand the psychological test score within the context of the person's life. The assessment task is to use test-derived sources of information in combination with historical data, presenting complaints, observations, interview results, and information from third parties to disentangle the competing hypotheses. The process of idiographic evaluation is far from simple and requires a high degree of skill and sophistication to be implemented properly (Meyer et al., 2001).

As forensic psychology is built upon the foundation of clinical psychology, so too is forensic psychological assessment built upon the foundations of clinical psychological assessment while adding important data-gathering steps that include third party record review and third party interviews. Clinical psychological assessment is composed of clinical interviews and psychological measurement. Clinical interviews often are unstructured and provide for the client to guide the therapist toward client-defined areas of relevance. Meyer et al. (2001) point out that clinical assessment, which often relies only on unstructured interviews and observations, is limited. When interviews are unstructured, clinicians overlook certain areas of functioning and focus more exclusively on presenting complaints. When interviews are highly structured, clinicians can lose the forest for the trees and make precise but errant judgments. Such mistakes may occur when the clinician focuses on responses to specific interview questions (e.g., diagnostic criteria) without fully considering the salience of these responses in the patient's broader life context or without adequately recognizing how the individual responses fit together into a symptomatically coherent pattern. Additional confounds derive from patients, who are often poor historians and/or biased presenters of information (Meyer et al., 2001, p. 135).

The Potential Power of Test Results

The authors of the *Standards for Educational and Psychological Testing* (American Educational Research Association, American Psychological Association, & National Council on Measurement in Education, 1999) have observed: "The greater the potential impact on test takers, for good or ill, the greater the need to identify and satisfy the relevant standards" (p. 112). Extending that obligation further, the greater the potential impact on consumers of psychological services, for good or ill, the greater the need to adhere to established standards; to be responsive to applicable guidelines; and to endeavor to identify and subsequently utilize the best methodology possible.

Choosing Assessment Instruments

The question to be asked (and correctly answered) is: Do the instruments you have elected to utilize reliably measure *functional* abilities that bear directly upon the matter before the court? Several authors have questioned the usefulness of many currently available assessment techniques. In describing assessment techniques such as the ASPECT and the Bricklin scales, LaFortune and Carpenter (1998) warn that: "[T]he validity of these measures is unestablished at best and seriously flawed at worst" and that their use "cannot be recommended" (p. 222). Similar concerns have been voiced by Otto and Edens (2003).

In this article, I describe a battery of tests suggested for use in child custody evaluations that focus attention on specific functional aspects of parental behavior, parent-child behavior, or inter-parental behavior. I am mindful of the cautions voiced by many authors regarding the inappropriate application of specific assessment techniques to custody assessment and the application of invalid assessment techniques to custody assessment (LaFortune & Carpenter, 1998; Otto & Edens, 2003; Otto, Edens, & Barcus, 2000). In this article, I offer a perspective about how to use psychological tests and measures in a child custody evaluation in an ethically responsible and functionally useful manner.

The criteria "frequency-of-use by surveyed mental health professionals" has not been used as an acceptable measure either of the reliability or of the validity of an assessment instrument in any statistics text or legal test (such as a Frye or a Daubert challenge) with which I am familiar. It is reasonably expected that evaluators will obtain, review, and critically examine the documentation concerning assessment instruments under consideration and that they will select only those whose reliability and validity is acceptable when used for the purpose intended.

Consider the following from the *Standards for Educational and Psychological Testing* (American Education Research Association et al., 1999): (1) Tests are to be accompanied by documentation that will provide test users with the information needed to make sound judgments about the nature and quality of the test, the resulting scores, and the interpretations based on the test scores (p. 67); (2) Presentation and analyses of validity and reliability evidence often are not needed in a written report, but the professional strives to understand, and prepares to articulate, such evidence as the need arises (p. 121); (3) The greater the potential impact on test takers, for good or ill, the greater the need to identify and satisfy the relevant standards (p. 112).

In 1971, a case came before the United States Supreme Court that had nothing whatsoever to do with custody work but the reverberations of which have been dramatically felt by evaluators. *Griggs et al. v. Duke Power Company*, 401 U.S. 424 (1971) was a case involving procedures employed in the selection, placement, and promotion of personnel in an industrial setting. In deciding the case, the court ruled that any testing procedures must be demonstrably reasonable measures of (or predictors of) job performance. Though no polls have been taken on the matter, it is my impression that there is agreement among experienced evaluators that it is advisable to conceptualize parenting as a job and to be guided by the *Griggs* decision. In particular, I believe there to be agreement that evaluators must focus their attention and their assessment efforts on functional abilities that bear directly upon the attributes, behaviors, attitudes, and skills that published research suggests are reliably associated with effective parenting. Examining an attribute in the absence of evidence of its connection to parenting effectiveness and related factors leaves a psychologist open to criticism on several fronts. For the custody evaluator, the data must always be directly or indirectly addressing questions about parenting effectiveness, child development, parent-child fit, or co-parenting.

Usefulness of Psychological Assessment Data

Forensic assessment can circumvent problems commonly associated with clinical assessment by imposing somewhat greater structure and greater direction on the accumulation of data. Data may be obtained from independent sources such as third party information, historical review, direct observations, and psychological test data. Elsewhere, I have described the usefulness of this robust methodology applied to child custody evaluations (Gould, 1998; 2004). In this article, I focus only on the use of psychological tests.

Meyer et al. (2001) identify several reasons why the use of psychological tests in a comprehensive psychological assessment provides a unique data set. Their criteria for the use of psychological tests in a clinical evaluation assessment are applied below to the use of psychological tests in a forensic assessment.

1. Use of a psychological test battery provides an empirically based set of data that allows for more precise measurement of individual characteristics than is usually obtained from interviews alone.[1] The use of multiple tests that comprise a test battery allows for cross checking of hypotheses. By incorporating multiple measures of multiple dimensions, the evaluator is able to gather a wide range of information to facilitate understanding the parent as well as to facilitate an understanding of the comparative strengths and limitations of each parent, both against each other and against a group of peers.
2. Another advantage to the use of a psychological test battery is the generation of data from a large number of personality, cognitive, emotional, or other dimensions simultaneously. Test batteries tend to be inclusive and cover a range of functioning domains, many of which may be overlooked during less formal evaluation procedures.
3. A third advantage is standardized administration and scoring procedures. Each parent is presented with a uniform stimulus that serves as a common yardstick to measure his or her characteristics. Standardization also may reduce legal and ethical problems because it minimizes the prospects that unintended bias may ad-

versely affect the parent and/or the evaluator's interpretation of the parent's responses.

4. A fourth advantage is the comparison of the parent's scores to context specific normative data, permitting each parent to be compared with a relevant group of peers. The information obtained from such normative comparison allows the evaluator to formulate refined inferences about the strengths and weaknesses of a parent compared with a relevant group of peers. For example, both the MMPI-2 and the MCMI-III have data reported for male and female custody litigants. Use of these norms allows the evaluator to consider the degree to which a particular parent's scores deviate from the norm group. An experienced evaluator is able to take the obtained data and examine subtle differences in the data that may be relevant to questions about individual functioning along relevant dimensions associated with parenting.

5. Manuals for psychological tests used in a forensic evaluation should have information about reliability and validity.[2] Such psychometric information allows the evaluator to consider the strength and limitations of the information obtained from the test. Without such information, evaluators have little ability to gauge the accuracy of the data they interpret when making judgments.

6. It is also important to note that the use of psychological testing in child custody evaluations is a community standard among psychologists (Ackerman & Ackerman, 1997; Bow & Quinnell, 2001; Quinnell & Bow, 2001) although the frequency of use of specific psychological tests has been recently challenged (Hagen & Castagna, 2001).

Multi-Trait/Multi-Method Assessment

Forensic assessment is premised upon the idea of seeking independent information that either confirms or disconfirms a hypothesis. A satisfactory forensic evaluation contains multiple sources of information from independent sources of data This is referred to as the multi-trait/multi-method model of assessment (Campbell & Fiske, 1959) and has been applied to forensic psychological evaluations in general (Heilbrun, 2001) and to child custody evaluations, in particular (Gould & Stahl, 2000).

A critical issue in the use of a multi-trait/multi-method model is the extent to which distinct assessment methods provide independent versus redundant information. It is important to recognize that more data does not always mean more accurate results. For example, when using tests that are intercorrelated, it is possible that the predictive power of the two tests combined is lessened compared with the predictive power of the psychometrically sounder test (Borum, Otto, & Golding, 1993). The idea behind multi-trait/multi-method assessment is to increase the predictive power of the data. An increase in predictive power is considered incremental validity. If a method does not increase the ability of the data to predict the behavior of interest, then there is no incremental validity derived from the use of the method.

It is critical to remember that the use of the same method obtained from different people may produce unique observations. For example, self-report questionnaires that are completed by parents, siblings, aunts, uncles, teacher, coaches, youth counselors, therapists, and other people outside the family system may provide very different descriptions of the identified behavior. Obtaining information from different people provides for a multidimensional description of the issue or trait being assessed and it allows for comparison to other sources of data.

CHOOSING PSYCHOLOGICAL TESTS AND MEASURES

Even those who caution us about the presentation of psychological science in the courtroom acknowledge the relative usefulness of objective psychological testing in a forensic context (Heilbrun, 1992; 1995; 2001). This is because a well-developed psychological test appears to meet many, if not all, of the psycho-legal criteria for presenting scientific evidence in court (see, e.g., Daubert v. Merrell Dow Pharmaceuticals [1993]; Kumho Tire Company Ltd. et al. v. Carmichael et al. [1999]).

An important aspect of the forensic use of psychological testing is that the test must be useful for the purpose for which it is being used. The tests we use must have been shown to have an empirical literature basis for its use in a particular type of situation. Similarly, when we offer opinions about test results, they must be framed within the appropriate interpretive context of that test. For example, the MacAndrews scale on the MMPI and MMPI-2 does not measure alcohol use or abuse but the propensity to be prone to use or abuse alcohol should the individual drink (Greene, 2000).

The MMPI-2 and the MCMI-III are tests of psychopathology and personality functioning. They are not tests of parenting capacity. Use of data from the MMPI-2 and the MCMI-III may be used to generate hypotheses about individual functioning that are subject to confirmation or disconfirmation of data from independent data sources. We can hypothesize that a person with a high score on MMPI-2 Scale 6 (Paranoia) may have difficulties with trusting others, but without independent information that confirms that this particular parent with a high Scale 6 displays difficulties trusting others and that these difficulties adversely affect his or her parenting of the child, we cannot know the meaning of the test score in the context of the parent's relationship with the child.

Because tests like the MMPI-2 and the MCMI-III are not developed for use in child custody evaluations, it is important that the evaluator go beyond citing a scale elevation. In my view, an evaluator should carefully check the specific items elevated on a scale. In a recent case, for example, a parent's high score on the Alcohol Potential Scale (APS) was the result of item endorsements that included:

1. If my family puts pressure on me, I'm likely to feel angry and resist doing what they want;
2. I've done a number of stupid things on impulse that ended up causing me great trouble;
3. Punishment never stopped me from doing what I wanted;
4. There are members of my family who say I'm selfish and think only of myself;
5. I seem to make a mess of good opportunities that come my way;
6. I am very good at making up excuses when I get into trouble;
7. I act quickly much of the time and don't think things through as I should.

When I conducted an interview focused on each of the items that elevated the APS scale, I discovered that the individual was endorsing items that reflected what her spouse had told her about her behavior during the marriage and items that reflected her belief that her husband's attempts to control her behavior were no longer going to limit her choices. The lesson is that evaluators need to critically evaluate not only scale elevations but also examine whether the specific endorsed items reflect aspects of the current custody dispute context. That is, evaluators need to critically examine the degree to which elevated scores are the results of artifacts of the custodial dispute and/or other factors that may be unrelated to parenting and co-parenting.

Currently, there are no tests of parenting capacity but there are tests that assess different aspects of parenting. Among the more commonly used parenting measures are the Parent-Child Relationship Inventory

(PCRI), the Parenting Stress Inventory (PSI), the Child Sexual Behavior Inventory (CSBI), the Child Abuse Potential Inventory (CAP), the Parenting Alliance Measure (PAM), and the Parenting Stress Survey (PSS). There are also useful measures of child behavior such as the Achenbach Child Behavior Checklist (CBCL), Conners Rating Scale (CRS), and the Behavior Assessment Scale for Children (BASC). There are also measures of a child's perception of a parent's parenting and disciplinary behavior.

The use of parenting measures or use of child behavior measures are useful for gathering data about specific areas of concern such as risk for physical violence as measured on the CAP or risk for abuse and neglect as measured on the PSI. In my view, it is important to use psychometrically sound measures that also have normative data against which to compare a parent or a child's responses to the population at large. At present, most of these measures do not have normative data for male and female custody litigants, so caution should be exercised when interpreting the meaning of the data. Currently, there is research in progress to develop normative data for custody litigants on several measures commonly used in custody evaluations (J. R. Flens, personal communication, September 20, 2004). When such normative information is unavailable, there are at least two options. The most conservative option is not to use the measure. The alternative is to administer and score the measure and to use the results only as a hypotheses generator. No conclusions should be drawn from these data. The data are used only to suggest other areas of parental or child functioning to examine using independent sources of information.

Test Choice and Daubert Challenge

Once an assessment tool is identified in your report as a psychological test and if you live in a state in which Daubert is accepted, I believe that you need to be prepared to defend the choice and the use of a test in Daubert challenge. Such a challenge may include explaining to the judge information about a test's underlying theory of science, whether it has been published in a peer-reviewed journal, status as a current standard among the psychological community, psychometric data about its reliability, validity, base rate estimates and its falsifability (Medoff, 2003).

If you base your opinion on a particular instrument in any way, that instrument's scientific validity for the purpose you used may be the focus of a Daubert challenge. If you base your opinion on a particular methodology, then it is the methodology that will be the focus of a Daubert challenge.

It seems to me that there are two ways to approach a Daubert challenge. The first way, described above, is to focus attention on each test used in your battery of tests. My experience is that most of the psychological tests and measures used in child custody evaluations might have difficulty surviving a Daubert challenge because the tests have not been developed for use in child custody assessments. Lesson: Don't base your opinion upon the results of a specific test or a specific set of tests.

The second approach to a Daubert challenge is to focus less attention on individual tests and more attention on the scientific methodology used in the evaluation process. Rather than examining each test used in the evaluation process, the evaluator describes the usefulness and breadth of data from alternative independent sources of information. As noted in the Daubert (1993) decision: *"Scientific methodology today is based on generating hypotheses and testing them* (emphasis added) to see if they can be falsified; indeed, this methodology is what distinguishes science from other fields of human inquiry" (p. 593).

It is important for the evaluator to describe how information from any one data source may be used to generate hypotheses about the parent, the child, or the family. It is important to describe how information from one source of data is used to confirm or disconfirm hypotheses generated from other independent sources of information. One view is that psychological test data are weighed no more heavily than collateral data or direct observational data. An alternative view is that psychological testing should be weighed more heavily than other sources of data because a well-developed test will have standardized norms, quantitative measurements, multiple validity studies, standardized observational conditions, and other psychometric properties. It is my opinion that how you weigh the usefulness of data from different information sources depends on the characteristics of each case. It is the convergence of independent sources of data that help to make one hypothesis more likely than another to be supported, and the weight we assign to each information source may vary from case to case depending upon the quality of the data and the way in which the data may be interpreted within the larger context of the family system.

Within this view of examining trends in data across methods, a less scientifically rigorous measure may be assigned a similar weight in decision making as a psychometrically sound measure. Both sources of information provide data from which hypotheses are generated for confirmation from alternative, independent data sources.

Daubert challenges are rarely used in child custody cases. If you practice in a Frye jurisdiction your task may be very different in defending your use of a psychological test or measure. There are several publications describing how psychologists and other mental health professionals use psychological tests in custody evaluations (e.g., Ackerman & Ackerman, 1997; Quinnell & Bow, 2001). Based upon a Frye standard, it is possible that the use of the House-Tree-Person test, Sentence Completion test, or TAT would be ruled admissible because of their general acceptance among evaluators as reported in these peer-reviewed articles. It is the contention of this article and, I would argue, it is the intention of the current APA Ethics Code (American Psychological Association, 2002) and the Specialty Guidelines for Forensic Psychologists (Committee on Ethical Guidelines for Forensic Psychologists, 1991) to focus attention on the reliability, validity, and relevance of tests and measures used in a forensic context. A test that is widely used by colleagues does not mean that the test is psychometrically sound.

An assumption built into the Frye standard is that a test would not be commonly used among professionals in a field if its reliability had not been previously demonstrated. As summarized in a recent Illinois State Supreme Court Decision (Donaldson v. Central Illinois Public Service Co. [2002]), "A technique, however, is not 'generally accepted' if it is experimental or of dubious validity. Thus, the Frye rule is meant to exclude methods new to science that undeservedly create a perception of certainty when the basis for the evidence or opinion is actually invalid" (Donaldson at 324).

Such is not the case with many assessment techniques used in the child custody field. Many clinical assessment techniques drawn from clinical practice have been used in child custody evaluations and, until recently, have been accepted as commonly used among custody evaluators despite their lack of reliability and relevance (Ackerman & Ackerman, 1997). The use of unreliable, clinically derived techniques such as human figure drawings, sentence completion tests, and other similar projective techniques may have earned a place in the scientific community and have undeservingly created a perception of reliability when, in fact, there is no basis for such belief. An assumption of the Frye standard that a principle or technique is not generally accepted in the scientific community if it is by nature unreliable does not appear to be reflected in custody evaluators' historical use of projective techniques. Unreliable methods and the interpretation of unreliable information that has been drawn from those unreliable methods have been used as a basis upon which evaluators have offered opinions about custodial placement and visitation access. Reliance upon unreliable techniques serves neither the families nor the courts. Fortunately, that is an increasing focus by child custody evaluators on the use of reliable and relevant assessment techniques (Bow & Quinnell, 2001).

PRACTICAL EXAMPLE OF THE USE OF TESTS IN CHILD CUSTODY EVALUATIONS

Over the past several years, I have included in the "Interpretation of Psychological Tests" section of my advisory reports (a) why I choose certain tests, (b) what information each test may provide, and (c) the relevance of the potential information gleaned from the test to the issues before the court. When discussing each test, I provide information about each parent's validity scale scores and I provide a discussion of the relevant scores from the tests.

I interpret the tests using the following strategy. I have parents complete the MMPI-2 and the MCMI-III on a computer and their results are scored using a Pearson-NCS scoring program. Most often, I use the Extended Score report rather than the Interpretive Report because I do not want to be placed in a situation where I am asked to testify about what specific scores the author of the Interpretive Report used in reaching his conclusions. I do not know what specific scale scores (or combination of scale and subscale scores) were used by the author of the Interpretive Report in rendering opinions and conclusions, and when testifying I do not want to be placed in a position of having to grope for answers to questions about the relationship between Interpretive statements from the MMPI-2 Interpretive Profile and test scores. The use of computer-generated interpretive reports may also raise ethical concerns given the current wording of the APA Ethics Code (2002) section 9.09 Test Scoring and Interpretation Services. In particular, paragraph b notes the following:

> Psychologists select scoring and interpretation services (including automated services) on the basis of evidence of the validity of the program and procedures as well as on other appropriate considerations. (See also Standard 2.01b, Boundaries of Competence)

I do not know if the authors of the recent APA Ethics Code revision intended the use of computer-generated testing interpretive reports to raise ethical issues, but the wording of Section 9.09 has been brought to the attention of the ethics board of the APA for clarification in a letter written by Leslie Drozd, PhD, Lyn Greenberg, PhD, and David Martindale, PhD. In what was believed to be a response to this letter as well as concerns expressed by others, Dr. Stephen Behnke (2004), the APA Ethics Director, penned a column in the APA *Monitor*, suggesting that evaluators should be able to answer the following questions regarding any CGTI program used: (1) Given the purpose for which the service is utilized, what evidence of the program's validity do I require so that I may benefit, and not harm, my client?; and (2) What information about a program need I have in order to take responsibility for what my assessment contains?

It is my opinion that it is not presently possible to answer these questions. The algorithms (i.e., program logic and decision rules) used to generate the interpretive statements in a computer-generated interpretation are not publicly available. Therefore, evaluators are unable to answer important questions about which data are used to generate specific statements found in the interpretive reports. Suffice it to say, however, the prudent child custody evaluator should be prepared to defend the use of computer-generated test interpretation reports if he or she chooses to base an opinion on the interpretive data found in the computer generated report.

When I write up the test results section, my first step is to visually inspect the printout. I look over all the numbers and I look over the critical items if they are included in the printout. Next, I compare the current results with those reported by Bathurst, Gottfried, and Gottfried (1997) for the MMPI-2 and I compare the current results with those reported by McCann, Flens, Campagna, Colman, Lazzaro, and Connor (2001) for the MCMI-III. In the third step, the validity scales of both tests are reviewed to determine the effect that any potential response style (e.g., fake good) may have on the overall test results. This also involves an understanding of how a favorable response style may result in a corrected profile. The presence of a corrected scale elevation could reduce the confidence and certainty I place in the interpretation of that particular scale, or the profile in general. In the third step, I review my textbooks on the MMPI-2 and MCMI-III. Often, I will use two or three texts and examine their explanations, looking specifically for differences in interpretations that might be relevant to the case at hand. In those rare instances in which I use an Interpretive Report, the next step is to use the Interpretive statements as if they were a third party source providing an outsider's view of the data. The final step is putting all the information together.

I also use tests and measures that assist in assessing factors that I believe are relevant to an understanding of each parent, each child, and the overall family context. I administer a measure of anger expression and anger management because I have found that so many parents involved in CCEs are angry and are often expressing their anger in inappropriate or dysfunctional ways. I administer measures of parenting communication and parenting alliance to help examine the degree to which these parents are able to engage in productive inter-parental communication and inter-parental cooperation. I administer several measures of parenting attitudes, parent-child relationship factors, and parental coping skills.

I want to gather information about how each parent views each child so I administer measures that assess child behavior. Often these measures are completed by teachers and other relevant people in the children's lives.

I administer structured questionnaires and psychological measures aimed at screening for familial violence, screening for factors associated with child abuse and neglect, and misuse of disciplinary techniques. When there are allegations of familial violence, my choice of psychological tests and measures is often guided by the use of peer-reviewed evaluation protocols developed to investigate allegations of familial violence (e.g., Austin, 2000, 2001; Bancroft & Silverman, 2002a, 2002b; Drozd, Kleinman, & Olesen, 2000).

When there are allegations of child sexual abuse, I administered measures developed to examine a child's observed sexual behavior and measures developed to investigate perpetrator-associated factors in cases of intra-familial child sexual abuse (cf. Kuehnle, 1996). I will also follow one of several peer-reviewed evaluation protocols developed to investigate factors associated with intra-familial child sexual abuse perpetrators (e.g., Lanyon, 2001).

It is my belief that evaluators too often limit themselves to psychological tests and measures that focus attention on broad concerns about psychopathology while ignoring a systematic examination of factors associated with family conflict, parental communication and cooperation, child development, and parent-child relationships.

Here is an example of how I describe the use of psychological tests and measures in my reports. I believe it is important to explain to judges why I have chosen specific tests and measures and to explain the relevance of each test to the concerns before the court. My introduction to the Interpretation of Results section in my report reflects this idea of explaining each test and why it was chosen.

First, I discuss my test selection. I include information about the test and its relevance for inclusion in the present evaluation:

> *Relevance of use of psychological tests and measures:* The use of psychological tests and measures in a child custody evaluation provide a genuinely empirical foundation for interpretation of data (Otto et al., 2001). Several of the tests such as the MMPI-2 and MCMI-III are measures of psychopathology or personality functioning. Measuring psychopathology or personality functioning is important in a child custody evaluation to rule out personality disorders, abnormal functioning, and other such individual factors that might adversely affect parenting of the child, and co-parenting with the other parent. The data from the MMPI-2 and MCMI-III provide an opportunity to compare the parent's responses against those of a sample of female custody litigants. That is, research examining the MMPI-2 and MCMI-III in child custody evaluations provides normative data against which to compare this particular parent's responses on a standardized measure of personality functioning. (Bathurst et al., 1997; McCann et al., 2001)

For each test and measure that is administered during the evaluation process, I provide an explanation to the Court about why I chose the specific test or measure. Too often, I have heard judges ask why a test is used in an evaluation and what information from the test is expected to be obtained. When you explain the relevance of choosing a specific test or measure, you are able to help the judge understand why the test was chosen and how the data generated from the test results may be used in generating hypotheses about parental, child, or family functioning. Here is another example of how I include a statement about the relevance of the tests and measures I choose to include in my evaluation:

> A parent's perceptions of the child as well as the parent's perception of her relationship with the child are critical aspects in any child custody evaluation. The Parent Child Relationship Inventory (PCRI) and the Parenting Stress Inventory (PSI) provide information about these dimensions. The PSI has the added dimension of being a useful screening tool for potential factors in the parent-child relationship that could result in parental abuse and/or neglect of the child.

Below is an example of how I provide a research based interpretation of test results and incorporate them into the clinical data obtained from other sources of information gathered during the evaluation procedure. I begin the report section by explaining to the reader to be wary about how test data are interpreted.

> Psychological test data is but one source of information in a child custody evaluation. The usefulness of psychological test data is that it provides a genuinely empirical foundation to the custody assessment, allowing comparison of a parent's scores to normative data. This is also its Achilles heel. The appearance of test-generated numbers may lead the reader to believe that test data are somehow more reliable and valid or should be given greater weight than other sources of information gathering. The appearance of a scientific test often gives the appearance of truth.
>
> Psychological truth in a child custody evaluation does not come from only one data source in a child custody evaluation. For example, the reader may read language from the MMPI-2 that is provocative in a psychological sense. In a legal sense, one might argue that the use of some MMPI-2 labels for certain scales is more prejudicial than probative. I warn the reader to be aware of any possible prejudicial effect on interpretation of the data that might result solely from meanings attributed to the scale names rather than meaning attributed to interpretation of the data. A person who scores highly, say, on the Schizophrenia scale may or may not be a mental health concern. It is only after reviewing data from multiple data sources that the evaluator (and reader) should be in a position to decide upon the weight and substance of each factor.

Next, I provide a statement about the limitation of psychological test data drawn from the work of Greenberg (1996).

> The psychological test interpretations presented below are hypotheses and should not be considered in isolation from other information in this matter. The interpretive statements are actuarial and expert predictions based upon the results of the tests. Personality test results reflect characteristics of persons who have provided test response patterns similar to those of the current individual. Although test results are presented in an affirmative manner, they are probabilistic in nature. The reader should interpret these findings cautiously. From test results alone, it is impossible to tell if these

patterns and/or deficits are directly or indirectly related to parental competencies. Therefore, the reader should examine the test interpretations for general trends and put limited weight on any one specific statement or set of statements without additional support from an alternative source of data such as information obtained from collateral information. In the integration and presentation of test data, where results were unclear or in conflict, I used clinical judgment to select the most likely hypotheses for presentation.

Finally, I provide a discussion of the results of each test and integrate the test results with information gleaned from other sources of data. As you will read, I attempt to frame my interpretation of test results both through the use of research results that informs my decision making and through the use of independent sources of information that help provide confidence for the convergence of the data upon a conclusion. The discussion segment described below is part of a much larger discussion that would appear in my reports in which I more fully describe interpretation of test results.

Results from the MMPI 2: According to Mr. Smith's MMPI-2 results, he approached the test (L = 61; F = 47; K = 78; S = 72) in a manner *similar* to the configuration of the normative data reported for a sample of male custody litigants (Bathurst et al., 1997). Mr. Smith approached the test in a manner similar to other male custody litigants involved in child custody litigation. As a result, his scores on the MMPI-2 clinical scales are likely to be underestimates of his true scores.

You will note that I provide the scale scores so that someone reviewing my work will know the specific scores enabling him or her to assess the accuracy of my interpretation. In those situations in which the data may suggest more than one reasonable explanation, I discuss each reasonable explanation and then I provide an argument about why I believe that one explanation is more persuasive than the other.

People whose scores on Scale 6 are similar to Mr. Smith's score are often characterized as likely to be suspicious, hostile, and overly sensitive. They may have a delusional or thought disorder. The most significant contribution to his increased suspiciousness comes from ideas of external influence. People who score in this range often externalize blame for their problems and project responsibility for their negative feelings onto others (Greene, 2000, p. 159). One might argue that it is somewhat common in child custody evaluations to feel that people are out to get you and that people are talking about you behind your back. However, even when comparing Mr. Smith to a normative sample of male custody litigants on Scale 6 ($T = 52.4$, $sd = 9.41$), his score is almost three standard deviations above the male custody-litigant average.

It is likely that there are two factors at work here. The first is that the divorce conflict has created an atmosphere where Mr. Smith rightly and accurately perceives a threat from others. In addition to this expected reaction, he is likely to have some usually suspicious traits under the best of circumstances. These suspicious traits may become further exaggerated during times of stress such as the custody dispute. One hypothesis to consider is that Mr. Smith's suspiciousness may decrease once the stress of the divorce and child custody issues have concluded. On the other hand, these traits may be somewhat more characterological in nature and will not dissipate following resolution of the divorce and custody action.

In the discussion of Mr. Smith's basic scale scores, I describe the parent's scores and compare his scores to the normative data about male custody litigants. I also provide hypotheses about what may be operating in this particular situation. Although I included only a brief example of what is a much longer report, I begin to introduce plausible rival interpretations in the above paragraph. Although not reported here, the full report contained a discussion of several other possible factors drawn from the MMPI-2 data and how they may be expressed through the father's parenting. I also review the specific items that elevated the scale score and investigate the reasoning behind the endorsed items through an interview format.

Integrated into my discussion of MMPI-2 results will be information from other sources obtained during the evaluation. For example, if I have collateral data or interview data that support the MMPI-2 data, I will briefly note the convergence of these data. If I have independent sources of data that do not confirm the MMPI-2 data, I will briefly note the lack of convergence of these data.

FINAL THOUGHTS

There are several issues that have not been thoroughly addressed in this article that briefly need mention. As a field of endeavor, we have yet to reach a consensus about how to weigh the relative contribution of testing results with other independent sources of data nor do we know what factors contribute to how test data are weighed. We do not yet know what data are ultimately more important in predicting the best psychological interests of the child.

We have yet to fully examine the relative merits of each independent information source used in CCEs. We do not know what psychological test data are most predictive of the best psychological interests of the child nor do we know how such data are best used in combination with other sources of data. These are areas ripe for future research and scholarship.

In summary, this article has described a comprehensive approach to the use of psychological tests and measures in a child custody evaluation. I described a model for the use of relevant psychological tests and measures to assess areas of concern in a specific family system. I also provided a practical example of how I report psychological test data in my advisory reports, including language pertaining to limitations of data and explanation of the relationship between choice of test and relevance to custody issues.

NOTES

1. It is important to consider the weight one assigns to the meaning of psychological test data. Caution needs to be used to insure that one does not place undue decision-making weight on the value of psychological test data compared to the decision-making weight placed on information obtained from other sources. Psychological test data may not include information about important contextual factors such as the nature and quality of co-parenting and parental communication.

2. It is likely that test manuals will not contain information relevant to child custody litigants and will not contain information about custody litigant samples.

REFERENCES

Ackerman, M. J., & Ackerman, M. (1997). Custody evaluation practices: A survey of experienced professionals (revisited). *Professional Psychology: Research and Practice, 28*(2), 137-145.

American Educational Research Association, American Psychological Association, & National Council on Measurement in Education. (1999). *Standards for educational and psychological testing.* Washington, DC: American Psychological Association.

American Psychological Association. (2002). Ethical principles of psychologists and code of conduct. *American Psychologist, 57*(12), 1060-1073.

Austin, W. G. (2000). Assessing credibility in allegations of marital violence in the high-conflict child custody case. *Family & Conciliation Courts Review, 38*(4), 462-477.

Austin, W. G. (2001). Partner violence and risk assessment in child custody evaluation. *Family Court Review, 39*(4), 483-496.

Bancroft, L., & Silverman, J. G. (2002a). *The batterer as parent: The impact of domestic violence on family dynamics.* Thousand Oaks, CA: Sage Publications.

Bancroft, L., & Silverman, J. G. (2002b). The batterer as parent: Assessing the impact of domestic violence on family dynamics. *Psychiatry, Psychology & Law, 9*(2), 284-285.

Bathurst, K., Gottfried, A. W., & Gottfried, A. E. (1997). Normative data for the MMPI-2 in child custody litigation. *Psychological Assessment, 9*(3), 205-211.

Behnke, S. (2004). Test-scoring and interpretation services. *APA Monitor, 35*(3), 58-59.

Borum, R., Otto, R., & Golding, S. (1993, Spring). Improving clinical judgment and decision making in forensic evaluation. *The Journal of Psychiatry & Law,* 35-76.

Bow, J. N., & Quinnell, F. A. (2001). Psychologists' current practices and procedures in child custody evaluations: Five years after American Psychological Association guidelines. *Professional Psychology: Research & Practice, 32*(3), 261-268.

Campbell, D. T., & Fiske, D. W. (1959). Convergent and discriminant validation by the multitrait-multimethod matrix. *Psychological Bulletin, 56,* 81-105.

Committee on Ethical Guidelines for Forensic Psychologists. (1991). Specialty guidelines for forensic psychologists. *Law and Human Behavior, 15*(6), 655-665.

Daubert v. Merrell Dow Pharmaceuticals, 113 S. Ct. 2786 (1993).

Donaldson v. Central Illinois Public Service Co., 199 Ill. 2d 63, 767 NE2d 314 (2002).

Drozd, L., Kleinman, T., & Olesen, N. (2000). *Alienation or abuse?* Proceedings of the Fourth International Symposium on Child Custody Evaluations (pp. 169-181). Madison, WI: Association of Family & Conciliation Courts.

Frye v. United States 293 F 1013 D.C. Cir. (1923).

Gould, J. W. (1998). *Conducting scientifically crafted child custody evaluations.* Thousand Oaks, CA: Sage Publications.

Gould, J. (2004). Evaluating the probative value of child custody evaluations: A guide for forensic mental health professionals. *Journal of Child Custody, 1*(1), 77-96.

Gould, J. W., & Stahl, P. M. (2000). The art and science of child custody evaluations: Integrating clinical and mental health models. *Family and Conciliation Courts Review, 38*(3), 392-414.

Greenberg, S. (1996, June). *Child custody evaluations.* Workshop sponsored by The American Board of Professional Psychology Summer Institute, Post Graduate Study in Psychology. Portland, OR.

Greene, R. L. (2000). *The MMPI-2: An interpretive manual* (2nd ed.). Boston, MA: Allyn & Bacon.

Griggs v. Duke Power, 401 US 424 (1971).

Hagen, M. A., & Castagna, N. (2001). The real numbers: Psychological testing in custody evaluations. *Professional Psychology: Research and Practice, 32*(3), 269-271.

Heilbrun, K. (1992). The role of psychological testing in forensic assessment. *Law and Human Behavior, 16*(3), 257-272.

Heilbrun, K. (1995). Child custody evaluations: Critically assessing mental health experts and psychological tests. *Family Law Quarterly, 29*(1), 63-78.

Heilbrun, K. (2001). *Principles of forensic mental health assessment.* New York: Kluwer Academic/Plenum Publishers.

Kuehnle, K. (1996). *Assessing allegations of child sexual abuse*. Sarasota, FL: Professional Resource Press.

Kumho Tire Company Ltd. et al. v. Carmichael et al., 256 U.S. 137 (1999).

LaFortune, K. A., & Carpenter, B. N. (1998). Custody evaluations: A survey of mental health professionals. *Behavioral Sciences & the Law, 16*, 207-224.

Lanyon, R. I. (2001). Psychological assessment procedures in sex offending. *Professional Psychology: Research & Practice, 32*, 253-260.

McCann, J. T., Flens, J. R., Campagna, V., Colman, P., Lazzaro T., & Connor, E. (2001). The MCMI-III in Child Evaluations: A Normative Study. *Journal of Forensic Psychology Practice, 1*(2), 27-44.

Medoff, D. (2003). The scientific basis of psychological testing: Considerations following Daubert, Kumho, and Joiner. *Family Court Review, 41*(2), 199-213.

Meyer, G. J., Finn, S. E., Eyde, L. D., Kay, G. G., Moreland, K. L., Dies, R. R. et al. (2001). Psychological testing and psychological assessment: A review of evidence and issues. *American Psychologist, 56*(2), 128-165.

Otto, R. K., & Edens. J. F. (2003). Parenting capacity. In T. Grisso (Ed.), *Evaluating competencies: Forensic assessments and instruments* (2nd ed; pp. 229-307). New York: Plenum Press.

Otto, R. K., Edens, J. F., & Barcus, E. H. (2000). The use of psychological testing in child custody evaluations. *Family & Conciliation Courts Review, 38*(3), 312-340.

Quinnell, F. A., & Bow, J. N. (2001). Psychological tests used in child custody evaluations. *Behavioral Sciences & the Law, 19*(4), 491-501.

Testing, One, Two, Three, Testing: An Attorney Perspective

Dianna Gould-Saltman

SUMMARY. This article addresses the attorney perspective on the use of psychometric testing in the context of family law child custody evaluations. Although attorneys, judicial officers and child custody evaluators "use" psychometric testing in family law matters, the ways in which each discipline uses the information gleaned from the results of these tests as administered to child custody litigants can differ substantially. This article distinguishes the attorney perspective from the mental health perspective in the use of the results of such tests. *[Article copies available for a fee from The Haworth Document Delivery Service: 1-800-HAWORTH. E-mail address: <docdelivery@haworthpress.com> Website: <http://www.HaworthPress.com> © 2005 by The Haworth Press, Inc. All rights reserved.]*

KEYWORDS. Testing, MMPI, psychometric instruments

DEFINING THE PARAMETERS OF THE ARTICLE

I am not a mental health professional.[1] I am an attorney. This article is intended to address the attorney perspective on the use of psychometric

Dianna Gould-Saltman is an attorney licensed to practice in California and is certified by the California State Bar Board of Legal Specialization as a Certified Family Law Specialist. She is a Fellow of the American Academy of Matrimonial Lawyers.
Address correspondence to Dianna Gould-Saltman at <dgsaltman@aol.com>.

[Haworth co-indexing entry note]: "Testing, One, Two, Three, Testing: An Attorney Perspective." Gould-Saltman, Dianna. Co-published simultaneously in *Journal of Child Custody* (The Haworth Press, Inc.) Vol. 2, No. 1/2, 2005, pp. 71-81; and: *Psychological Testing in Child Custody Evaluations* (ed: James R. Flens, and Leslie Drozd) The Haworth Press, Inc., 2005, pp. 71-81. Single or multiple copies of this article are available for a fee from The Haworth Document Delivery Service [1-800-HAWORTH, 9:00 a.m. - 5:00 p.m. (EST). E-mail address: docdelivery@haworthpress.com].

Digital Object Identifier: 10.1300/J190v02n01_05

testing[2] in the context of family law child custody evaluations. I do not intend to address in depth the comparative utility of one test over another, the application of these tests outside the context of child custody evaluations, or the various debates among professionals about the value of particular tests. What I hope to address is the way in which attorneys view psychometric testing, which may be fundamentally different than it is viewed by mental health professionals or, for that matter, judicial officers.

PRACTICALITIES

For the most part, lawyers (and judges who come from the ranks of lawyers) are linear thinkers. We like things organized and disdain "multi-tasking." After having gone from high school to college to law school to bar examination, we are quite familiar with "tests." The use of tests in the context of our family law work accomplishes a number of things in our minds. Tests break things down to numbers, and we understand numbers. It allows us to quantify the sometimes unquantifiable. It allows us to compare people and aspects of people in ways which mere personal observation can not always do, at least in the limited time and under the limited conditions allotted in litigation.

Tests give the sense of objectivity to counterbalance the much more subjective clinical portion of a custody evaluation. Even tests which are not "objective" in the clinical sense can seem objective to the attorney because it somehow allows us to compare apples to oranges.

Tests also provide a short cut through some of the denser aspects of custody evaluations. Rarely does an attorney subpoena the underlying tests and responses to determine whether tests were properly interpreted, applied, or summarized. More often, a shorter summary of the battery of tests is incorporated in an overall evaluation report in a way that tends to highlight ways in which the testing supported the conclusions of the evaluator based on other measures (clinical sessions, interactions sessions, interviews with collateral witnesses, etc.). Where an attorney might not feel comfortable with a two-page summary of 20 hours of interviews, attorneys seem to accept a two-page summary of what may be 100 pages of test questions and responses.

Testing has its drawbacks, of course. While, ideally, a well-crafted child custody evaluation report will provide the parties and counsel information they can use to enter into a child-centered parenting arrangement, testing implies more than one evaluator's opinion: it identifies personality "flaws," from the litigant's perspective. While a litigant might be able to overlook an adverse "opinion" and focus on the recommendations at hand, purportedly objective "findings" that are adverse often result in a litigant feeling more defensive, the other party taking the offensive, and the battle lines being drawn. Evaluations come in the context of litigation far more often than any more collaborative dispute resolution venue.

Few lawyers, fewer judicial officers, and almost no litigants understand the complexities of each instrument, the interplay between instruments, or the relevance of any particular instrument to parenting ability. Few attorneys understand each instrument well enough to be able to meaningfully cross-examine an evaluator regarding the use or interpretation of the results of each one. Even when another mental health professional is used to assist the attorney in preparing to cross-examine an evaluator, the analysis is imperfect. Assuming each professional is proficient in his or her own field but not necessarily proficient in the other fields, a mental health professional is looking at psychometric testing from the perspective of its intended use, its extrapolated use for a new population, and the idiosyncrasies of the instrument. An attorney, trained as a litigator, is looking for loopholes: ways to bolster the positive information for the client and to point out the negative information about the other side. It is an advocate's position informed by the hired mental health expert but filtered through the advocate's lens. The judicial officer, trained as an advocate but converted to a neutral position, is seeking relevant information that will assist in determining the best interests of the child in a way that offers more than merely hearing testimony from the litigants and witnesses could provide.[3]

The issue of using psychometric testing is complicated by the evaluator's own obligation to conduct a child custody evaluation at a level which at least meets the requisite standard of care in the community. If the community in which the evaluator practices expects that psychometric testing will be used to identify or rule out psychopathy, or to generate or confirm hypotheses, an evaluator who determines that psychometric testing will provide no additional benefit to the parties' or to the evaluator's own analysis of the custody situation may find himself or herself pressured to conduct such testing *pro forma*. Ackerman and Ackerman (1997) conducted a survey of tests used in custody evaluations and compared them to the types and frequency of use noted 10 years earlier by Keilin and Bloom (1986). In both surveys the MMPI (or MMPI-2) was the most frequently used test and the Rorschach the second most frequently used test, but the frequency with which the MMPI (or MMPI-2) was administered during custody evaluations had increased 20% and the use of the Rorschach had increased 6%. The MCMI-II and MCMI-III, which didn't exist when Keilin and Bloom conducted their 1986 survey, was used by over one-third of custody evaluators by 1997.

TYPES OF INSTRUMENTS

For purposes of this discussion I am defining "objective" personality tests as those for which there are quantified criteria for "scoring." I am defining "projective" tests as those requiring the evaluator to apply subjective or semi-subjective criteria to interpret the responses. I am aware that there is a great deal of controversy regarding whether some instruments are really "objective" or "projective" and that there may be substantial cross-over between categories. Examples of objective tests include the Minnesota Multiphasic Personality Inventory-2 (MMPI-2) and the Millon Clinical Multiaxial Inventory III (MCMI-III).

Many judicial officers do not distinguish the relevance to parenting between different types of instruments. Most do know that the MMPI-2 is the most widely used test in child custody evaluations but, other than a result which identifies a likely pathology, they do not necessarily tie in the results to parenting competency. Yet the MMPI-2 is probably the most well-liked test among lawyers because it offers "hard numbers" rather than ephemeral concepts. Objective tests, such as the MMPI-2, require forced choices (true or false, for example) and so offer an easy comparison between test takers. Projective tests, which allow for more "open-ended" questions and narrative answers, are not as easy to use to compare test takers. Both projective and objective tests have some "key" for interpretation of the answers to allow some uniformity of interpretation. Both types of tests have been used over and over in custody litigant populations, but most were not designed to assess parenting abilities in custody litigant populations. Therefore, the results of these tests may be somewhat consistent but not necessarily relevant.

Many evaluators use other instruments which were designed to assess parenting skills but which are neither objective nor projective "tests." Many of these instruments are surveys or inventories designed to address parenting strengths and weaknesses but whose responses are interpreted by the evaluator (for example, the Parent Child Relationship Inventory, the Parent Stress Index, and the Parent Awareness Skills Survey). Interestingly, Ackerman and Ackerman (1997) found that while 92% of respondents used the MMPI-2 and 48% used the Rorschach, most other tests and related instruments were used far less but their devotees used them often.[4]

There appears to be disagreement among evaluators as to whether testing is to be used to generate hypotheses, to confirm hypotheses, or both. From an attorney perspective, testing (and obtaining the results) before clinical interviews for the purpose of generating hypotheses has the potential to result in cross-examination as to confirmatory bias. One could easily imagine a cross-examination question such as, "If you believe in your testing and your testing showed X, isn't it likely, doctor, that you marshaled all the data you gathered thereafter such that it stacked up in favor of the hypothesis you'd already generated? Wouldn't it have been frustrating if, after all that 'objective' testing, your clinical and investigatory data refuted your hypothesis and you had to explain the difference?"

On the other hand, using the testing to confirm hypotheses developed from clinical interviews and collateral data could call into question the interpretation of the testing results, especially those from projective tests and non-test instruments. One could imagine hearing, "Doctor, once you'd invested all the time in the interviews and developed some hypotheses, wouldn't it be easy to interpret the results of the testing so that they conformed to your hypotheses, except for perhaps the *really* significant spikes on the objective tests? More importantly, what steps did you take to assure that you didn't or couldn't subconsciously do so, and are you positive that you didn't?"

SPECIFIC INSTRUMENTS AND THEIR UTILITY

Since experts may only be appointed when the trier of fact needs expert information that is beyond common knowledge and which information could not be garnered by the testimony of other witnesses, does testing enhance the reliability of the opinion offered by the expert? Some have expressed concern that the expert testimony of mental health experts in child custody litigation neither assists the trier of fact nor offers reliable opinion based upon scientifically valid data (see Hagen, 1997). This does not appear to be the direction courts are taking, and there is a trend toward applying scientific principles to child custody evaluations (see Gould, 1998).

OBJECTIVE PERSONALITY TESTS

A vast majority of custody evaluations that involve testing involve the MMPI-II, and thus attorneys are more likely to be familiar with this instrument. Attorneys expect to be required to address the use of this instrument if a matter is litigated (Karp & Karp, 2003).

Objective tests are inherently attractive to attorneys for a number of reasons. The scales are known and well-documented. While the MMPI was not originally created to evaluate either a custody litigant population or to address parenting skills and deficits, there has been some research to address how these instruments have been used with custody populations and what the results have been (Bathurst, Gottfried, & Gottfried, 1997). Attorneys who regularly practice family law will likely be more familiar with testing than family law judicial officers before whom they appear, particularly if the family law bench is a "rotation," as it is in many jurisdictions. It is likely that the only explanation for the test results the judicial officer will get will be from the report itself (unless a litigant can afford to, and chooses to, pay for the evaluator or another mental health professional to testify) and from the attorneys. The scales have colloquially familiar names such as the "hysteria" scale, the "paranoia" scale, and the "lie" scale. While family law attorneys may know that the names of these scales do not necessarily correlate to the colloquial meaning of the words "hysteria," "paranoia," and "lie," it is less likely that a judicial officer will have that understanding; thus the results can be explained in a context that sheds the best light on the client. Most importantly, an objective test allows the attorney to have a sense that he or she is "comparing apples to apples," because the litigants are being given the same questions, the same testing conditions, and are being scored by the same person (or computer) using the same criteria. Objective tests are accepted by attorneys as generally more valid and reliable than projective tests.

The danger here is that the psychometric test results are generally incorporated in the body of the overall custody evaluation report. Unless the parties have separate experts to whom the raw data and test answers are provided, or the attorney who received the data by court order has a means of interpreting the data, the only thing a judicial officer will know are those portions of the psychometric tests which the evaluator deemed relevant or significant enough to incorporate in the evaluation report. While it is possible that objective test results that confound the observational and interview data may be included in the report (and is likely if there are significant anomalies which require explanation), most of the objective test results which will be in a report are those that either confirm or direct the analysis of the evaluator.

PROJECTIVE PERSONALITY TESTS

While no individual projective test is used as often as the MMPI-2 in custody evaluations, many, if not most, evaluators use some projective tests or a combination of them. These include the Rorschach (ink blot), Thematic Apperception Test (TAT), Sentence Completion Test, Draw-A-Person Test, and House-Tree-Person Test. These tests require the test taker to provide more free-form responses to intentionally ambiguous criteria, from which the evaluator draws conclusions and makes assessments.

Projective tests probably offer more information about a test taker's thinking (complex vs. simple, for example) by allowing the test taker to create the answer rather than requiring a forced choice. Mental health professionals trained to administer these tests have criteria by which to analyze the responses, but even within those criteria, there is a lot of room for subjective interpretation.

There is a lot of room for cross-examination when evaluators have relied strongly on projective tests in drawing conclusions about parenting. There is room for criticism in the understanding of either the test taker or the evaluator of the task, the response, the interpretation, or the circumstances of the testing. Even the timing of the testing, or the timing of the analysis of the results (i.e., before or after clinical interview, before or after receiving information from critical collateral sources) can affect the results.

INTELLIGENCE TESTS

Few attorneys take exception to the administration of intelligence tests in the context of a custody evaluation if there is reason to do so. However, if intelligence sufficient to understand the process, meaningfully participate in the evaluation, and understand and implement parenting duties is not in question, even the administration of intelligence tests to parents may not be appropriate. Most attorneys will not be concerned about the administration of age-appropriate and/or developmentally appropriate intelligence tests to children in the context of a custody evaluation. Most realize that it is important for an evaluator to gauge a child's understanding of the process and ability to meaningfully participate. In cases where a child's cognitive abilities are at issue, or the parents disagree on this, intelligence tests for children may be critical to the evaluation process and appropriate recommendations which serve the interests of the child.

INSTRUMENTS WHICH ARE NOT "TESTS"

Arguably, instruments which are not "tests" may provide the best, most relevant information to an evaluator. Surveys and questionnaires which directly address parenting skills, concerns, values, and levels of understanding may be most relevant and provide the evaluator the most accurate picture of a parent's ability to parent the child in question. Because the instrument will not necessarily have undergone critical review and replication, it may not have the same inherent reliability as an instrument that has. If an evaluator uses such an instrument, it is still important to have it reviewed by other professionals to assure that the questions are not ambiguous, that they are easily understood, and that the results are not analyzed to generalize beyond that which the instrument purports to measure. Such instruments may be best used to generate hypotheses and to "start the discussion" but should not be used as the sole or even the primary basis upon which to draw conclusions.

SHOULD ATTORNEYS OR JUDICIAL OFFICERS REQUEST CERTAIN TESTS?

The extent to which an expert's evaluation is requested can be directed by the Court's order. The order may be based on the specific relief requested by the moving party, the Court's need for information bearing on the best interests of the child(ren), or something broader than the former and more discreet than the latter. Attorneys and judicial officers have the ability, jointly, to craft an order directing the evaluator to address the evaluation in specific ways.

Sometimes, maybe most times, there is a need to limit the evaluation based on financial constraints, time constraints or both. If the attorneys and the Court do not believe that testing would assist the Court, the evaluator, or the parties in assessing the issues before the Court, why require testing? In some cases there are specific issues which almost call out for testing: Is there an issue of intellectual capacity and should intelligence tests be performed? Is there an issue of abuse and should the CAPI or something like it be administered? Are there allegations of insufficient parenting abilities or understanding and should the PASS be given?

There is a certain symmetry here when evaluators, in an abundance of caution, administer tests for which there are no presenting issues, and attorneys or judicial officers have little interest in tests unless they serve to get to the heart of the "problem" faster.

CONCLUSION

Attorneys and child custody evaluators have similarities in that they both interview litigants (sometimes the same litigants) and obtain information that will ultimately serve as the basis for a settlement or the presentation to the Court. Attorneys' style of interview tends to be fact-driven and interrogatory. Evaluators' styles tend to be open-ended and exploratory. Each professional is a product of his or her training. Attorneys can compare what an evaluator does by interviewing litigants or witnesses directly to what the attorney does in interviewing those same people.

Psychological testing is an area in which attorneys and child custody evaluators do not have confluence. Attorneys don't do anything that is "like" testing, although most attorneys have gone through plenty of tests over the course of their academic careers. The attorney's orientation to testing will, therefore, be by comparing what is being done *to* the client to what has been done *to* the attorney, not what the attorney *does*.

Testing results are also perceived by attorneys as "evidence." They are the support used by the evaluator to back up the conclusions reached by the evaluator. Attorneys do one of two things with "evidence": they embrace it if it is consistent with their clients' position, or they rebut it if it is not. Evaluators should understand that, while most child custody cases will settle prior to trial, for those which do not, attorneys are trained to question and test each piece of evidence to place the client in the best possible light under the circumstances. For this reason it is incumbent on a custody evaluator to critically select those instruments which the evaluator can justify using in a particular case under the given circumstances, with the expectation that the evaluator will be asked to do just that.

NOTES

1. In the interest of complete disclosure, I do hold a Bachelor of Arts in psychology from the University of California, Irvine.

2. By "testing," I am including both purportedly objective instruments such as the MMPI-2 and MCMI-II as well as subjective instruments, such as the PASS and PSI.

3. The Court generally only appoints an expert when the matter requires information that is beyond common knowledge. California *Evidence Code*, Section 730, under which most experts are appointed by the Court in California, for example, provides:

> When it appears to the court, at any time before or during the trial of an action, that expert evidence is or may be required by the court or by any party to the action, the court on its own motion or on motion of any party may appoint one or more experts to investigate, to render a report as may be ordered by the court, and to testify as an expert at the trial of the action relative to the fact or matter as to which the expert evidence is or may be required. The court may fix the compensation for these services, if any, rendered by any person appointed under this section, in addition to any service as a witness, at the amount as seems reasonable to the court. Nothing in this section shall be construed to permit a person to perform any act for which a license is required unless the person holds the appropriate license to lawfully perform that act.

Similarly, *Federal Rules of Evidence*, Rule 702, after which many states have tailored their rules of evidence, provides:

> If scientific, technical, or other specialized knowledge will assist the trier of fact to understand the evidence or to determine a fact in issue, a witness qualified as an expert by knowledge, skill, experience, training, or education, may testify thereto in the form of an opinion or otherwise, if (1) the testimony is based upon sufficient facts or data, (2) the testimony is the product of reliable principles and methods, and (3) the witness has applied the principles and methods reliably to the facts of the case.

4. For example, the Bender-Gestalt was used by only 9% of respondents to the survey, but those respondents used it 82% of the time. Likewise, the PASS was used by only 8% of respondents but those respondents used it in 94% of their child custody evaluations.

REFERENCES

Ackerman, M. J., & Ackerman, M. (1997). Custody evaluation practices: A survey of experienced professionals (Revisited). *Professional Psychology: Research and Practice, 28*(2), 137-145.

Bathurst, K., Gottfried, A. W., & Gottfried, A. E. (1997). Normative data for the MMPI-2 in child custody litigation. *Psychological Assessment, 9,* 205-211.

CAL. EVID. CODE § 730.

FED. R. EVID. 702.

Gould, J. (1998). *Conducting scientifically crafted child custody evaluations.* Thousand Oaks, CA: Sage Publications.

Hagen, M. (1997). *Whores of the court: The fraud of psychiatric testimony and the rape of American justice.* New York: Regan Books.

Karp, C. L., & Karp, L. (2003). *MMPI.* Retrieved August 18, 2004, from http://aaml. org/MMPI.htm

Keilin, W. G., & Bloom, L. J. (1986). Child custody evaluation practices: A survey of experienced professionals. *Professional Psychology: Research and Practice, 17,* 338-346.

THE USE OF THE MMPI-2
AND THE RORSCHACH
IN THE CHILD CUSTODY CONTEXT

How Can the MMPI-2
Help Child Custody Examiners?

Alex B. Caldwell, Jr.

Alex B. Caldwell, Jr. obtained his PhD in 1958 from the University of Minnesota. He is Clinical Professor Emeritus, U.C.L.A. Departments of Psychology and Psychiatry, where he has been on the faculty for 45 years. He has taught MMPI interpretation across the country and internationally and has received numerous awards for his work. He created a uniquely detailed and specific MMPI/MMPI-2 interpretation system and formed Caldwell Report to make the results professionally available. He regularly consults with mental health professionals on related issues, occasionally testifying when the test results are crucial to litigation.

Address correspondence to: Alex B. Caldwell, PhD, Caldwell Report, 5839 Green Valley Circle, Suite 203, Culver City, CA 90230 (E-mail: Caldwell.alex@comcast.net).

The author would like to express special appreciation to Stuart Greenberg for careful readings of drafts of this paper and for many very constructive suggestions. Also much gratitude goes to Roger Greene for the various analyses that he generously contributed to this article.

[Haworth co-indexing entry note]: "How Can the MMPI-2 Help Child Custody Examiners?" Caldwell, Jr., Alex B. Co-published simultaneously in *Journal of Child Custody* (The Haworth Press, Inc.) Vol. 2, No. 1/2, 2005, pp. 83-117; and: *Psychological Testing in Child Custody Evaluations* (ed: James R. Flens, and Leslie Drozd) The Haworth Press, Inc., 2005, pp. 83-117. Single or multiple copies of this article are available for a fee from The Haworth Document Delivery Service [1-800-HAWORTH, 9:00 a.m. - 5:00 p.m. (EST). E-mail address: docdelivery@haworthpress.com].

SUMMARY. The paper explores what hypotheses we can infer from the MMPI-2 regarding parenting behaviors and what are the significant limitations on our inferences. The first half looks at the MMPI-2 from a child custody view: is there a foundation from which the test can generate expectations regarding five basic issues, i.e., the quality of attachment and bonding, potential for antisocial behavior, temper control, alienation of affection, and chemical abuse and dependence. The second half looks at custody from an MMPI-2 point of view: what is the range of possible variables that will generate useful hypotheses regarding parent-child interactions and family systems? The effects of the circumstances of litigation on score elevations are considered, including recommended limits as to how much elevation can be dismissed as only contextual. "Occasion validity" (are these scores trustworthy) is distinguished from "Attribute validity" (what do the scores tell us). The clinical application of an objective interpretation system is discussed, including the courtroom credibility of explicit convergent validity. *[Article copies available for a fee from The Haworth Document Delivery Service: 1-800-HAWORTH. E-mail address: <docdelivery@ haworthpress.com> Website: <http://www.HaworthPress.com> © 2005 by The Haworth Press, Inc. All rights reserved.]*

KEYWORDS. MMPI, child custody

There have been many responses to the basic question of whether the MMPI-2 *can* help or not in child custody evaluations. Some clinicians have asserted flatly that it should not be used. They argue that the test was developed on severe psychiatric patients and not on custody clients, so it is simply inappropriate. Others have emphasized that there is no established body of parent-child MMPI or MMPI-2 research to cite in support of a custodial opinion or recommendations. In contrast to these arguments is the near universal use of the test in custody examinations, estimated to be around 90% by Ackerman and Ackerman (1997) in both their data and those of Keilin and Bloom (1986). This use does not prove validity, of course, but it suggests a widespread belief that it can potentially be of help.

This paper was written to elaborate and extend an approach to the MMPI-2 that I believe many clinicians have been following, at least in general concepts. The common goal is to generate as many workable hypotheses and as much useful information from the test scores and profile patterns as is reasonably possible. In pursuit of this, I will discuss a variety of parenting-relevant variables that I believe can be estimated, with satisfactory accuracy, using available scores from the MMPI-2. I will start by looking at the MMPI-2 from the custody perspective, i.e., can the test generate practical hypotheses in examining the so-called Big Five: attachment, antisocial behavior, temper control, alienation, and chemical abuse and dependence. This will be followed by an analysis of custody from an MMPI-2 perspective, what are the range and variety of topics about which the MMPI-2 can help focus our examinations. These are the component parts of the custody report I have developed: a discussion of several parental role-modeling variables, and then by other variables that I believe to be potentially informative regarding significant aspects of parenting behaviors and family systems. I will discuss the issue of situational pressures and temporal fluctuations in the context of adversarial custody disputes later, as the influence functions across the variables. Lastly, I will discuss normative and validity questions regarding the interpretive custody report I have developed.

FROM THE CUSTODY-PARENTING PERSPECTIVE: CAN THE MMPI-2 SPEAK TO THE MAJOR ISSUES?

Attachment/Bonding

A basic judgment in a child custody examination is of the depth and dependability of the parent-child bonding, the attachment from which the love flows, the solid anchor of caring, and the development of the child's own eventual capacity to bond to others as an adult. All of the recurrently listed descriptors of people with primary elevations on scale 4-Pd (the multifaceted and complex behavioral shifts in the direction of asocial and amoral psychopathy) relate to problems of impaired bonding: egocentric, impulsive, demanding, manipulative, callous, uses others as objects, financial irresponsibility, etc. (e.g., see Gilberstadt & Duker, 1965, pp. 57-60). If one posits (1) a genetic vulnerability, (2) unwantedness in infancy, childhood, and possibly in utero, and (3) chronic and intense strife in the childhood home as all contributing substantially to elevations on scale 4-Pd, then one understandably has a quite broad construct (Caldwell, 2001a). Its expressions are very diverse, from persistently problematic relationships to failures of conscience to the callous side of criminal activity. I consider it to be a single, broad construct with expressions that range from highly subtle and disguised to flagrantly evident. For further comments, see Caldwell (2001a).

The behavioral continuum identified by the Pd scale can be defined in part by the characteristics of those with extreme elevations. Keeping in mind that the population and its contextual demands are radically different, Megargee and Bohn (1979) provide descriptions of mostly two- and three-scale code types on federal prisoners, and this was updated for the MMPI-2 by Megargee, Carbonell, Bohn, and Sliger in 2001. Of their 10 male types (nine of which replicated among female inmates in 2001), their "Delta" group was defined by a singular, high spike on scale 4-Pd. This group produced a sharp picture of the extreme of this scale. Among numerous related qualities, these subjects came from the most unfavorable childhood backgrounds the authors had encountered among their prisoner types with the highest or second highest scores on lifelong attributes of "Family incohesiveness," "Parent-child tension," and "Social deviance of the siblings" and almost no socializing or nurturing parental or family influences (pp. 253-254). In prison they bonded to no one, they were assaultive when thwarted (although not actively seeking out violence), and they left prison notably unchanged. Their central 4-Pd core is a lifelong inability to bond. Note that the heritability factor for 4-Pd in the Minnesota twin data (DiLalla, Carey, Gottesman, & Bouchard, 1996) was just over 60%, which is directly consistent with the markedly impaired bonding throughout their families.

It should be emphasized that depth of attachment problems come in all degrees; in the normal range it may be no more than an unsatisfying adjustment in a particular area of the person's life, e.g., a bit too much focus on the person's self-interests and ambitions to the disregard or subtle occasions of indifference to or emotional neglect of children and spouses, an occasional coldness in personal or work relationships, or just instances of more than expected egocentrism and of taking advantage of others. Low scorers have been described as having notably stable long-term attachments and as sexually unassertive (Meehl, 1951). Drake and Oetting (1959) observed low scores on scale 4-Pd to be "indicative of conformity with the mores of the social group" (p. 22). Thus, impairments of bonding and attachment are well assessed by scale 4-Pd across a wide range of levels.

For interpretive purposes, it should be considered that the 4-Pd scale is strongly affected by the revised norms for the MMPI-2. That is, the same raw score (and no items were deleted from 4-Pd in the revision process) yields a *T*-score eight to ten points lower throughout the range from the mid-T-40s to the T-70s for women and up to T-90 for men, and the differences are only slightly smaller above those ranges. The typical nine-point downward shift throughout this working range, consistently more than any other scale in this range, often leads to a substantial underestimation of the importance of a 4-Pd score both absolutely and via displacement to a lower rank in the code. In hindsight there appears to have been an overrepresentation of 4-Pd in the volunteer sample (Caldwell, 1997b), so in comparison to them everyone looks less disposed to 4-Pd behaviors.

It is difficult to ascertain how much of a custody litigant's 4-Pd score reflects state versus trait characteristics. Obviously, custody litigants are in the very midst of the severing of a life-central attachment, and a sizable proportion of them are having it severed against their wishes. Further, they are also confronted with the potential forced disruption of much of their parent-child attachments. From a more trait, or chronic, perspective, a custody litigant whose attachments are to whatever degree unstable or shallow is not going to volunteer that that is the case, very possibly trying hard to impress the examiner with the opposite. The estimation of this issue is then from other sources and primarily historical data unless there are obvious lapses of "being there for a child" in the person's narration (which can go surprisingly easily unnoticed by the self-justified narrator) or be otherwise evident in the parent-child interaction. Thus, it is difficult to know from the MMPI-2 scores alone what a prominent 4-Pd elevation–mildly to moderately elevated–most meaningfully reflects: chronic attachment problems, primarily the acute state of currently conflict-reduced attachments to the spouse and children, rage at the other spouse's attachment-destroying actions and litigation, or new attachment fears that the litigant is facing as a possible outcome of the legal process. In any case, an elevated scale 4-Pd generates a variety of hypotheses with regard to attachment that are critical to examine further.

Potential for Antisocial Behavior

Otto, Buffington, and Edens (2003) stressed that one of the most consistent findings regarding child development has been that parents who show antisocial behaviors tend to have children who show a variety of significant adjustment problems. These typically are externalizing actions such as aggression and delinquency. They cited that, "when predicting antisocial behavior at age 32, Farrington (2000) reported that having a criminally-convicted parent when the individual was between ages eight and ten was the single strongest predictor among a host of risk factors (odd ratio = 3.7)" (p. 31). Otto also stressed that the effects of antisocial parental behaviors are apt to reach well into the adulthood of their children.

The aggression, irresponsibility, deceitfulness, general non-conformity, impulsivity, and lack of remorse that define Antisocial Personality Disorder (DSM-IV; American Psychiatric Association, 1994) are also the prototypic descriptors for profiles that code as "4-8-9" (the three highest scales in any order; the tendency is still there although the picture is more mixed if these three scales are first, second, and fourth or first, third, and fourth). These three scales were also the three specific "activators" of juvenile delinquency in the extensive longitudinal studies of Hathaway and Monachesi (1963).

Again defining the extreme, Megargee et al.'s (2001) "Foxtrot" code type, with an elevated 9-4-8 mean code, identifies prison predators who need to be segregated because of their exploitative and abusive danger to other inmates. Interpretively, the Pd adds the callousness, the Ma adds the pressured impulsivity and drives the aggression, and the Sc turns it all mean or even sadistic (e.g., Megargee's Foxtrot data and the cases coded 489–in any order and especially if coded 4896–in the Atlas [Hathaway & Meehl, 1951]); at the extreme it can involve the pleasure of being in control of the cruelty rather than the helpless victim one was as a child). In contrast, at mild elevations (e.g., around *T*-60 on the MMPI-2) one sees people who manage adequately but at the expense of less than optimal long-term gratification in one or more areas of their lives. There may be some emotional exploitation or subtle intimidation of those around them, occasional deceits and manipulations, a heightened degree of sexual aggressiveness, and fewer self-restraints than others would wish.

Bosquet and Egeland (2000) studied parenting behaviors of a sample of women in a low-income housing project (92% unmarried) according to their scores on the Antisocial Practices (ASP) content scale of the MMPI-2. When their children were 13 and 24 months old, the mothers with elevations on ASP at *T*-70 or higher (45 of 141, 32% of their subjects) were observed to be significantly less understanding and more hostile and harsh in their parenting styles than mothers in their two other groups from the same setting. They demonstrated higher levels of insensitive and angry parenting behavior during stressful laboratory tasks, were more physically and antisocially coercive, and demonstrated more physically abusive behaviors in both home and laboratory settings.

Unfortunately this data is of almost no *direct* applicability to custody litigation in that these women were typically of less than high school education, and they were very open and candid with elevated scores on scale F and low scores on scales L and especially K (directly opposite to the great majority of litigating parents). For example, custody litigants taking the MMPI-2 do *not* say true (the scored response) to ASP items such as that they would sneak into a movie theater without paying if they could get away with it, that nearly anyone would lie to keep out of trouble, or that they have hoped that criminals would get away with it if they are really clever. Of 554 unselected female child custody litigants (the group is described in the "As compared to what norms?" section below), 79% scored below *T*-50 on ASP, 95% below *T*-60, and 99% below *T*-70; only five individuals of the 554 exceeded *T*-70. Even slightly fewer of a sample of 550 male litigants reached each of these thresholds. Thus, the *T*-70 criterion of Bosquet and Egeland (2000) is an effective "no-show" among custody litigants, although high ASP scores would be highly meaningful in the rare instances when they do occur.

I believe there is, however, an important *indirect* applicability of this data. The MMPI-2 mean profile of their high ASP subjects was '98-*456*, a very distinct 9'84 if the (approximate mean) raw scores are transposed onto the original MMPI norms. This is, of course, the same combination of 4, 8, and 9 discussed above, and the elevated ASP group mean profile of Bosquet and Egeland (2000) was clearly different from their two comparison groups, who were drawn from the same social, economic, and residential circumstances. It should be remembered that the K scale and K-correction were originally added to the MMPI in order to minimize errors of overinterpretation when the person was self-critical as well as errors of underinterpretation when the person responded defensively and the elevations were suppressed; there is a striking contrast between the unsophisticated low-K candor of the Bosquet and Egeland (2000) group and the typically much more educated and defensive custody litigants. Note that all three of scales 4, 8, and 9 are K-corrected.[1] The K of persons in custody disputes reflects both their characteristic degree of self-favorableness *plus* the defensiveness added by the context. That extra amount of "contextual K" generates a larger K correction than is standard for the "normal subject" norms. On the other hand, it may also be the case that the same contextual demands to disavow pathology also reduce the clinical scale raw scores, thus making the *T*-score appropriate (our best estimation) even when it is almost all K-correction. Thus, whether antisociality is defined by high numbers of ASP content scale items in open and self-critical subjects or is defined by variations of the K-corrected 4-8-9 codes, an antisocial response pattern in a relatively straightforward *or* in a guarded and defensive litigant urges careful examination.

What is possibly surprising is that the occurrences of primarily 4-8-9 scale elevations are hardly more prevalent in the custody cases than in the MMPI-2 normative sample. It seems likely that high school dropout and undependable to poor financial management would operate as selective factors against being able to invest tens of thousands of dollars in custody litigation. In any case, my experience is that well-defined antisocial personalities are relatively rare events in the custody litigation arena, but that when they do occur (even just a little over *T*-55) and the behaviors and attitudes are clinically confirmed, then the indications of antisocial potential appear clearly adverse for parenting. As with any hypotheses generated from the MMPI-2, indications of such antisocial potentials would need to be confirmed from non-test information. But high-K antisocial litigants can be very facile in rationalizing and externalizing any past problematic behaviors or interpersonally destructive actions, so their self-justifications should be taken with great caution. If confirmed, antisocial tendencies are like an infectious social disease that quickly distorts family systems and damages relationships all around.

Temper Control

Temper outbursts, and domestic violence at the extreme, appear to be more a matter of code types and pattern effects than of the scales individually, both as to the likelihood of problematic or destructive tantrums and as to the nature of the outbursts. The codes most typically associated with temper control issues are 46/64, 49/94, and 69/96.[2] The other crucial pattern is comprised of the variations of the 34/43 code. At least moderately elevated (or less elevated but notably defensive) profiles coded 46 and 64 are typically a good fit to Paranoid Personality Disorder (DSM-IV; American Psychiatric Association, 1994) or occasionally to Delusional Disorder–effectively the same pathology–without a generalized cognitive disorganization. Often acting as tyrants in the home, they protect against coercion of their wills by becoming the coercers. Relative to the low frequency of overtly abusive tempers across all custody litigants, I see 46/64 as equally or more directly alerting as to the possibility of abusive temper outbursts than any other code type.[3] There may be a tendency in the 46/64 individual to excuse the other person until too much unfairness or hurtful punishment leaves the person with "no choice" but to react. Even then there may be a denial of any personal anger, only a justification that the offending person must be stopped from hurting others. Thus, when "forced" to act by too much unjust treatment or unnecessary pain, the reaction is to put an immediate stop to what is intolerable, whatever that takes.

For code 96/69, there is a low threshold for a vigilant arousal, and provocative challenges to their expectations and personal security quickly put them on edge. There is a reluctance to take action for which others could end up retaliating, except for what they perceive as "coercive" or relatively extreme circumstances. But the threat of their anger can be strongly and persistently intimidating. For code 49/94, the problem is primarily poor frustration tolerance, especially the rejection of quid pro quo expectations, and then for an eruption of anger when blocked or thwarted. The higher the 4-Pd, the more tenuous the controls; as noted, beware the underestimation of elevation on 4-Pd and its associated behaviors in the MMPI-2 norms. In psychiatric inpatient samples, subjects with elevated 86, 89, and overlapping profiles can be dangerous at unpredictable moments and in unexpected ways, but these patterns are quite rare among custody litigating parents.

Those with mildly to moderately elevated 43/34 codes typically deny feeling anger or hostility, and they appear to hold in or repress resentments until too many negative feelings come out "all at once." For example, the 34/43 clinic patient (usually requiring an at least moderately elevated profile) may grab an upsetting or too-critical person by the throat, and, if sufficiently enraged or inebriated, squeeze tragically hard (in the custody context this is a low probability event that is *not* "more likely than not," but an alert to a possible reaction to a perception of extreme provocation). In parallel studies, Davis and Sines (1971) and Persons and Marks (1971) showed that these and other behavioral characteristics were the same in association with the 34/43 code whether the person was being seen in the clinic or in prison. A parallel carryover to the custody context has not been independently demonstrated, although clinical cases are quite consistent with this. The longstanding denial and overcontrol of hostility in this group is typically pushed toward the extreme by what is effectively an almost absolute prohibition against admitting it in the custody litigation context. For example, over 80% of custody litigants say true to the item: "I have very few quarrels with members of my family," despite their life circumstances (Greenberg, 2004).

A preliminary inspection of limited available data suggested that the scales just discussed are also the most pertinent to domestic violence, an extension of the control conflict issues that underlie intra-familial temper outbursts. My present opinion is that, relative to other profiles, those profiles with scale 6 highest or second highest are in the longer term potentially the most dangerous; when they feel "forced to react," they can do so in extreme ways. High 6-Pa profiles that have a distinct "6-8 V" configuration (off-target beliefs or "twisted" ideation in the absence of corresponding uncertainty) and with values of 70 or more, especially if over 80, on the Goldberg Neurotic-Psychotic Index[4] (Goldberg, 1965) probably mark those who are the *relatively* greatest risks for dangerous domestic violence. Although usually short of being fixedly delusional, these latter often seem to be operating on a different "wavelength" from other people; they start from different premises or beliefs and consistently make idiosyncratic interpretations of the meaning of important events. Assault and, at the rare extreme, homicide by those with 43/34 variants seems more chancy, depending more on the circumstances of the moment than on planning or scheming. The convergence of one of these patterns with a history of explosive or realistically scary temper outbursts would, of course, be the relatively strongest alert to a careful consideration of such a risk in one's recommendations. Any test-based prediction of dangerous or violent behavior (rare events) must always be made with caution, however; we must keep in mind the dictum that past behavior is the best predictor of future behavior.

Additionally, we are much more willing to believe men to be violent than women. This expectation is confounded, however, by the fact that it is also men who more often report feeling situationally "persecuted" by spouses who are divorcing them and by the spouses' attorneys who are perceived to be holding visitation with the children hostage in exchange for a generous financial settlement. The epitome of the examination dilemma is that a false allegation of domestic violence or child sexual abuse can contribute in the accused to elevations on scales 4-Pd and 6-Pa and possibly to the very 6-4 code that is associated with someone who is suspect to commit such acts. The prudent examiner must never forget the obligation to consider *all* data from *all* reasonable perspectives (Committee on Ethical Guidelines for Forensic Psychologists, 1991; Greenberg, 2004; Shuman & Greenberg, 2003).

Alienation of Affection

Although one can never say from the MMPI-2 alone that an alienation of the other parent's affection has occurred, I do believe it is possible to identify characteristics that make a parent reactive to such issues. In my experience, this has consistently been anchored in scale 6-Pa, both as total scale score and with particular weight on the Pa3 subscale, moral righteousness. This is an expression of the general scale 6-Pa disposition to dichotomize others as either "for me or against me." (If one is already strongly disposed to see others as "for me or against me," then the reality that the opposing litigant's attorney *is* "against me" only intensifies the issue. But in many respects this is the opposing counsel's job and obligation, unless perhaps restrained by his/her own client.) The high-scale 6-Pa parent can become acutely sensitized to a child's comments that favor or praise the former spouse. This may then lead to a perception that the other spouse is attempting to alienate the child's affections, and indeed the alienating spouse is often the first to accuse the other spouse of alienating behaviors. The "self-protective" efforts to counteract this perception can then have directly alienating effects against the other parent. Thus, the alienating efforts and actions are likely to derive from sincere perceptions, which may be anywhere from accurate to seriously inaccurate, that what the other spouse is doing must be countered.

Such a sequence may, of course, never have been triggered. The high 6-Pa person may have a greater than base rate likelihood to feel held in a trap by the other parent in a disadvantageous position with respect to how little she or he can offer the children, tending to incline them toward the other parent. Nevertheless, the test indications mark a readiness to make "for me/against me" perceptions; the actual occurrence of alienating demands and pressures is then a matter for clinical determination. Test respondents who are low on this variable would be relatively more apt to see it as important for the child or children to have positive identifications with each parent and that an overwhelmingly negative image of either of one's parents is potentially quite problematic for the child's developing self-identity. If "My mommy (or daddy) is a terrible person" is drilled into a child, then the child can easily wonder, "What does that make me?" This issue might be helpful and constructive for the potentially alienating parent to be aware of, although the balance between reality and self-serving judgments in dealing with this can be precarious.

Chemical Abuse and Dependence

The interest of the court is in the exposure to current parental chemical consumption and abuse that can jeopardize the status of a child. Courts do not typically penalize people who have been consistently abstinent. In contrast, the best of the MMPI and MMPI-2 alcoholism scales, the MacAndrew (1965) Alcoholism scale (*MAC*, now *MAC-R* on the MMPI-2), was developed to assess the relative presence or absence of a long-term disposition to become *dependent* on alcohol (as contrasted to intermittent alcoholic binges). This disposition has been shown to be present well before the development of problems with alcohol: Kammeier, Hoffman, and Loper (1973) demonstrated elevated *MAC* scores in entering liberal arts college freshmen at the University of Minnesota an average of about 13 years prior to detox treatment. Chang, Caldwell, and Moss (1973) showed that *MAC* scores did not go down after a year in a California Department of Corrections facility for alcoholics. The scale also marks a vulnerability to difficulties with agents that relieve mood distress such as heroin, cocaine, and other opiates, but it is of little if any use with such addictions as tobacco, marijuana, psychedelics, stimulants, overeating or other idiosyncratic food habits, etc. The *MAC* and *MAC-R* have worked less well in medical populations (Malinchoc, Offord, Colligan, & Morse, 1994). I am not aware of any direct research on the scale in custody litigants, although given the unusual subtlety of the scale items, there is no obvious reason to expect it to work poorly in the latter population.

The potential utility of the scale then is to estimate at least relative degrees of vulnerability to abuse chemical agents. For example, when one parent calls the other an alcoholic and the other minimizes or denies it, the *MAC* score helps weigh the extent of follow-up; if the raw score is at or over 24, especially if it is at or over 28, then such an accusation should be taken quite seriously, but if it is below 24, more so if below 20 to 22, then the accusation is likely to be exaggerated (except possibly for just binging). There are other problems, of course, in terms of false positives and false negatives. Along with the fact that no such scale is perfect, false positives may be due to decisions not to drink, e.g., strict religious beliefs, a parent of the litigant in question who had dreadful drinking habits, an early and acutely embarrassing drunken episode, etc., which can lead to a firm, lifelong determination not to drink. False negatives include episodic or binge drinking patterns (as noted, the *MAC* is primarily about daily dependence), a surge of alcohol consumption in a period of great stress or depression, or other situational fluctuations as well as, of course, whatever test misses may occur in either direction. But scores below 20 are rarely (and below 16 very rarely) associated with chronic daily dependence on alcohol or opiates. With such a low score, I would recommend treating an accusation of excessive drinking with skepticism in following it up in the examination.

To protect against some occasional false negatives, I give some weight to the Addiction Admission Scale (*AAS*; Weed, Butcher, McKenna, & Ben-Porath, 1992), this being the set of MMPI-2 items that explicitly report problems with chemical agents. There are some cases with *MAC* scores a little below raw 24 that are picked up just by looking at the *AAS* item count or asking about the extensively overlapping Critical Items. These items would also flag a careful inquiry into the circumstances and habits of chemical intake.

FROM THE MMPI-2 PERSPECTIVE: WHAT IS THE RANGE OF POSSIBLE CONTRIBUTIONS TO OUR UNDERSTANDING OF INDIVIDUAL PARENTS AND FAMILY SYSTEMS?

Table 1 lists the parenting and custody-determination relevant variables that I believe can be assessed from the test. Note that after validity, they are sequenced from more general personality attributes that could substantially affect family systems to specific parent-child issues. Five of the last six variables correspond to the five basic areas of parenting already discussed. I will review these approximately in order, starting with the four validity-related variables as a single group. Discussing all of the 26 listed variables would, however, go far beyond the available space. I will discuss selected variables that bear most strongly on custody examinations. Descriptions of all of the variables with comments on the most contributory scale weights are available from Caldwell Report (Caldwell, 2001b).

The Boundaries of "Occasion" Validity

"Validity" is already an overextended term. We talk and write reports about whether this particular individual test outcome is "valid" with practical implications that are notably different from our thinking and writing about our research-focused types of validity, e.g., construct, face, concurrent, predictive, convergent, etc. For example, the questions as to whether scale 4-Pd measures what it is supposed to–and what *is* that?–are very different from whether or not this person mangled the test and produced invalid and useless results. I am using "Occasion" validity to identify answers to the question, *Can we depend on the results obtained on this particular occasion*? The questions as to behavioral outcomes and construct meaning are discussed subsequently as "Attrib-

TABLE 1. MMPI-2 Variables Potentially Relevant to Parenting and Custody

Test Validity

    1. Morally proper responding

    2. Subtle intentional minimizing

    3. Atypical and deviant responding

    4. Genuinely positive self-esteem and self-confidence

Personal Style

    5. Cheerful vs. guilt issues, depressed

    6. Energy level: slow pace vs. high energy

    7. Denying and repressive vs. frank and candid

    8. Level of health concerns

    9. Awareness of his/her potential for interpersonal provocation

    10. Oriented toward own agenda vs. incorporates others' interests

    11. Social shyness vs. extroversion

    12. Level of day-to-day organization

Adult Role Modeling

    13. General emotional threshold

    14. Potential for self-centered actions vs. other centered reactions

    15. Externalizing vs. internalizing

    16. Linear focus under stress vs. strained reasoning

    17. Interpersonal functioning: anxious vs. self-comfortable

    18. Ability to forgive and forget

Control Issues

    19. Under-controlled and ascendant vs. self-constrained and rule-bound

    20. Low vs. high decision control needs

    21. Potential for antisocial conduct

    22. Possible temper control problems

    23. Vulnerability to chemical dependency

Parent-Child Interaction Potentials

    24. Quality of parent-child bonding

    25. Risk of alienation of affection

    26. Presentation as parent: role-played virtue vs. sincerity

ute" validity. An explicit differentiation between "Occasion" validity and "Attribute" validity facilitates both hypothesis generation and examination as well as subsequent reports and testimony.

The MMPI-2 has more different scales to help answer Occasion validity questions than any other personality test ever created. Scales L, F, and K date back to the early 1940s, but they have always had troublesome ambiguities as to the sources of their elevations. Is L elevated by a sincere moralistic properness or by an unwillingness to report "anything that can be used against me?" Is F elevated by genuine psychopathology and severity, or is it elevated by exaggeration and "faking sick"? Is K elevated by a high level of sophistication in a sincere respondent, or is it a measure of "faking healthy," a relatively subtle, deliberate minimizing of one's problems and conflicts? In each of these cases the first alternative is the possibility of a subtle but extensive biasing of the scores in the absence of any deliberate desire or significant conscious attempt to do so, called "self-deception" by Paulhus (1984). Each second alternative is then a willful attempt to alter the test results in some desired direction, or "impression management" in Paulhus' terms. Greene (2000a) uses "over-reporting" and "under-reporting" in a more generic sense without specifying the presence or absence of an intent to distort.

Can we tell these apart? Such a separation is often guesswork on the basis of scales L, F, and K alone. A too-general presumption of deliberate impression management can easily lead to mistaken rejections of test data when the respondent actually was sincere. I believe that we can relieve those uncertainties to a substantial and very helpful degree. Two "fake good" scales that were developed on the basis of instructions to consciously distort one's responses in self-favorable ways have consistently emerged from the meta-analyses as both sensitive and specific (e.g., see Baer & Miller, 2002). These are the Social Desirability scale (Sd) of Wiggins (1959) and the Malingering Positive scale (Mp) of Cofer, Chance, and Judson (1949).[5] Although they correlate +.75 (on the 52,543 cases in the Caldwell Data set developed by Roger Greene; Caldwell, 1997a), the Sd scale has more items asserting that one is an estimable citizen with high standards, as persevering, as doing many things of public benefit, as having strong moral values and positive religious beliefs, and that one is energetic and socially responsible. Thus, Sd is closer to the moral properness of the L scale. The Mp scale essentially denies a diversity of problems: one presents as having many interests, as feeling entirely self-confident, as having few fears and no angry impulses nor any problems with religion, and as having high values, unflinching honesty, a dedicated life, and socially estimable talents. Mp is then closer to the problem minimizing of the K scale than is Sd. But together they are of great help in discriminating when the elevations on L and K are due to intentional distortion, or, in the absence of elevations on Sd and Mp, the elevations on L and K derive from sincere responding, whatever else the source of such a "tilt" of the person's responding.

A third and unexpectedly important scale measures the person's level of socioeconomic status identification (SES): the Ss scale of Nelson (1952). From the Caldwell Data set (Caldwell, 1997a), this scale turns out to have major importance in understanding the K scale, the correlation of Ss with K being +.65, which is well above the +.50 of Mp and the +.28 of Sd with K. In addition, Ss is barely correlated with Mp (+.17) and virtually not at all with Sd (.05). (The correlation of the F scale with Ss at $-.77$, about 60% of the variance, is also of major importance clinically but rarely pertinent in custody litigant profiles.) Note that the contributions of Ss versus Mp and Sd to K are almost completely independent and simply additive. When cross examined on a particularly high K score with a challenge that it proves the person was highly defensive, it becomes possible to assert a flat "no" when Mp and Sd are not elevated; this may be to the consternation of the cross examining attorney who previously had always understood K to be just a measure of defensiveness.

Are there cutoff points beyond which a profile should be rejected as hopelessly "occasion invalid"? There certainly are in the look-bad direction, e.g., a profile including a raw F of 30+ (out of 60 possible items) is just not interpretable. In this case, one not only has no idea, even with the K correction, what the elevations really "should be," and, at least equally seriously, no idea what the *code type* really should be. In the "look good" direction, I am, however, very reluctant to simply cut off a "uselessly invalid extreme." There are effective cutoffs in the literature that optimally separated those instructed to fake good from those who took the test "straight," but the "fake" and "straight" distributions still showed enough overlap to sustain highly cautious interpretations rather than throwing the data away. In particular, any elevations based on self-negative item content (e.g., 1-Hs, 2-D, the obvious half of 3-Hy, the predominant, obvious parts of 4-Pd and 6-Pa, and all of 7-Pt and 8-Sc) that are obtained *despite* a strong attempt to fake good are apt to be all the more important clinically (each response having overcome the person's resistance to being self-negative).

I do not believe there is any absolute "occasion invalid" cutoff on K. It can be close to 30 out of 30 possible items without significant elevations on Mp or Sd; this is usually associated with a high to very high score on the Ss scale, and elevations on Welsh R also add to K. (Over T-60 is very high on Ss given the high SES of the MMPI-2 normative sample; T-70 virtually never occurs.) In these instances, the K correction is adjusting for the *unintentional*[6] bias of Ss, that higher SES subjects consistently internalize more favorable self-images, just as people raised in poverty typically internalize negative elements in their self-images. For the L scale, there is also no clear "occasion invalid" cutoff; the higher the L, the stricter the presentation of moral propriety. Dahlstrom, Welsh, and Dahlstrom (1972) provide a thorough discussion of the suppression of profile elevation on seven of the eight clinical scales when raw L is 10 items or more; this is maximal for scale 8-Sc (as compared to the other clinical scales), and the suppression of 1-Hs is minimal.

Given these considerations, how do we evaluate the effects of the intense situational demands to make perceivably "custody desirable" or "excellent parenting" responses? The litigants feel at times desperately pressed to look trusting and friendly (e.g., 3-Hy Subtle, Ego Resiliency or ER-S; Block, 1965), socially outgoing (low 0-Si), emotionally in control of themselves (R, Ego Control or EC-5 [Block, 1965], O-H), nurturing (Mf), highly responsible (L, Sd), as having a high level of moral rectitude (subscale Pa3, Responsibility or Re; Gough, McClosky, & Meehl, 1952), etc. To analyze the test-taking attitude, I recommend starting the interpretation with three steps: (1) Did the person pay attention and fill in the responses reliably (e.g., VRIN and TRIN)? (2) Were the responses biased (e.g., L, F, and K)? and (3) Where did any biasing come from? The last proceeds by monitoring the extent of conscious, deliberate under-reporting or understatement of conflicts and distress on the Sd and Mp scales. If these are not elevated, then, allowing for the behavioral and attitudinal implications of L and K, we can generally take the clinical scales at face value and interpret them accordingly. If, however, Sd and Mp are substantially elevated, e.g., much over T-60, then we are alerted to the directions of trying to "look good" discussed below in the section on litigation sources of variance. Even if present, they may be so to varying degrees; this can to some degree be estimated from the profile by what is not much elevated as well as what is nevertheless elevated as well as from interview and collateral information. In the highly defensive (maximal impression management) subject, it becomes a matter of integrating test hypotheses with examiner judgment, based on all available information, as to what directions of biases the person took in setting out to distort the test results. To facilitate this, the quantifications of the 26 variables in the Caldwell Custody Report are extensively adjusted within the algorithms for the individual variables as to degrees of defensiveness. In summary, with carefully defensive examinees we simply need all the relevant test *and* non-test information we can obtain in order to make the best possible judgment as to what the person's scores most truly tell us about him/her.

What Personal Style or Long-Term Characteristics Potentially Influence Parenting and Family Systems?

Depression. Otto, Buffington, and Edens (2003) identified the impact of parental depression on child development as one of the most widely researched areas in developmental psychopathology. In particular, maternal depression has repeatedly been shown to have adverse effects on child development (Cummings & Davies, 1999; Downey & Coyne, 1990; Field, 1995; Hammen, 1997; Lovejoy, Graczyk, O'Hare, & Neuman, 2000; Oyserman, Mowbray, Meares, & Firminger, 2000). This has been reported to lead to parent-child relationship insecurities, to both internalizing and externalizing conduct problems, and to difficulties in social adjustment and school achievement.

Because the MMPI-2 depression scale contains a variety of subtly as well as obviously depressive items, it is especially suited to the evaluation of defensive litigants. It is much more difficult to fake (in either direction) than explicit and transparently obvious depression inventories, and hence should be much more credible in court. When scale 2-D is somewhat elevated but in the normal range, the evaluator may need to look for such minimal or disguised qualities as being earnest and subdued, as having a slightly painful or ironic sense of humor, as taking many responsibilities quite seriously, or as being a "too nice" and self-sacrificing person. This is especially true if K is elevated in a sophisticated subject and the unhappiness is hidden and rarely if ever explicit. If an unhappily negative observation is followed by such assertions as, "I guess that's how I am," or "That's just how life is," that covertly depressive quality would merit note.

Parenting behaviors that may merit investigation include amount (or lack) of support offered, extent of criticalness and inductions of guilt, intrusions of personal preoccupations, expressions of pessimism and discouragement toward the child, reduced overall communication, and tensions and struggles around expressing frustrations and resentments.

Repression and Denial. Is the person repressed, prone to look the other way, avoiding of directly facing and then being done with interpersonal conflicts? The litigant sample from Roger Greene shows virtually a full standard deviation shift in this direction for litigants, mainly as a function of elevations on scale 3-Hy and in particular the subtle Hy items (Greene, 2000b). These responses are, however, related to needs to present oneself as trusting, non-resentful, and non-suspicious so that the effects of short-term presentation (beware elevations on Sd and Mp) vs. enduring personal style would need to be sorted out. Does the person have a long-term history of a subtly naive trust of others, of being a bit Pollyanna, a hesitance to confront upsetting behaviors by others, a sometimes unexpected friendliness with strangers, and perhaps a characteristic distaste for crime and violence? Note that occasionally intense emotional outbursts (e.g., of saved up hurts) would not be ruled out. Does the person's role modeling have inhibitory effects on the children?

Level of Day-to-Day Organization. I do not know of any parenting-specific data on disruption or disorganization of daily functioning, and it is the exception in relatively educated and well-to-do litigants, but when Barron's (1953) ego-strength or *Es* scale is much below *T*-50, and certainly if at all below *T*-40, the parent's ability to manage all the demands and difficult contingencies of parenting is apt to be seriously compromised. Each task tends to be perceived as another unwanted demand or burden, and important actions and even basic responsibilities may get left undone or be abandoned. As an issue for examination, this would particularly matter in dispositions by community children's social services. Note that the interactions among these variables are important to keep in mind. For example, the combination of an elevated depression score and low Es would especially undermine the capacity to initiate and complete routine parenting responsibilities. Examples of the importance of this would be: (1) if it is going to be a big struggle for an unevenly organized father to have to manage a second job in order to keep up with alimony and child support payments, or (2) if an occasionally disorganized mother is going to have to return to the workforce while trying to manage children part or all of the time. If the person is depressed *and* disorganized, such a load feels onerous if not enormous. With lower Es scores, the anticipation of who will manage to do what for the children would need to be carefully thought through.

Narcissism. Indications of narcissism from the MMPI-2 seem to have two differentiable aspects. One is the *egotistical narcissism* (variable 14, potential for self-centered actions) that corresponds most directly to the DSM-IV definition (American Psychiatric Association, 1994). This has a primarily hypomanic coloring including the following criteria: (1) grandiose sense of self-importance, (2) preoccupied with fantasies of great successes, (3) believes that he or she is unique or special, (4) requires excessive admiration, (5) has a sense of entitlement, (8) is often envious of others or believes that others are envious of him or her, and (9) shows arrogant, haughty behaviors or attitudes (p. 661). Only criteria (6) and (7) seem appreciably to also overlap scale 4-Pd: (6) interpersonally exploitative, i.e., takes advantage of others to achieve his or her own ends, and (7) lacks empathy: is unwilling to recognize or identify with the feelings and needs of others (p. 661). These criteria would clearly best fit a moderately elevated 9-4 MMPI code or an even mildly elevated 9-4 MMPI-2 code. The history and input from less biased observers should confirm the inflation of the self-image, the demands that his/her opinions be agreed to by others, and in general an increased level of affective and verbal- or motoric-energy pressures. On the other hand, if there were evidently inflated self-assertions together with high scores on the conscious defensiveness scales (Mp and Sd, see section on "occasion validity"), then the self-esteem may well be overstated for situationally manipulative reasons.

The second indication is of *self-interest narcissism* (variable 10, oriented toward own agenda). This is basically the contribution of 4-Pd to a variety of codes and profiles. This is the pursuit of (usually) short-term self-interests. Such pursuits can be beneficial to some who are close to the individual but emotionally hurtful and practically harmful to others who are in the person's way. But the benefits to loved ones and friends may be about as much coincidental as (or even more than) they are an act of love. This is the *"unsocialized"* aspect of scale 4-Pd (from the "asocial/amoral" phrase), that the person can at times (when threatened) be destructively disregardful of the interests of others. In terms of MMPI-2 scale scores, this does not require the activation or pressure of scale 9-Ma; in some instances it may be describable as a passive-aggressive or passive-dependent neglect of doing things that matter a lot to someone else but are ungratifying nuisances or just boring to the self-interested narcissist. For example, profiles marked by elevations on scales 2-D together with 4-Pd particularly fail to get around to actions that benefit others but not themselves (as well as pursuit of their own longer term interests).

Externalizing/Internalizing. Does the parent consistently see problems as external to the self and due to other people vs. seeing them as personal and internal deficiencies? A refinement of Welsh's (1952) ratio provides an estimation of how much the person is disposed to see problems in life as due to a lack of consideration or even the ill will of others, and nothing will get better unless others change. Some externalizers can be quick to assert, "I certainly admit a mistake if I make one," but no one can remember when they ever did. Litigants are infrequently self-blaming internalizers. Note that too much other-blaming can become problematic if not damaging to a child, whether the child rebels against or internalizes the blame.

Threshold of Emotional Expression. Is the person emotionally constricted and contained, more limitedly and briefly engaging feelings, or is the person readily emotional and openly reactive on a more-or-less continuous basis? Several scales influence these behaviors, including L, K, Welsh's *R* (Welsh, 1965), and Block's Ego Control scale, *EC-5* (Block, 1965). Averaged data for over 1,100 custody litigants (Greene, 2000b) suggest that they lean considerably in the less emotional to at times tightly constricted direction, although intense outbursts of too-long held in feelings may occur. A potential outcome to be examined is the increased inhibition of spontaneous emotional expression in the child.

Low vs. High Decision Control Needs. Does the person apparently need to exert control over all family decisions? Needs to make one's own decisions are anchored in the difference of the scale Do (Dominance/autonomy; Gough, McClosky, & Meehl, 1952) minus the Dy scale (Dependency; Navran, 1954). The pressure to impose one's decisions is then marked by the pairwise codes among scales 3-Hy, 6-Pa, and 9-Ma. The other parent may feel he or she has distressingly little say in most large and small decisions, at least not without an ever-pending veto.

The five most often decisive issues were discussed in the first half of this paper. The following paragraphs summarize lines of examination inquiry that correspond to the variables as previously defined.

Evaluation of Potential for Antisocial Conduct. The most definitive confirmation of antisociality is likely to be historical, especially two or more arrests for "with-victim" crimes, and even one such arrest would obviously be significant. Similarly, having been sued for some sort of aggressive or exploitative action would be noteworthy. The relevance of arrests for victimless crimes would depend more on the circumstances. In face-to-face contact, if the interviewer were to find himself/herself privately asking any of the following questions, they would be typical for the 4-8-9 type: (1) "Is this person trying in some subtle (or even more overt) way to intimidate me?" (2) "Does this person seem to manipulate for the sake of manipulating, even beyond personal gain?" (3) "Is this person too glib or scarily facile in telling me whatever he/she believes I want to hear?" and, (4) "Does this person coldly look me right in the eye–perhaps with an oddly blank expression–even at the very moment I think he/she is stretching the truth, or when outright lying to me?"

Assessing Temper Control Issues. The assertion of an explosive potential would need historical confirmation or other clinical verification. Is anger (as far as is known) entirely expressed verbally? Has the person ever overtly threatened physical harm? Been physically menacing? Is there any consistency in which events have been the immediate precipitations of such acts? Has the person recently lost a job or is otherwise unemployed? (Major life downturns can greatly reduce the threshold for temper outbursts.) Has anything gotten broken in anger? Has anyone been struck, or otherwise physically hurt or injured?

Elevations on the Overcontrolled-Hostility scale (O-H; Megargee, Cook, & Mendelsohn, 1967) are problematic both in custody examinations and in general. Although the scale originally showed that most murderers are different from other inmates (much more overcontrolled and non-confrontational in prison as well as in general), the prediction of homicide is virtually always a wrong prediction because the base rate is far too low. So what does O-H measure? Behaviorally, it appears to overlap (and is probably potentiated by) the 34/43 code, that is, that resentments are persistently held in and often explicitly denied. *Low* O-H subjects can be annoyed and upset over minor aggravations, express it openly, and quickly forget about it (more strictly self-controlled family members are apt to remain uncomfortable about the undercontrolled outpouring much longer after). Examination questions to explore overcontrol could be of the sort: "How does she react to criticism (i.e., holds it in)?" "What does he do if someone keeps putting him down (doesn't object or show anger)?" "Has she ever blown up a lot more intensely than one would have expected for the provocation?" "Have you ever been uncomfortable because he *didn't* show his annoyance?" If the latter answers are yes, are backed up by cogent examples, and can be judged not to be the product of ulterior motives, then the person is likely to need help in anger release (the "flip" side of anger management).

Questions as to Chemical Abuse and Dependence. The emphasis is, as previously stressed, on current dependence on alcohol and other chemicals. Observer reports are obviously vital. In direct examination, if the examinee responded positively to any alcohol and drug Critical Items, they would be natural openers to inquiry about abuse and dependence. Again, if raw *MAC-R* is 24 or higher, caution is indicated lest the person too easily "explain away" problematic habits, with great caution if *MAC-R* is at or over 28. The same Critical Items can be used or reworded for inquiry with the opposite parent and others who are interviewed. Older children's comments can be illuminating, especially if spontaneously offered when not in the presence of the opposite parent and without any evidence of coaching or of simply parroting the other parent.

Evaluating the Level of Bonding and Attachment. Useful questions to ask of those who know the person would be probes for times when others would likely have anticipated the problematic or hurtful consequences of their actions on others, but the parent in question did not so moderate his/her behavior. Does the person have a history of making questionable moral choices? Have there been occasions of seeming indifference to the distress that his/her actions caused others? A child may be questioned (in appropriate-to-the-child wording) such as, is Daddy/Mommy "sometimes right there for you" but sometimes he/she just doesn't pay attention to you when you really wish he/she would? The inquiry is for ethical-moral shortcomings and lapses of "really being there" for the child.

Exploring Alienation of Affection. Questioning about alienation is itself sensitive lest the litigant be quickly alert to whether the examiner will himself/herself take sides, i.e., "against me." The degree of underlying malice is an interview judgment. More neutral third parties can be very helpful in reporting the frequency of criticism and urgency of insistence on what is wrong with or bad about the other parent, especially any observations of a putting down of the other parent in public situations. Genuinely voluntary complaints by the child or children (no indications of coaching) that one parent criticizes the other uncomfortably much would, of course, get special weight.

The Role-Playing of Parental Virtue and Sincerity. Does a parent go to an extreme in role-playing the image of being an "ultra-good" parent? Particularly characteristic of the 34/43 code, this is typically the recitation of all the good things the person does for the child or children with what then becomes an evident shortage of events or expressions of unqualified affection. One may hear, e.g., "I take the kid to all these lessons, I make sure the kid sees the dentist, he (or she) is clean and well dressed," etc. If asked, "Do you ever just sit and hold her?" the answer may subtly imply "Who has time? I have my own life" (although such an attitude may well not be openly verbalized in the custody examination context). As 4-Pd is increasingly elevated, the examiner should be alert to elements of duplicitous deception, often as "white lies" about the self, the other spouse, or a child's problems. It is curious that the family conflict items on scale 4-Pd (subscale Pd1, Family Conflict) are readily suppressed by elevations on scale K (a raw score of zero is not unusual!) even though family conflict issues are so centrally why the person is being seen. In contrast, most of the problematic conduct items (subscale Pd2, Authority Conflict) have more factual, historical content and are minimally K-suppressed (perhaps because "They might prove I was lying"). One would hardly expect a custody litigant wanting the children to respond positively to feelings of alienation from others or from his or her own feelings, so the K-correction is then obviously important to scale 4-Pd in relation to the management of "an ideal parent" impression.

WHAT MMPI-2 VARIANCES ARE ATTRIBUTABLE TO THE CONTEXT OF LITIGATION?

Child custody fights often involve very deep hurts and unforgiving resentments. Spouses feel betrayed and abandoned by their once beloved spouses and, sometimes, by their children. Subsequent-marriage spouses have reported feeling the new mate might as well still be married to the first spouse because so much energy, attention, and money continue to be directed at that other person. Some affects change considerably, and others persist. What aspects or proportions of the MMPI-2 scores are reasonable to attribute to those intense affects in the litigation context? Which scales are more subject to rapid change when there are major shifts in the person's circumstances? These are not precisely answerable questions, but there are tendencies that can be noted.

The litigants being forensically examined for custody are only a small and select subset of the total of those adults who get divorced (far less than 10%; Greenberg, 2004); some couples have no children, others have grown children, and, in addition, most with children reach more amicable separations. I believe that the relatively modest but prevalent elevations on scales 3-Hy, 4-Pd, and 6-Pa (Bathurst, Gottfried, & Gottfried, 1997) are additive combinations of pre-existing sensitivities with situational tensions and stresses that, together, push the litigious attitudes.[7] A person who already has the vanities and self-righteousness associated with the 34, 36, and 46 pairings among these three scales is more vulnerable to feeling deeply pained (scale 3), abandoned and unwanted (scale 4), and wrongly treated (scale 6) in the process of separation and divorce. Given the defensiveness with which they approach the test, which, as discussed in the "occasion validity" section, is between a one-half to one full standard deviation shift on the average (Caldwell,

2001b), the increments of elevation generally appear to be small, but they are regularly present. For example, if one starts with a mild elevation on scale 4-Pd, coming from unstable or somehow limited attachments to one's own parents in one's childhood, such sensitivities would naturally be incremented in the midst of a wounded and angry breakup. Similarly, preexisting tendencies to deny ill intentions and personal shortcomings (the subtle side of 3-Hy) and a readiness to focus on what is acceptable or unacceptable conduct within a marriage (scale 6-Pa and especially subscale Pa3) would easily be accentuated in such a breakup.

Limits on such effects are, of course, somewhat arbitrary and hard to set. But I am not aware of ever having seen a *T*-score over 70 on 4-Pd on the MMPI-2 where there was not a definite longer-term history of corresponding moral and interpersonal struggles as well as internal questions as to personal goals and feelings. Thus, I believe an attempt to dismiss an MMPI-2 *T*-score on 4-Pd beyond *T*-70 as entirely attributable to the immediate stress of litigation is seriously misleading if not outrightly fallacious; whenever such a dismissive stance is anticipated, the opposite examiners and counsel may need to prepare a chronology of episodes of subtly if not overtly unsocialized disregard of the feelings of others and of morally questionable choices.[8]

There has never been a publication regarding the exact extent or size of such *T*-score shifts specifically due to ongoing custody litigation, the prior unstressed testing rarely if ever being available. In clinical contexts, the mood- and anxiety-reflective scales such as 2-D, 7-Pt, and 9-Ma have been observed to shift abruptly and widely, and 8-Sc can occasionally be driven up sharply by bewildering trauma and panic or by organic brain injury. I have also seen 3-Hy change sharply with the onset of threats, e.g., gross public rejection, or with the dramatic relief of such threats. The other scales, however, seem to move up and down more slowly, and 1-Hs and 4-Pd typically seem to change slowly on retesting occasions.

From my experience, I would consider a five *T*-score increment to be a fairly typical litigation-generated shift on any of the eight basic clinical scales, and more than ten *T*-score points would be a large shift, except where it might be expected from severe or extreme life and identity threatening traumas. Granted, custody litigants commonly experience their struggles to be deeply upsetting and upending, but an argument to dismiss much more than 10 points of elevation on any given scale as only due to the circumstances of litigation should require the demonstration of substantial co-occurring attitudinal and emotional changes, which many relatively neutral observers would be able to agree to be

clearly noticeable and to have been triggered directly by the circumstances of the litigation. That is, the person is currently showing a significantly different emotional makeup than was characteristic prior to
the litigation. In sum, an elevation over *T-70 on any of the eight basic
clinical scales* would almost always reflect some degree of pre-litiga-
tion disposition, as usually would an elevation over *T-65.* I reiterate
these numbers are from my experience; I know of no data that would directly confirm or disconfirm them. My underlying belief is that what are
already vulnerable and sensitive aspects of personality are likely to
show larger changes under corresponding stresses, and that steady and
untroubled personality characteristics will be less susceptible to change,
so that, barring a unique and never-before-experienced trauma, elevated
litigant *T*-scores are likely to represent mostly *additive effects* of prior
dispositions plus current stresses, especially on scales 3-Hy, 4-Pd, and
6-Pa.

AS COMPARED TO WHAT NORMS?

To develop a system to represent scores on a variety of custody-relevant dimensions, including those discussed in this paper, one must have
a reference set. The basic set is the MMPI-2 normative sample, the
2,600 males and females used for the means and standard deviations
(Butcher, Dahlstrom, Graham, Tellegen, & Kaemmer, 1989). But custody cases may well differ from the MMPI-2 sample. Roger Greene
(2000b) has accumulated a sample of over 1,100 MMPI-2 response protocols from custody litigants. These custody cases are a set that Greene
obtained from litigants seen by his colleagues, and they are otherwise
unselected beyond being acceptably valid protocols and the referrals to
the particular examiners who provided them. He generously provided
me with the means and standard deviations of these subjects on the 26
variables included in my final MMPI-2 Custody Report. In this way, every person taking the MMPI-2 for custody examination purposes can be
compared to *both* the normal and the litigant samples, and those two
samples can be compared to each other. The mean profiles (by gender)
in Greene's sample are slightly more elevated than those of Bathurst et
al. (1997), but otherwise almost a tracing of their mean profiles with the
usual litigant predominance of scales 3-Hy, 4-Pd, and 6-Pa.
   A few comments may be of interest as to how the litigants differ from
the MMPI-2 normative sample, although the latter is already a much
more educated sample (like the litigants) than would correspond to the

U.S. Census. Cutting at one-half standard deviation (*T*-55) or more for both male and female litigants, they are (or present themselves to be): more deliberately defensive (emphasizing the Mp [Cofer, Chance, & Judson, 1949] and Sd [Wiggins, 1959] *conscious* defensiveness scales, see the "occasion validity" section); more repressed and denying; relatively lacking in awareness of how they upset others; more emotionally restrained and constricted; prone to hold onto resentments and perhaps exceptionally slow to forgive; responsible and self-controlled; high needs to be in control of everyone's decisions; and prone to role-play an exaggerated amount of virtue as a parent.

Interestingly, although their mean scores are slightly elevated, they do *not* quite meet the half standard deviation threshold for such variables as: consistently shallow bonding; potential for antisocial conduct (quite average); possible serious temper problems; externalizing and other blaming; and risk of alienation of affections (just on the margin).

They are also below the MMPI-2 normative sample mean on vulnerability to chemical dependency, more extroverted than average, and report little socially interfering anxiety. If one looks at the first list of more descriptive items, and imagines a married couple *both* possessing those characteristics, one gets an image of how, when an initially idealized relationship goes sour, the two parties are ill equipped to resolve their differences amicably and peacefully.

WHAT IF THE PROFILE "DOES NOT FIT"?

No personality test is, of course, infallible. The Internet can be accessed for advice on how to take the MMPI-2, and some examinees can be quite creative. What if no profile interpretation from any source on the MMPI will generate a description that seems to match the person in front of you about whom you have accumulated a mass of information? What then?

In some instances, especially when the available data indicate considerably more psychological problems and disturbance than the very unelevated profile suggests, the story is told by the Mp and Sd scales. If one or both are over *T*-70, then the MMPI-2 scores can largely be set aside as too suppressed by conscious defensiveness. This will occasionally apply when the Mp and Sd scales are around *T*-65 or a bit higher. The litigant will know he/she deliberately set out to "look as good as possible" (which is *not* the case when L and K are elevated but Mp and Sd are not). Sometimes the person will accept that such an extreme effort to "look good" actually will operate seriously against him/her ("It makes you look like you have something to hide"), and they will retake the test with a more straightforward attitude. Sometimes faking is flatly denied, and that closes that door; you report the defensiveness.

Once in a while the story is told by a score around T-65 or higher on the Control scale, Cn (Cuadra, 1953). This is the ability to put up a façade–often highly convincing–that may cover over urgently or even dangerously aggressive impulses. A high Cn score urges a careful search of collateral information as to expressions of aggression that have never emerged in direct interviews. On the other hand, the preponderance of litigant scores on Cn are low, so this will only infrequently explain profile pathology that is not evident in face-to-face contact.

There may still be times, hopefully rare, when the test looks valid and yet inexplicably unlike the examinee. Here the test data would have to be set aside without a resolution as to what went wrong. The unexpectedly different self-presentation on the test may need to be described, perhaps with comments as to what would argue against it or what would be consistent with any part of it. One then simply explains to the trier of fact what one believes the preponderance of evidence to be.

THREE FACES OF ATTRIBUTE VALIDITY

Construct Validity

The custody-related variables discussed depend substantially on the history of construct development in the MMPI/MMPI-2 literature. The eight basic clinical scales, however, were originally constructed on an entirely empirical basis to match eight diagnoses descended in part from the emphasis on meticulous observation by Kraepelin and many others; despite the etiologic speculations of the time, precise and detailed observation was strongly emphasized. Consequently, the core concepts for each of the MMPI-2 clinical scales remain in dispute, and etiologies by code type have only been very minimally explored. I offered my own evolutionary/adaptational hypotheses in Caldwell (2001a). For example, that article includes the argument for the centrality of unwantedness/impaired bonding (along with intense family stress and problematic genes) as to the etiologic origins of elevations on scale 4-Pd. Some of the best support for the primarily code type construct inferences (e.g., temper control, control over decisions, etc.) can be found in such early sources as Hathaway and Meehl

(1951), Gilberstadt and Duker (1965), and Marks and Seeman (1963). The relation of the *MAC* and *MAC-R* scales to alcohol and drug abuse has been studied for several decades.

The development of this actuarial, computer-generated system started with the identification of constructs that are potentially relevant to parenting. They must not only be conceptually useful and practical, but they also must be quantifiable from the MMPI-2 items, scores, and codes. Trial weights were assigned, and many trial runs were needed to refine these in order to allow for unanticipated scale combinations and infrequent vagaries of scores and odd outcomes that are hard to anticipate. Then we sought feedback from a variety of sources. The refinement of the validity of the constructs remains an ongoing process that has no absolute end point.

Predictive Validity

Writing algorithms to specify the selected variables accurately becomes a much more difficult task when the average baseline of the respondents is close to a full standard deviation more defensive than the basic MMPI-2 normative sample. Most of these variables have built-in "defensiveness modifications" in the formulas that adjust the weights (expressed as *T*-scores relative to the MMPI-2 normative sample), and those weights then select the intensity of the wording. The wording, in turn, may reflect relative levels of ambiguity due to high levels of defensiveness. The contrasting wording for low scores turned out to be not just an absence of the qualities characterizing the high scorers. Instead it is often an unexpected polarity and, at first glance, a seemingly different focus from what would be expected from the emphasis associated with a high score on that variable.

If there were appropriate data available, each variable could have its own probability value, but these values would vary somewhat from one subset of clients to another. Well-educated and relatively well-to-do clients will answer differently from less educated and economically poorer subjects–note the large divergence regarding the ASP content scale discussed above (a cutoff selecting about one-third of their research sample and less than one percent of litigants). Therefore, even if exact quantitative *p* values were derivable from a well-studied group, they presumably should not be reported because they could lead to misguided emphases in a somewhat dissimilar group. Thus, ultimate validation of the accuracy and fit of these variables will depend on estimated levels of likelihood that vary at least a little from one subgroup to the next.

I perceive my function in this context as an "actuarial consultant." This is a "professional-to-professional consultation," and this latter concept is basic to the APA ethical code (American Psychological Association, 2002) for computer-generated test interpretations. The material is broadly "actuarial" in Meehl's (1954) sense that it is derived from data characteristic of objectively matched cases, and it summarizes the specific attributes associated with various scores and combinations of scores without any prior regard to the individual to whom it is to be applied. This gives it the virtue of having no bias with regard to the immediate case. Judges and juries have appreciated the point that every word and every sentence in the report was written well before the person in question was given the test.

Convergent Validity

Functionally, the narrative content of the Custody Report should be considered as the summary of a series of hypotheses. They are behaviors and attitudes that have characterized clients with similar test results, so they are of increased (or decreased) likelihood for this particular person. The "connecting of the dots" between these hypotheses and the individual is indeed the clinical challenge and the clinical art. These convergences, then, are the demonstration that personal potentials identified from the individual's own independent responses to a set of true and false statements are then confirmable through, and confirming of, the interview-based, observational, and collateral information obtained.

I believe the demonstration of (1) the convergence of parenting-relevant test data–given no case bias in the origin of the predictions nor any input of information about the person or his/her circumstances–combined with (2) the examiner's careful accumulation of information assessing the accuracy and practical consequences for the children of the hypotheses generated and confirmed is the most forensically credible presentation we can make. That "the case information directly matches the actuarial expectations that are entirely neutral to this case" is a convincing assertion, and it locks in hard-to-impeach support of the recommendations we make. Given the often extreme emotions and biases of perception in such litigation, the anchoring of the evaluator's perceptions and recommendations in a truly objective and case-unbiased source can be like a breath of fresh air in the courtroom. At least that has been my hope in devoting years of work to the use of the MMPI-2 in custody examinations.

NOTES

1. The K correction is a complex issue. The development of the K scale itself involved a long series of possible scales, both involving instructions to fake (currently called Analog Research Group designs, ARG) and groups known or suspected of having distorted thresholds for symptom admission (currently Differential Prevalence Group or DPG designs). The core set of K items was a DPG scale, a sample of patients with inappropriately normal profiles (probably the first DPG design in history). Although the data presented in the "Boundaries of 'occasion' validity" section show that K is adjusting the scores considerably more for sophistication than for deliberate defensiveness, an extreme degree of K-type defensiveness can push scales 4-Pd, 8-Sc, and 9-Ma up. Nevertheless, my experience is that the K-correction per se rarely produces a 4-8-9 profile (raw 8-Sc usually being almost totally suppressed by a very high K). In some cases, however, the score on 8-Sc may be increased by an identity-devastation when the spouse is leaving ("dumping") them for someone else and threatening to take the children as well. This effect would need to be considered in a careful clinical examination. Although experiences may seem "strange and peculiar" (8-Sc) to the person who feels personally broken, relatively rapid healing may occur if the person is awarded sufficient time with the children to maintain a substantial attachment with them.

2. Years ago I compared notes with Phil Marks on four individuals who had schemed to explode bombs, which we viewed as an extreme temper tantrum. Each of the four had a profile defined by all three of scales 4, 6, and 9 highest, obviously not a favorable three-scale code.

3. Even if there were data to confirm this code type as the *relatively* greatest risk, this is *not* to say that such abusive reactions are "more likely than not." To assert in a report or in court that "abuse is likely" would seriously misrepresent the low base rates of such behavior. Rather, the issue is that the hypothesis of *relatively* increased risk of abuse should alert the examiner to take special care to evaluate any abusive events in the examinee's history and to be alert that others, e.g., the child or children, may be intimidated with regard to talking about it.

4. This value is the difference of the T-scores on three scales minus two others, i.e., $(L + 6\text{-Pa} + 8\text{-Sc}) - (3\text{-Hy} + 7\text{-Pt})$.

5. Nichols and Greene (1991) updated the Mp scale by creating a composite of the scale with items from the Sd scale as well as a few items from L, K, and S. Although the composite probably works a little better than either singly, I prefer to retain the information contained in the contrast between Mp and Sd.

6. I prefer "unintentional" to Paulhus' "self-deception" since, while SES has very large effects, I do not see variations of Ss scores as self-deceptive.

7. These 3-4-6 elevations are much more evident and substantial when the scores are transposed onto the original MMPI norms. Their elevations, as discussed earlier with regard to scale 4-Pd, are masked by selective reductions of elevation on the MMPI-2 norms, and the reductions of these three scales are notably maximal precisely within the typical custody litigant range. It would be a plausible but not independently testable hypothesis that the numerous couples who were actively recruited and who volunteered for a psychological research study (the MMPI-2 normative sample) already had persisting marital issues and conflicts. These could well have served to motivate their participation, so that a

considerable disproportion of scores fell in this range, in turn suppressing elevations on these three scales within the normal range.

8. A recent case in which a 4-Pd elevation over *T*-90 was successfully dismissed as entirely attributable to the stress of litigation prompted my concern (his history was so bad and lifelong that his own family asked to testify against him). I believe we need some limits as to what is dismissible, although these need to be broad because individual circumstances can vary so widely.

REFERENCES

Ackerman, M. J., & Ackerman, M. C. (1997). Custody evaluation practices: A survey of experienced professionals (revisited). *Professional Psychology: Research and Practice, 28*, 137-145.

American Psychiatric Association. (1994). *Diagnostic and statistical manual of mental disorders* (4th ed.). Washington, DC: Author.

American Psychological Association. (2002). *Ethical principles of psychologists and code of conduct.* Washington, DC: Author.

Baer, R. A., & Miller, J. (2002). Underreporting of psychopathology on the MMPI-2: A meta-analytic review. *Psychological Assessment, 14*, 16-226.

Barron, F. (1953). An ego-strength scale which predicts response to psychotherapy. *Journal of Consulting Psychology, 17*, 327-333. For the best integration of the scale development articles, see Dahlstrom, W. G., & Dahlstrom, L. (1980). Basic readings on the MMPI: A new selection on personality measurement, pp. 267-285. Minneapolis: University of Minnesota Press.

Bathurst, K., Gottfried, A. W., & Gottfried, A. E. (1997). Normative data for the MMPI-2 in child custody litigation. *Psychological Assessment, 9*, 205-211.

Block, J. (1965). *The challenge of response sets: Unconfounding meaning, acquiescence, and social desirability in the MMPI.* New York: Appleton-Century-Crofts.

Bosquet, M., & Egeland, B. (2000). Predicting parenting behaviors from antisocial practices content scale scores of the MMPI-2 administered during pregnancy. *Journal of Personality Assessment, 74*, 146-162.

Butcher, J. N., Dahlstrom, W. G., Graham, J. R., Tellegen, A., & Kaemmer, B. (1989). *MMPI-2: Manual for administration and scoring.* Minneapolis: University of Minnesota Press.

Butcher, J. N., Graham, J. R., Williams, C. L., & Ben-Porath, Y. S. (1990). *Development and use of the MMPI-2 content scales.* Minneapolis: University of Minnesota Press.

Caldwell, A. B. (1997a). *MMPI-2 data research file for clinical patients.* Unpublished raw data.

Caldwell, A. B. (1997b). Whither goest our redoubtable mentor, the MMPI/MMPI-2? *Journal of Personality Assessment, 68*, 47-68.

Caldwell, A. B. (2001a). What do the MMPI scales fundamentally measure? Some hypotheses. *Journal of Personality Assessment, 76*, 1-17.

Caldwell, A. B. (2001b). *Guide for understanding, presenting, and defending the custody report.* Culver City: Caldwell Report.

Chang, A. F., Caldwell, A. B., & Moss, T. (1973). Stability of personality traits in alcoholics during and after treatment as measured by the MMPI: A one-year follow-up study. *Proceedings of the 81st annual convention of the APA, 8*, 387-388.

Cofer, C. N., Chance, J. E., & Judson, A. J. (1949). A study of malingering on the MMPI. *Journal of Psychology, 27*, 491-499.

Committee on Ethical Guidelines for Forensic Psychologists. (1991). Specialty guidelines for forensic psychologists. *Law and Human Behavior, 15*, 655-665.

Cuadra, C. A. (1953). *A psychometric investigation of control factors in psychological adjustment.* Doctoral dissertation, University of California (Berkeley). Also reprinted in Welsh, G. S., & Dahlstrom, W. G. (Eds.) (1956). *Basic readings on the MMPI in psychology and medicine.* Minneapolis: University of Minnesota Press.

Cummings, E. M., & Davies, P. T. (1999). Depressed parents and family functioning: Interpersonal effects and children's functioning and development. In T. Joiner & J. C. Coyne (Eds.), *The interactional nature of depression: Advances in interpersonal approaches* (pp. 299-327). Washington, DC: American Psychological Association.

Dahlstrom, W. G., Welsh, G. S., & Dahlstrom, L. E. (1972). *An MMPI handbook: Vol. I. Clinical interpretation* (rev. ed.). Minneapolis: University of Minnesota Press.

Davis, K. R., & Sines, J. O. (1971). An antisocial behavior pattern associated with a specific MMPI profile. *Journal of Consulting and Clinical Psychology, 36*, 229-234.

DiLalla, D. L., Carey, G., Gottesman, I. I., & Bouchard, T. J., Jr. (1996). Heritability of MMPI personality indicators of psychopathology in twins reared apart. *Journal of Abnormal Psychology, 105*, 491-499.

Downey, G., & Coyne, J. C. (1990). Children of depressed parents: An integrative review. *Psychological Bulletin, 108*, 50-76.

Drake, L. E., & Oetting, E. R. (1959). *An MMPI codebook for counselors.* Minneapolis: University of Minnesota Press.

Farrington, D. P. (2000). Psychosocial predictors of adult antisocial personality and adult convictions. *Behavioral Sciences and the Law, 18*, 605-622.

Field, T. (1995). Psychologically depressed parents. In M. H. Bornstein (Ed.), *Handbook of parenting, Vol. 4: Applied and practical parenting* (pp. 85-99). Mahwah, NJ: Erlbaum.

Gilberstadt, H., & Duker, J. (1965). *A handbook for clinical and actuarial MMPI interpretation.* Philadelphia: Saunders.

Goldberg, L. R. (1965). Diagnosticians vs. diagnostic signs: The diagnosis of psychosis vs. neurosis from the MMPI. *Psychological Monographs, 79* (Whole No. 602).

Gough, H. G., McClosky, H., & Meehl, P. E. (1952). A personality scale for dominance. *Journal of Abnormal and Social Psychology, 46*, 360-366.

Greenberg, S. A. (2004, March). *The "not me" scale: Forensic implications of K item disavowal on the MMPI-2.* Invited Master Lecture to the Society for Personality Assessment. Miami, FL.

Greene, R. L. (2000a). *The MMPI-2: An interpretive manual* (2nd ed.). Boston: Allyn & Bacon.

Greene, R. L. (2000b). MMPI-2 data research file for child custody litigants. Unpublished raw data.

Hammen, C. (1997). Children of depressed parents: The stress context. In S. A. Wolchik & I. N., Sandler (Eds.), *Handbook of children's coping: Linking theory and intervention* (pp. 131-157). New York: Plenum Press.

Hathaway, S. R., & Meehl, P. E. (1951). *An atlas for the clinical use of the MMPI.* Minneapolis: University of Minnesota Press.

Hathaway, S. R., & Monachesi, E. D. (1963). *Adolescent personality and behavior: MMPI patterns of normal, delinquent, dropout, and other outcomes.* Minneapolis: University of Minnesota Press.

Kammeier, M. L., Hoffmann, H., & Loper, R. G. (1973). Personality characteristics of alcoholics as college freshmen and at the time of treatment. *Quarterly Journal of Studies on Alcohol, 34,* 390-399.

Keilin, W. G., & Bloom, L. J. (1986). Child custody evaluation practices: A survey of experienced professionals. *Professional Psychology: Research and Practice, 17,* 338-346.

Lovejoy, M. C., Graczyk, P. A., O'Hare, E., & Neuman, G. (2000). Maternal depression and parenting behavior: A meta-analytic review. *Clinical Psychology Review, 20,* 561-592.

MacAndrew, C. (1965). The differentiation of male alcoholic outpatients from nonalcoholic psychiatric outpatients by means of the MMPI. *Quarterly Journal of Studies on Alcohol, 26,* 238-246.

Malinchoc, M., Offord, K. P., Colligan, R. C., & Morse, R. M. (1994). The common alcohol logistic-revised scale (CAL-R): A revised alcoholism scale for the MMPI and MMPI-2. *Journal of Clinical Psychology, 50,* 436-445.

Marks, P. A., & Seeman, W. (1963). *The actuarial description of abnormal personality.* Baltimore: Williams & Wilkins.

Meehl, P. E. (1951). Observations in graduate seminar.

Meehl, P. E. (1954). *Clinical versus statistical prediction: A theoretical analysis and a review of the evidence.* Minneapolis: University of Minnesota Press.

Megargee, E. I., & Bohn, M. J. (1979). *Classifying criminal offenders: A new system based on the MMPI.* Beverly Hills: Sage Publications.

Megargee, E. I., Carbonell, J. L., Bohn, M. J., & Sliger, G. L. (2001). *Classifying criminal offenders with the MMPI-2: The Megargee system.* Minneapolis: University of Minnesota Press.

Megargee, E. I., Cook, P. E., & Mendelsohn, G. A. (1967). Development and validation of an MMPI scale of assaultiveness in overcontrolled individuals. *Journal of Abnormal Psychology, 72,* 519-528.

Navran, L. (1954). A rationally derived MMPI scale for dependence. *Journal of Consulting Psychology, 18,* 192.

Nelson, S. E. (1952). The development of an indirect, objective measure of social status and its relationship to certain psychiatric syndromes (Doctoral dissertation, University of Minnesota). *Dissertation Abstracts International, 12,* 782. (See discussion in Caldwell, 1997b.)

Nichols, D. S., & Greene, R. L. (1991, March). *New measures for dissimulation on the MMPI/MMPI-2.* Paper presented at the 26th Annual Symposium on Recent Developments in the Use of the MMPI (MMPI-2/MMPI-A). St. Petersburg Beach, FL.

Otto, R. K., Buffington, J. K., & Edens, J. F. (2003). Child custody evaluation: Research and practice. In A. Goldstein (Ed.), *Handbook of psychology.* New York: Wiley.

Oyserman, D., Mowbray, C. T., Meares, P. A., & Firminger, K. B. (2000). Parenting among mothers with a serious mental illness. *American Journal of Orthopsychiatry*, *70*, 296-315.

Paulhus, D. L. (1984). Two-component models of socially desirable responding. *Journal of Personality and Social Psychology*, *46*, 598-609.

Persons, R. W., & Marks, P. A. (1971). The violent 4-3 MMPI personality type. *Journal of Consulting and Clinical Psychology*, *36*, 189-196.

Shuman, D. W., & Greenberg, S. A. (2003). Expert witnesses, the adversary system, and the voice of reason: Reconciling impartiality and advocacy. *Professional Psychology: Research and Practice*, *34*(3), 219-224.

Weed, N. C., Butcher, J. N., McKenna, T., & Ben-Porath, Y. S. (1992). New measures for assessing alcohol and drug abuse with the MMPI-2: The APS and AAS. *Journal of Personality Assessment*, *58*, 389-404.

Welsh, G. S. (1952). An anxiety index and an internalization ratio for the MMPI. *Journal of Consulting Psychology*, *16*, 65-72.

Welsh, G. S. (1965). MMPI profiles and factor scales A and R. *Journal of Clinical Psychology*, *21*, 43-47.

Wiggins, J. S. (1959). Interrelationships among MMPI measures of dissimulation under standard and social desirability instructions. *Journal of Consulting Psychology*, *23*, 419-427.

What the Rorschach Can Contribute to Child Custody and Parenting Time Evaluations

Robert E. Erard

SUMMARY. Personality assessment can indirectly help custody evaluators answer important questions about parental competence and the fit between parents' psychological resources and children's needs. It is preferable to use testing to check hypotheses derived from the case information rather than the reverse. The Rorschach makes it possible to assess implicit motives, coping capacities, and need states, thus complementing and supplementing self-attributed personal characteristics from the MMPI-2 and other self-report data. It also offers idiographic infor-

---

Robert E. Erard, PhD, practices clinical and forensic psychology in private practice. He has authored and co-authored articles on the release of raw test data, the forensic use of the Rorschach, and child custody mediation. He has presented workshops and symposia on ethics in clinical and forensic assessment, conducting child custody evaluations, MMPI-2/Rorschach integration, and the Rules of Evidence. He is a past President of the Michigan Psychological Association and the Michigan Inter-professional Association on Marriage, Divorce, and the Family.

Address correspondence to: Robert E. Erard, PhD, Psychological Institutes of Michigan, P.C., 26111 West Fourteen Mile Road, Suite 104, Franklin Village, MI 48025 (E-mail: rerard2000@ameritech.net).

The author would like to thank Dr. Jay Flens for proposing this article and Dr. James Livingston for his thoughtful suggestions.

[Haworth co-indexing entry note]: "What the Rorschach Can Contribute to Child Custody and Parenting Time Evaluations." Erard, Robert E. Co-published simultaneously in *Journal of Child Custody* (The Haworth Press, Inc.) Vol. 2, No. 1/2, 2005, pp. 119-142; and: *Psychological Testing in Child Custody Evaluations* (ed: James R. Flens, and Leslie Drozd) The Haworth Press, Inc., 2005, pp. 119-142. Single or multiple copies of this article are available for a fee from The Haworth Document Delivery Service [1-800-HAWORTH, 9:00 a.m. - 5:00 p.m. (EST). E-mail address: docdelivery@haworthpress.com].

Available online at http://www.haworthpress.com/web/JCC
Digital Object Identifier: 10.1300/J190v02n01_07

119

mation for individualizing assessments. Concerns about admissibility and charges that the Rorschach "overpathologizes" litigants are addressed, and suggestions are offered for making optimal use of the Rorschach in child custody work. *[Article copies available for a fee from The Haworth Document Delivery Service: 1-800-HAWORTH. E-mail address: <docdelivery@haworthpress.com> Website: <http://www.HaworthPress.com> © 2005 by The Haworth Press, Inc. All rights reserved.]*

KEYWORDS. Rorschach, child custody evaluation, forensic, norms, MMPI

Nearly all child custody and parenting time evaluations involve some kind of psychological testing (Ackerman & Ackerman, 1997; Keilin & Bloom, 1986; Quinnell & Bow, 2001). Survey data indicate that custody evaluators spend an average of about five hours in this activity (Ackerman & Ackerman, 1997; Bow & Quinnell, 2001; Keilin & Bloom, 1986), comprising about 25-30% of the total time they spend conducting the evaluations (not including report writing).

One reason that testing is such a common feature of these evaluations is, of course, that the people who write orders for them expect it to be done. Indeed, it is by no means unusual for evaluators to receive court orders that require "testing" without even mentioning the critical context in which it is embedded (i.e., the need for evaluation and recommendations for custody or parenting time). In recent surveys (described in Ackerman, Ackerman, Steffen, & Kelley-Poulos, 2004), between 73.9% and 85.5% of attorneys and judges expected psychological testing of parents or children to be administered by custody evaluators. In another survey (Bow & Quinnell, 2004), the mean ratings by attorneys and judges of psychological testing on a 1-5 scale of importance were 4.0. It is certainly plausible, nay likely, that consumers of custody and parenting time evaluations tend to overestimate both the validity and the relevance of psychological tests for this kind of legal decision-making. Their aura of scientific objectivity and precision and simply the fact that psychological tests are one source of data that cannot be duplicated in ordinary courtroom procedures probably play a large part in determining their popularity among legal professionals.

While there are many good scientific, ethical, and legal reasons not to base child custody recommendations entirely or even primarily on the results of psychological tests (APA COPPS, 1994; Bricklin, 1999;

Brodzinsky, 1993; Gould, 2004; Grisso, 1990; Heilbrun, 1992; Melton, Petrila, Poythress, & Slobogin, 1997; Roseby, 1995; Stahl, 1999; Weit-Weithorn & Grisso, 1987), most psychologists concur with legal professionals in considering at least some personality testing of the parents to be a critical component of the generally accepted multisource, multimethod approach to data gathering (APA COPPS, 1994; Matarazzo, 1990; Weithorn & Grisso, 1987). Of course, psychologists know that there are few complex questions that can be confidently answered on the basis of psychological testing, unless they are integrated into a broader psychological assessment.

THE USE OF PERSONALITY TESTING IN CHILD CUSTODY EVALUATIONS

Personality testing of parents in child custody evaluations typically includes the MMPI-2 (Butcher, Graham, Ben-Porath, Tellegen, and Dahlstrom, 2001): 91.5% in the Ackerman and Ackerman (1997) survey and 94% in Quinnell and Bow (2001); the Rorschach, which is used somewhat less often: 47.8% in Ackerman and Ackerman (1997) and 44% in Quinnell and Bow (2001); and the MCMI series (Millon, Millon, and Davis, 1994: 34.3% in Ackerman and Ackerman (1997) and 52% in Quinnell and Bow (2001).

Whereas test selection by custody evaluators has often been surveyed, the professional literature offers somewhat less guidance about how custody evaluators ought to go about deciding which tests to use. Some authors (Brodzinsky, 1993; Underwager & Wakefield, 1993) have offered many instructive examples of how testing has been misused, but discussions of what specific contributions particular tests can make to the evaluation process are more challenging to find. Part of the problem is that, as Ellis (2000) has observed: "The majority of tests that are well validated and standardized have no direct bearing on parenting issues. The newer tests that have been developed to measure parenting skills or parent-child attachment . . . have not yet been rigorously validated" (p. 145).

Otto and Collins (1995) reviewed the MMPI/MMPI-2 literature and found no particular profile that identified parents as abusers or that was associated with abuse. Still more to the point, they were unable to identify any single scale or pattern of scales that was directly related to effective or ineffective parenting. A similar survey of the literature on the

Rorschach or the MCMI-III would scarcely be expected to yield more promising predictors of abuse or parental effectiveness.

Even though they are only indirectly informative about the specific psycholegal questions at issue in a child custody case, there is still good reason to use general personality measures. As noted in the *Standards for Educational and Psychological Testing* (American Educational Research Association, American Psychological Association, & National Council on Measurement in Education, 1999), " . . . many tests measure constructs that are generally relevant to the legal issues even though norms specific to the judicial . . . context may not be available" (p. 129). Putting the case more concretely, Graham (2000) has observed that if a person has been described in his or her personality testing as "impulsive, unstable, unpredictable, and aggressive and as having very poor judgment, this would certainly be relevant to how this person might be expected to function in the parental role" (p. 376).

The particular relevance of personality testing in child custody evaluations is largely attributable to the social contexts in which divorce cases are selected for child custody evaluations. Because custody evaluations are costly, time-consuming, stressful, and emotionally draining, they tend to be ordered only in exceptional family law cases. These are primarily cases in which serious questions have been raised concerning parental fitness or the capacity of the parents to cooperate.

While parental unfitness may be the result of cognitive or physical limitations or a lack of relevant experience, most allegations of unfitness (or relative unfitness) that are referred for psychological evaluation involve problems such as emotional instability, self-centeredness, antisocial attitudes and behaviors, deficient empathy, aggressiveness, poor impulse control, and irrational beliefs or thought processes–in short, clinical personality issues. Questions concerning the capacity of parents to cooperate also tend to extend beyond the usual "irreconcilable differences" or "destruction of the objects of matrimony" that lead to divorce; the usual concern is about whether some basic characteristics of the parents' individual makeup–their personalities–are very likely to prevent such cooperation over time. Somewhat less frequently, evaluations are also ordered because of concerns about the fit between one or both parents' characteristic motives, values, and cognitive and emotional resources (again–their personalities) and the specific needs and characteristics (often, but not always, the personalities) of their children.

Thus, there is really no need to bemoan the fact that there are currently no psychological tests that are known to predict validly what custody or parenting time arrangement will be in the best interest of a particular child. Even though this is most often the ultimate issue that the expert has been asked to address, it is simply not the sort of question one should expect a personality test to answer. What constitutes a child's "best interest" is, in the final analysis, not a psychological question, but a question of value to be determined over time in a socio-legal decision-making process guided by community standards along with statutes and case law.

What personality testing in particular can answer are often highly relevant intermediate questions along the way to an opinion about a child's best interest: questions about parents' capacity to regulate their affects and tolerate frustration, how sensitive they may be in understanding someone else's feelings or a contrasting perspective, how realistic their expectations of themselves and others seem to be, whether they allow themselves to experience a full range of emotions and to respond to such feelings in others, what kinds of characteristic defenses and coping strategies they use when encountering intense emotional demands, how well they adapt to breaks in routine and changes in circumstances, and how much of their attention is focused on their own needs and feelings vs. those of other people. Questions of similar importance can be asked of personality testing in children: What cognitive, emotional, and social resources does the child have for coping with the particular strains of this divorce? How much stress or insecurity is the child experiencing and where is it showing up in her functioning? Is the child experiencing a developmental lag or succumbing temporarily to situational stress (Roseby, 1995)? How independent and adaptable is this child likely to be in a setting of rapidly shifting routines and environments? How mature is this child's cognitive and social judgment in appraising his home environment? How sensitive does this child seem to be to family issues involving aggression, loss, sexuality, or unpredictability in the home environment?

In addition, personality tests bring to custody evaluations a kind of scientific anchoring for the subjectivity of clinical judgment. Features of personality tests such as standardized methods and conditions for gathering information, the availability of standardized norms and comparison groups, and the use of scientifically validated rules for preliminary interpretation offer the evaluator (and by extension, the trier of fact) a means of checking and quantifying subjective impressions and applying nomothetic decision rules to the data.

Unfortunately, it turns out that the degree of scientific certainty is usually greatest for relatively trivial and obvious questions and usually weakest for especially complex, subtle, and interesting questions. As Edwin Schneidman (2004) puts it, "In all scientific endeavors, there is always a trade-off between precision and relevance, and we should be very wary of losing relevance for specious accuracy (even if it brings kudos and money)" (p. 133). While two qualified psychologists looking at the same personality test results will generally agree in broad outline about their meaning, the specific application of those results to a particular context of legal decision-making involves a significant degree of subjective judgment.

TESTS AS SOURCES OF "HYPOTHESES"

It is currently fashionable for custody evaluators (perhaps in imitation of the several standard computerized test report narratives that do so) to describe their findings from personality testing as "hypotheses," rather than as facts or even opinions. It is often not clear what they expect the readers of these reports to *do* with such hypotheses. Ordinarily, one thinks of hypotheses as propositions that are going to be tested through some future research, but surely to leave it up to the finder of fact to devise some means of testing these "hypotheses" is an abdication of the expert's own responsibility to offer reasonable conclusions as to whether or not these "hypotheses" apply in the instant case.

This is not to deny that it is sometimes a reasonable procedure in conducting an evaluation to use psychological tests as a source of hypotheses to be confirmed or refuted by other sources of data, such as personal and family histories, clinical observation, interview data, documentary records, collateral sources, and the like. Once such hypotheses have been confirmed to some reasonable degree of certainty, however, they ought to be offered as opinions. Alternatively, if they are not strong enough to stand on their own and cannot be confirmed by other data, there is no good reason to include them in the evaluation report–as "hypotheses" or otherwise. Mere speculation has no useful role to play in the courtroom.

Irrelevant test findings are equally out of place. As Bricklin (1999) has observed, evaluators should consider whether information about the conceptual target that a test aims to measure, even if highly accurate, would make a difference regarding some decision: "If the answer is it would not, there is no reason to analyze a score's value" (p. 125). What is most important is to avoid what Roseby (1995) has called a "pathology hunt," where minor discrepancies from test norms are used to hold custody litigants to higher standards of mental health than are generally applied to the non-litigating population.

However common it may be to derive clinical hypotheses from the test data and then look for factual confirmation, it is nevertheless probably not the best procedure in child custody evaluations. If the evaluator's goal is (as it should be) to conduct a legally relevant evaluation, it stands to reason that the most important hypotheses to consider ought to originate in the factual and conceptual problems posed by the case itself (see Krishnamurthy, 2004).

In such an approach, one begins with the matter to be decided (e.g., whether a change of custody is in the best interest of the children, how parenting time should be divided, whether supervised parenting time is indicated) and then proceeds to the factually relevant questions. Such questions will often involve an evaluation of psychologically relevant factual allegations made by the parents that form an essential part of the legal basis for their pleadings. These may include claims about psychological characteristics of the other parent that might be associated with abuse or neglect of the children (such as low frustration tolerance, antisocial attitudes and behaviors, substance abuse) or that may interfere with the other parent's capacity to co-parent (e.g., obsessive or delusional preoccupations about a former spouse that are being shared with the children).

Personality testing of children may also usefully address questions raised about the children's particular needs and vulnerabilities (e.g., whether a child's need for routine or current attachment status are such that a proposed parenting time arrangement would be too disruptive; whether a child's emotional brittleness at home and poor school performance bespeak a maladaptive reaction to an untenable family situation; whether a child's rigid adherence to one parent's view of reality over the other's is associated with anxiety about losing that parent's love; whether a child is emotionally and socially resilient enough to adapt well to a relocation to a distant country, far away from one of her parents). From such questions, meaningful and relevant hypotheses can be derived about what sorts of data one should expect to see (and not see) in the personality testing and elsewhere.

Thus, the usual flow of inquiry is reversed. Rather than looking for discrepancies from population norms in the testing and generating a variety of possible concerns–shotgun style–and finally trying to shoehorn them into the legal issues posed by the case, one begins with the most important concerns flowing from the legal issues and generates differential hypotheses to be answered by the available data, including, of course, the testing.

Such hypothesis generation and testing are iterative. Each tentative observation and conclusion leads to further possibilities and new conceptualizations, which are subjected to further testing and confirmation. In this process, factual data from the family history and direct clinical observation come first, whereas testing and its associated theoretical constructs are used to refine one's understanding of what the factual findings mean. As Fischer (1994) has proposed, "Our primary data are particular life events. Test scores, theoretical constructs, and research literature are all derived, secondary data through which the assessor modifies and refines his or her perception of life events–both those that are reported by the client and those that occur during the assessment" (p. 46).

In contrast to the test-centered approach, one that begins with hypotheses generated by the actual and implicit referral questions has two main advantages. First, it is more likely to emphasize the most relevant data, rather than what may be most psychometrically salient, thereby demonstrating in a transparent fashion what the findings mean in the context of the legal proceedings. By framing test results in terms of actual issues in the case, it becomes easier to construct a "narrative bridge" (Brodsky, 2004, p. 21) between the technical findings and the actual experience of the litigants. Second, from a Bayesian standpoint, such an approach maximizes inferential validity by keeping the conditional probabilities in the proper sequence. For example, instead of asking, given an elevated Scale 8 on the MMPI-2 or a high X-% on the Rorschach, "What is the likelihood that this father uses poor judgment in making decisions about his child?" the evaluator asks, "Given observational and historical data suggesting that father makes poor decisions in his parenting, is there test evidence that would tend to confirm that this is part of a more general problem with perceiving events realistically and conventionally?"

WON'T THE MMPI-2 SUFFICE?

Many forensic psychologists limit their personality testing to self-report measures such as the MMPI-2. There are several advantages in choosing this instrument. It is almost universally accepted by clinicians, researchers, and courts as a reliable and valid clinical personality test. It takes little clinician time to administer and is easy to score with automated methods. While the MMPI-2 lends itself to conceptually sophisticated and nuanced interpretations by masters of the instrument, even journeyman test users can routinely obtain reasonably valid results using cookbook methods.

In contrast, effective use of the Rorschach Comprehensive System (Exner, 1993) requires establishing an effective "testing relationship" with the subject and paying close attention to subtle indications to begin and end response inquiry. Administration and scoring alone often require two or more hours of clinician time. The Rorschach requires mastery of highly complex scoring rules and of interpretive routines that require simultaneous analysis of a wide array of variables and scoring configurations. Novices using cookbook methods may easily commit substantive interpretive errors. Maintenance of expertise in using the Rorschach for forensic purposes also generally requires many hours of devotion to developments in the literature concerning emerging scoring and interpretive methods, empirical foundations and range of application, and academic controversies. Why would anyone think it is worth the trouble?

Part of the answer has to do with the limitations of self-report tests, such as the MMPI-2. Particularly in high stakes situations, such as child custody evaluations, self-serving misrepresentations (Lanyon, 2001) in litigants' statements about themselves are more or less the norm. Custody litigants taking self-report tests tend to ask themselves: "Would a parent who deserves to be awarded custody answer this question true or false?" Thus, it is hardly surprising that Bagby, Nicholson, Buis, Radovanovic, and Fidler (1999) found that " . . . Underreporting of symptoms in child custody litigation evaluations represents a real and significant challenge to psychologists using the MMPI-2 in their assessments of such litigants" (p. 28). Similar concerns have been voiced by Ollendick and Otto (1984), Siegel (1996), and Bathurst, Gottfried, and Gottfried (1997). While validity indicators can detect many naïve attempts at impression management, within-normal-limits profiles can be misleading in custody cases even in the absence of defensiveness on the validity scales (Graham, 2000). The Rorschach can often detect serious pathology that the MMPI-2 will miss (Ganellen, 1994, 1996).

When MMPI-2 results are treated as "hypotheses" to be confirmed by other "convergent data," a still more subtle snare awaits the unwary evaluator. Most of the other types of data available to custody evaluators for comparison to MMPI-2 data, such as answers to questionnaires and in structured interviews, descriptions of personal history and family life, self-assessments of parenting skills and values, and answers on tests such as the Personality Assessment Inventory (Morey, 1996) and the MCMI-III, are treated as multiple sources, but they are all mono-method approaches in the sense that they are primarily based on self-report. Even data gathered from the other party, the children, and collateral sources shares several important method characteristics with verbal self-report data; all of it requires verbal formulation and conceptualization from the speaker (method similarity) and all of it involves at least some dim awareness of how what is said may help or hurt the cause of a given party (demand characteristics). When "convergent validity" is established almost exclusively through self-report information, a great deal of noise is introduced into the data in the form of illusory correlations based on method similarities (Meyer, 1996, 1997, 1999) and demand characteristics.

The Rorschach often leads to interpretations at variance with those derived from MMPI-2 data (Archer & Krishnamurthy, 1993). This has sometimes led critics (e.g., Wood, Nezworski, & Stejskal, 1996) to argue that the Rorschach must be inaccurate or not very useful. However, its lack of routine correlation with self-report data is in fact one of its most important virtues in forensic work. Because the Rorschach does not rely on verbal self-report data and instead involves direct observation of performance under standardized conditions by the evaluator, it can be an effective means of introducing method variance into the evaluation process.

The two tests often complement each other, and the use of both together can provide incremental validity, particularly with regard to findings about personality functioning (Archer & Krishnamurthy, 1993; Blais, Hilsenroth, Castelbury, Fowler, & Baity, 2001). Ganellen (1996) has written an excellent guide to the joint use of the MMPI-2 and the Rorschach, and Weiner (1999) offers a striking case example of how the tests may profitably be used together in a child custody evaluation.

When heteromethod convergence is achieved between self-report measures and Rorschach findings, a high degree of confidence in such findings is often justified. When the results are divergent or even contradictory, this too can be clinically useful, because it may prompt the evaluator to look more carefully at all available data in an effort to resolve the apparent contradiction. In some cases, the resolution may be found in adjusting one's interpretation of the meaning of a scale or variable (e.g., an elevated MMPI-2 Scale 8 with a normal Perceptual-Thinking Index on the Rorschach may reflect profound alienation and social insecurity rather than psychosis). In other cases, it may be that the subject was less defensive or more engaged on one test or the other (Ganellen, 1994; Meyer, 1999; Meyer, Riethmiller, Brooks,

Benoit, & Handler, 2000; Shapiro, Leifer, Marton, & Kassem, 1990). In still others, what might appear to be a personality trait on one test may be revealed as more likely the product of situational influences on the other (e.g., "paranoid" attitudes, suggested by MMPI-2 Scale 6 = 67, in the Rorschach context of T = 1, PTI = 0, COP = 3, AG = 0, and high M + %, are more likely to be interpreted as situational distrust).

Robert Bornstein (2001, 2002) has offered an intriguing analysis of the differential contributions of self-report and performance (projective) methods. According to Bornstein (2001), the Rorschach Comprehensive System is designed primarily to assess three things: implicit motives (need states that the subject cannot describe directly), cognitive/perceptual style, and aspects of the individual's coping style such as stress tolerance and coping resources.

The concept of process dissociation has to do with the first of these: implicit motives. Bornstein cites McClelland, Koestner, and Weinberger (1989), who proposed that implicit motives predict an individual's spontaneous behavior in less structured situations. Tests that tap into implicit motives like the Rorschach:

> provide a more direct readout of motivational and emotional experiences than do self-reports that are filtered through analytic thought and various concepts of self and others. . . . Implicit motives are more often built on early, prelinguistic affective experiences whereas self-attributed motives are more often built on explicit teaching by parents and others as to what values or goals it is important for a child to pursue. (McClelland et al., 1989, pp. 698-699)

Bornstein (2002) reviews research contrasting measures of self-attributed motives with performance-based measures of implicit motives in several areas, including achievement motivation, intimacy, power, and dependency. Borrowing the concept of "process dissociation" from the learning and memory literature (where it has classically been applied to the problem of implicit vs. explicit memory), he explains how implicit and self-attributed motivations can be determined to represent different aspects of the same construct by demonstrating converging behavioral predictions, modest positive intercorrelations, and differential effects of moderating variables. He offers evidence that by administering self-report (e.g., MMPI) and performance (e.g., Rorschach) measures of a particular motive or need state to the same individual and studying their discontinuities, clinicians can obtain a more complete picture of that person's underlying and expressed strivings.

A further advantage of including the Rorschach along with the MMPI-2 is the wealth of idiographic information it can offer, above and beyond the formal scoring relationships. While caution should be exercised in using idiographic data to make predictive statements, findings from a disciplined Rorschach content and sequence analysis, when integrated with biographical and nomothetic data, can help individualize the assessment (Fischer, 1994) by enriching the evaluator's understanding of the dynamics, habitual defenses, coping capacities, resiliency, preoccupations, and other aspects of the inner life of the person being tested (Bricklin, 1999; Peebles-Kleiger, 2002; Weiner, 2000).

IS THE RORSCHACH STILL WELCOME IN THE COURTROOM?

In child custody and parenting time cases, the Rorschach seems to be competing with the MCMI-III for second place among the most commonly used personality tests, where it used to be firmly ensconced just below the MMPI-2 in popularity (see Quinnell & Bow, 2001). Despite the Rorschach's unique advantages, some evaluators are reluctant to use it because they are afraid that Rorschach testimony may be found inadmissible in the courtroom. In support of such fears, they refer to a spate of articles over the past half dozen years attacking the use of the Rorschach in forensic practice.

From the standpoint of the legal system, if the Rorschach were in serious danger of being expelled from the courtroom, one might expect to see some trend in this direction in the nation's appellate courts. Meloy, Hansen, and Weiner (1997), using a Lexis search, found 494 appellate citations of the Rorschach between 1945 and 1995, with specific discussions of the use of the test in 194 cases. In nearly 90% of these cases, "the admissibility and weight of the Rorschach data were not questioned by either the appellant or the respondent and were important enough to be mentioned and discussed in the legal ruling by the court of appeal" (p. 60). While some courts questioned the specific relevance of findings from the testing, the validity of the method itself was attacked in only two cases.

Lower court decisions are not usually published, but Weiner, Exner, and Sciara (1996) surveyed 93 forensic psychologists about nearly 8,000 of their cases from across the U.S., 3,052 of which were child custody cases. The use of the Rorschach was challenged in only six cases, and in only one case was Rorschach-related testimony ruled inadmissible. This survey is currently being updated to see whether anything has changed in 2004.

Some Rorschach critics (Garb, 1999; Grove & Barden, 1999; Grove, Barden, Garb, & Lilienfeld, 2002; Wood, Nezworski, Garb, & Lilienfeld, 2001) are pinning their hopes that the Rorschach will eventually be banned from the courtroom on the current requirement in all federal courts and many state courts that judges make their own determinations about the scientific reliability of the methods on which experts base their testimony, following the U.S. Supreme Court cases, *Daubert v. Merrell Dow Pharmaceuticals* (1993) and *Kumho Tire v. Carmichael* (1999). While it may be true that psychologists who use the Rorschach Comprehensive System and other psychological tests will increasingly be called upon to justify their methods using the criteria set forth under *Daubert* (Medoff, 2003), this need not be very difficult if they have become conversant with the literature broadly defending the psychometric credentials of the Comprehensive System (e.g., Acklin, 1999; Meyer, 2000; Meyer & Archer, 2001; Rosenthal, Hiller, Bornstein, Berry, & Brunell-Neuleib, 2001; Viglione, 1999; Viglione & Hilsenroth, 2001) and defending the specific applicability of the Rorschach in forensic settings (Gacono, Evans, and Viglione, 2002; Hamel, Gallagher, & Soares, 2001; Hilsenroth & Stricker, 2004; McCann, 1998; Ritzler, Erard, & Pettigrew, 2002a, 2002b; Weiner, 1999, 2002), along with the work of the various critics cited earlier.

DOES THE RORSCHACH OVERPATHOLOGIZE?

One of the most virulent criticisms of the use of the Rorschach Comprehensive System in forensic settings is the claim that reliance on the standard Exner norms (Exner, 2001) leads to overpathologizing interpretations. In a number of U.S. and international samples of normal or "control" subjects, the average non-patient may appear to be psychologically unhealthy when compared to the Exner normative sample (see, for example, Shaffer, Erdberg, & Haroian, 1999; Wood, Nezworski, Garb, & Lilienfeld, 2001). Based on comparison to the Exner norms, more of these non-patients than expected could reasonably be considered to be narrow-minded and emotionally avoidant, to have mildly impaired reality testing, to be narcissistic, and to have limited capacity for warmth or emotional closeness with others. Some authors (Hunsley & DiGiulio, 2001; Wood, Nezworski, Garb et al., 2001;

Wood, Nezworski, Stejskal, & McKinzey, 2001; but see Meyer, 2001; Weiner, 2001a) have therefore questioned whether the Rorschach should even be used until newer, more representative norms have been established by research.

Several explanations have been offered for the failure of many local, so-called normal samples to pass Exnerian muster, including differences in recruiting and screening procedures (Exner's are rather strict and may be biased toward particularly ego-involved, self-censorious, high-functioning volunteers–see Weiner, 2001a, 2001b), statistical drift (aggregated data from local convenience samples tend to differ systematically from national published norms–see Meyer, 2001), differences in the demographic characteristics between samples, increased stringency in the Comprehensive System scoring rules over time, local differences in administration (especially in inquiry) and in scoring, and a tendency for the population to become increasingly neurotic over time (see generally, Meyer, Viglione, Erdberg, Exner, & Shaffer, 2004).

Thus, the differences between the Exner norms and other samples are probably the product of several factors, some reflecting real population differences and others artifactual. The fact remains, however, that most contemporary studies using the Rorschach with non-patients obtain mean scores that fall somewhere between Exner's non-patient norms and Exner's outpatient samples (Meyer et al., 2004).

In response to questions about the continuing relevance of the Exner norms, John Exner is about to publish a new normative sample. Preliminary results (Exner, 2002) seem to fall somewhere in between the original norms and contemporary local samples on several key variables. Most variables commonly associated with serious symptoms or personality disorders (e.g., PTI, DEPI, CDI, HVI) remain reassuringly rare in Exner's new normative data.

Four considerations seem to be particularly important in considering Rorschach norms and the assessment of psychopathology in child custody work. The first is: How representative are the Exner norms of scores likely to be obtained from nonpatients presenting for assessment? It is probably useful to think of the Exner norms as representing "healthy normals" as opposed to "people plucked at random off the street." A sample consisting of the latter can be expected to contain a fair amount of psychopathology. For example, in the MMPI-2 restandardization sample, which is closer to the "person-in-the-street" population, 39% of the "normal" men and 43% of the "normal" women have clinically significant elevations on at least one MMPI-2 clinical scale (Shaffer & Erdberg, 2004). When compared to international Rorschach samples, the Exner normative sample looks about 0.4 standard deviations healthier than the rest (Meyer et al., 2004). In other words, the Exner norms seem "off" by about 4 T-score points, about the same as the difference between the MMPI and the MMPI-2 norms. It is likely that the new Exner norms will carve away at these differences.

Second, it is crucial to bear in mind that responsible Rorschach users do not draw sweeping conclusions about psychopathology based on simple difference scores between particular Rorschach variables and their non-patient normative references. While such discrepancies, when sizable, are usually taken into consideration when interpreting a Rorschach, no diagnostic or interpretive statement is justifiable by such findings alone. As Exner (1993) has taken pains to explain:

> There is no simple checklist of Rorschach signs that automatically can be translated as representative of aspects of personality or behavior. . . . That supposition is *pure nonsense*, and the unwitting interpreter who is bound to that procedure would be better to avoid the use of the Rorschach in assessment work. The test is far too complex for a simplistic sign approach, and the validity of the interpretation will depend largely on the extent to which the interpreter achieves the full measure of data integration in forming the description of the subject. (p. 332)

Third, custody evaluators should try to become familiar with typical scoring patterns in the population of particular interest to them– viz., custody litigants. The effort to describe custody norms is already well underway for the MMPI-2 (Bagby et al., 1999; Bathurst et al., 1997) and the MCMI-III (Halon, 2001; Lampel, 1999; McCann, Flens, Campagna, Collman, Lazzarro, & Connor, 2001). Several preliminary studies have described typical Rorschach findings in custody cases (Bonieskie, 2000; Hoppe & Kenney, 1994; Lee, 1996; Singer, 2001), but so far none has made its way into the peer-reviewed literature. Because the purpose (and thus, meaning to the subject) of the testing is different from the ordinary clinical or research situation and because custody litigants may be facing unusual situational stressors, such comparisons may offer insight into what is usual and unusual for the situation of the custody litigant. Still, specialized norms only take us so far. As Graham (2000) has warned, the standard norms should remain the principal basis for comparison in all personality testing until extra-test correlates of scores for specialized groups are developed.

Fourth, psychologists who use the method described earlier, of looking first to the historical and observational data in the context of questions relevant to the legal determination and then using the testing for checking hypotheses and enriching one's understanding of the real-world issues, will tend to minimize any tendencies to misperceive or exaggerate pathology based on discrepancies from norms.

HOW TO USE (AND HOW NOT TO USE) THE RORSCHACH IN CHILD CUSTODY CASES

Rorschach protocols used for forensic purposes should always be administered and scored according to the rules of the Comprehensive System in order to meet acceptable criteria for psychometric reliability and validity. Users of the Rorschach in child custody matters should be reasonably conversant with both the classic and contemporary scientific literature on the test and regularly attend workshops or symposia on its forensic applications.

They should strive to maintain a high level of expertise in administering and scoring the instrument, since standardized administration and scoring are the foundation of valid use. They ought to regularly check their administration and scoring competence (see Standard 5.9, *Standards for Educational and Psychological Testing*, AERA et al., 1999) by reviewing the instructions and examples from the most current *Workbook* (Exner, 2001) and testing themselves against the exercises in the Appendix. Donald Viglione's (2002) recent guide to difficult scoring problems is also an invaluable resource.

There is good evidence that well-trained Rorschach scorers can achieve high levels of interrater reliability (Meyer, Hilsenroth, Baxter, Exner, Fowler, Piers et al., 2002). Even so, because even very experienced Rorschach users make occasional scoring or calculation errors, the use of a scoring program such as the RIAP 5 (Psychological Assessment Resources, Inc., Odessa, FL) or ROR-SCAN (Phil Caracena, Laredo, TX) is often helpful in preventing careless mistakes.

The forensic use of the associated interpretive programs is more problematic in two respects. First, as caveats in the narrative boilerplate of both commercial programs emphasize, an adequate interpretation for a given individual cannot be based on the formal scoring alone. Second, forensic experts who use such interpretive programs as part of the basis for their opinions may be ethically and legally required to produce them upon request, even though they may easily be mischaracterized by cross examiners.

Just as some MMPIs are more interpretable and useful than others, the same is true for Rorschachs. The most clinically reliable Rorschachs are those in which the test taker has understood the task and demonstrated adequate engagement with it, which can be determined by a combination of clinical observation and statistical features (particularly *R* and Lambda). Rorschachs in which test takers have demonstrated an abnormal "set," offered too few or too many responses, or failed to use a reasonable range of common determinants must, like MMPIs with questionable validity scale patterns, be interpreted with considerable caution, if at all.

Interpretation can be validly approached in a variety of ways, but for most users, systematic application of the interpretive procedures of the Rorschach Workshops *Primer* (Exner, 2000), along with careful attention to interpretable test behavior, projective content, and sequence analysis, following Irving Weiner's (2000, 2003) carefully delineated principles, is the optimal procedure.

Of particular importance in forensic work are Weiner's (2000) cautions (*inter alia*): (1) that examiners must first obtain a meaningful understanding of the underlying personality processes in a particular case before drawing clinical inferences about the test taker, (2) that they must try to attend to adaptive capacities as well as maladaptive tendencies, (3) that they should frame interpretive statements at appropriate levels of confidence, and (4) that they need to take the test taker's cultural context into consideration.

To these might be added the warning that in custody work, the Rorschach should not be used for fishing expeditions into every conceivable area of psychopathology. Rather, as discussed earlier, examiners should begin with an understanding of the unresolved issues from the "story" of the case and come to the Rorschach with meaningful questions that it may be well suited to answer.

In contrast to the finite number of appropriate uses of the Rorschach, there are, of course, an infinite number of ways *not* to use it. Those of particular concern (because they are not as rare as they should be in child custody work) include: (1) relying on unscored or incorrectly scored Rorschachs or otherwise departing from the fundamental procedures of the Comprehensive System; (2) interpreting Rorschachs exclusively according to computerized interpretive programs; (3) attempting to determine the actual quality of relationships between parents and children based on Rorschach responses; (4) basing opinions about the best interests of the children exclusively or even primarily on

Rorschach results; (5) basing psychodiagnostic conclusions about litigants or family members (particularly children–see Hamel, Shaffer, & Erdberg, 2000) on the Rorschach alone; (6) determining whether children are victims of sexual abuse or whether parents are abusers primarily from the Rorschach (Kuehnle, 1996); and (7) presuming a fixed, universal significance for particular Rorschach plates or response contents.

Another common, but less obvious, problem is the assumption of a fixed, universal meaning for certain Rorschach determinants and indexes. For example, a Reflection response (Fr/rF) does not always signify a Narcissistic Personality Disorder; an absence of Texture (T/TF/FT) does not always point to a cool, unaffectionate parent; three or more white space (S) responses do not always signify an angry, defiant person; a reasonable number of Human Movement (M) responses does not guarantee a capacity for accurate empathy; not all test takers who produce Lambda greater than 1.0 have Avoidant Personality Disorder; many people who are clinically depressed do not elevate DEPI; even some people with an Adjusted D greater than or equal to 0 lack an adequate capacity to manage stress; not everyone who produces a Vista (V/VF/FV) response loathes herself; and many, if not most, physically abusive parents do not produce Aggressive Movement (AG) responses. The meaning of Rorschach scores and indexes in a particular case must be determined contextually–both by comparing them to and integrating them with convergent and contrasting data elsewhere in the Structural Summary and by considering their particular meaning in the life history and recent experiences of the test taker.

The Rorschach is a sensitive instrument that can allow child custody evaluators privileged access to important data about test takers' coping capacities, cognitive and perceptual style, internal representations of self and others, and implicit motives and need states, using a methodology that does not rely on the test taker's self-attributed personal characteristics. When it is applied within its own proper scope by a well-trained, experienced examiner, it is a formidable resource for coloring in the lines of a thorough personality assessment.

REFERENCES

Ackerman, M. J., & Ackerman, M. C. (1997). Custody evaluation practices: A survey of experienced professionals (revisited). *Professional Psychology: Research and Practice, 28,* 137-145.

Ackerman, M. J., Ackerman, M. C., Steffen, L. J., & Kelley-Poulos, S. (2004). Psychologists' practices compared to the expectations of family law judges and attorneys in child custody cases. *Journal of Child Custody, 1*(1), 41-60.

Acklin, M. W. (1999). Behavioral science foundations of the Rorschach test: Research and clinical applications. *Assessment, 6*(4), 319-324.

American Educational Research Association, American Psychological Association, & National Council on Measurement in Education (AERA, APA, & NCME). (1999). *Standards for educational and psychological testing.* Washington, DC: American Educational Research Association.

American Psychological Association Committee on Professional Practice Standards (APA COPPS). (1994). Guidelines for child custody evaluations in divorce proceedings. *American Psychologist, 49,* 677-680. Available at www.apa.org/practice/childcustody.html

Archer, R. A., & Krishnamurthy, R. (1993). A review of MMPI and Rorschach interrelationships in adult samples. *Journal of Personality Assessment, 61,* 277-293.

Bagby, R. M., Nicholson, R. A., Buis, T., Radovanovic, H., & Fidler, B. J. (1999). Defensive responding on the MMPI-2 in family custody and access evaluations. *Psychological Assessment, 11,* 24-28.

Bathurst, K., Gottfried, A. W., & Gottfried, A. W. (1997). Normative data for the MMPI-2 in child custody litigants. *Psychological Assessment, 9*(3), 205-211.

Blais, M. A., Hilsenroth, M. J., Castelbury, F., Fowler, J. C., & Baity, M. R. (2001). Predicting DSM-IV Cluster B personality disorder criteria from MMPI-2 and Rorschach data: A test of incremental validity. *Journal of Personality Assessment, 76*(1), 150-168.

Bonieskie, L. M. (2000). An examination of personality characteristics of child custody litigants on the Rorschach. *Dissertation Abstracts International, 61*(6-B), 3271.

Bornstein, R. F. (2001). Clinical utility of the Rorschach Inkblot Method: Reframing the debate. *Journal of Personality Assessment, 77*(1), 39-47.

Bornstein, R. F. (2002). A process dissociation approach to objective-projective test score interrelationships. *Journal of Personality Assessment, 78*(1), 47-68.

Bow, J. N., & Quinnell, F. A. (2001). Psychologists' current practices and procedures in child custody evaluations: Five years after the American Psychological Association guidelines. *Professional Psychology: Research and Practice, 30,* 261-268.

Bow, J. N., & Quinnell, F. A. (2004). Critique of child custody evaluations by the legal profession. *Family Court Review, 42,* 115-127.

Bricklin, B. (1999). The contribution of psychological tests to custody-relevant examinations. In R. M. Galatzer-Levy and L. Kraus (Eds.), *The scientific basis of child custody decisions* (pp. 120-156). New York: Wiley.

Brodsky, S. L. (2004). *Coping with cross-examination and other pathways to effective testimony.* Washington, DC: American Psychological Association.

Brodzinsky, D. M. (1993). On the use and misuse of psychological testing in child custody evaluations. *Professional Psychology: Research and Practice, 24,* 213-219.

Butcher, J. N., Graham, J. R., Ben-Porath, Y. S., Tellegen, A., & Dahlstrom, W. G. (2001). *Minnesota Multiphasic Personality Inventory-2 manual for administration, scoring, and interpretation* (Rev. ed.). Minneapolis: University of Minnesota Press.

Daubert v. Merrell Dow Pharmaceuticals Inc., 125 L. Ed. 2d (1993).

Ellis, E. M. (2000). *Divorce wars: Interventions with families in conflict.* Washington, DC: American Psychological Association.

Exner, J. E. (1993). *The Rorschach: A comprehensive system* (3rd ed., Vol. I). New York: Wiley.

Exner, J. E. (2000). *A primer for Rorschach interpretation.* Asheville, NC: Rorschach Workshops.

Exner, J. E. (2001). *A Rorschach workbook for the Comprehensive System* (5th ed.). Asheville, NC: Rorschach Workshops.

Exner, J. E. (2002). A new nonpatient sample for the Rorschach Comprehensive System: A progress report. *Journal of Personality Assessment, 78,* 391-404.

Fischer, C. B. (1994). *Individualizing psychological assessment* (2nd ed.). Hillsdale, NJ: Erlbaum.

Gacono, C. B., Evans, F. B., & Viglione, D. J. (2002). The Rorschach in forensic practice. *Journal of Forensic Psychology Practice, 2*(3), 33-54.

Ganellen, R. J. (1994). Attempting to conceal psychological disturbance: MMPI defensive response sets and the Rorschach. *Journal of Personality Assessment, 63,* 423-437.

Ganellen, R. J. (1996). *Integrating Rorschach and the MMPI-2 in personality assessment.* Mahwah, NJ: Erlbaum.

Garb, H. N. (1999). Call for a moratorium on the use of the Rorschach Inkblot Test in clinical and forensic settings. *Assessment, 6*(4), 313-317.

Gould, J. W. (2004). Evaluating the probative value of child custody evaluations: A guide for forensic mental health professionals. *Journal of Child Custody, 1*(1), 77-96.

Graham, J. R. (2000). *MMPI-2: Assessing personality and psychopathology* (3rd ed.). New York: Oxford University Press.

Grisso, T. (1990). Evolving guidelines for divorce/custody evaluations. *Family and Conciliation Courts Review, 28,* 35-41.

Grove, W. M., & Barden, R. C. (1999). Protecting the integrity of the legal system: The admissibility of testimony from mental health experts under Daubert/Kumho analyses. *Psychology, Public Policy, and Law, 5*(1), 224-242.

Grove, W. R., Barden, C., Garb, H. N., & Lilienfeld, S. O. (2002). Failure of Rorschach-Comprehensive-System-based testimony to be admissible under the Daubert/Kumho Standard. *Psychology, Public Policy, and Law, 5*(1), 216-234.

Halon, R. L. (2001). The Millon Clinical Multiaxal Inventory-III: The normal quartet in child custody cases. *American Journal of Forensic Psychology, 19*(1), 57-75.

Hamel, M., Gallagher, S., & Soares, C. (2001). The Rorschach: Here we go again. *Journal of Forensic Psychology Practice, 1*(3), 79-88.

Hamel, M., Shaffer, T. W., & Erdberg, P. (2000). A study of nonpatient preadolescent Rorschach protocols. *Journal of Personality Assessment, 75,* 280-294.

Heilbrun, K. (1992). The role of psychological testing in forensic assessment. *Law and Human Behavior, 16,* 257-272.

Hilsenroth, M. J., & Stricker, G. A. (2004). Consideration of challenges to psychological assessment instruments used in forensic settings: Rorschach as exemplar. *Journal of Personality Assessment.*

Hoppe, C., & Kenney, L. (1994, August). *A Rorschach study of the psychological characteristics of parents engaged in child custody/visitation disputes.* Paper presented at the 102nd Annual Convention of the American Psychological Association, Los Angeles.

Hunsley, J., & DiGiulio, G. (2001). Norms, norming, and clinical assessment. *Clinical Psychology: Science and Practice, 8,* 378-382.

Keilin, W. G., & Bloom, L. J. (1986). Child custody evaluation practices: A survey of experienced professionals. *Professional Psychology: Research and Practice, 17,* 338-346.

Krishnamurthy, R. (2004, March 12). Representing intricacies of personality in MMPI-2 interpretation. In C. G. Overton (Chair), *Achieving complexity and depth in personality test interpretation.* Symposium conducted at the Society for Personality Assessment Annual Scientific, Miami, FL.

Kuehnle, K. (1996). *Assessing allegations of child sexual abuse.* Sarasota, FL: Professional Resource Exchange.

Kumho Tire v. Carmichael, 119 S. Ct. 1167 (1999).

Lampel, A. K. (1999). Use of the Millon Clinical Multiaxial Inventory-III in evaluating child custody litigants. *American Journal of Forensic Psychology, 17,* 19-31.

Lanyon, R. I. (2001). Dimensions of self-serving misrepresentation in forensic assessment. *Journal of Personality Assessment, 76*(1), 169-179.

Lee, M. (1996). *The use of the Rorschach in child custody evaluations.* Paper presented at the 2nd Child Custody Symposium of the Association of Family and Conciliation Courts, Washington, DC.

Matarazzo, J. D. (1990). Psychological assessment versus psychological testing: Validation from Binet to the school, clinic, and courtroom. *American Psychologist, 45,* 999-1017.

McCann, J. T. (1998). Defending the Rorschach in court: An analysis of admissibility using legal and professional standards. *Journal of Personality Assessment, 70*(1), 125-144.

McCann, J. T., Flens, J. R., Campagna, V., Collman, P., Lazzarro, T., & Connor, E. (2001). The MCMI-III in child custody evaluations: A normative study. *Journal of Forensic Psychology Practice, 1*(2), 27-44.

McClelland, D. C., Koestner, R., & Weinberger, J. (1989). How do implicit and self-attributed motives differ? *Psychological Review, 96,* 690-702.

Medoff, D. (2003). The scientific basis of psychological testing: Considerations following Daubert, Kumho, & Joiner. *Family Court Review, 41*(2), 199-214.

Meloy, J. R., Hansen, T. L., & Weiner, I. B. (1997). Authority of the Rorschach: Legal citations during the past 50 years. *Journal of Personality Assessment, 69*(1), 53-62.

Melton, G., Petrila, J., Poythress, N., & Slobogin, C. (1997). *Psychological evaluations for the courts* (2nd ed.). New York: Guilford.

Meyer, G. J. (1996). The Rorschach and MMPI: Toward a more scientifically differentiated understanding of cross-method assessment. *Journal of Personality Assessment, 67,* 558-578.

Meyer, G. J. (1997). On the integration of personality assessment methods: The Rorschach and MMPI. *Journal of Personality Assessment, 68,* 290-330.

Meyer, G. J. (1999). The convergent validity of MMPI and Rorschach Scales: An extension using profile scores to define response and character styles on both methods and a reexamination of simple Rorschach response frequency. *Journal of Personality Assessment, 72*, 1-35.

Meyer, G. J. (2000). On the science of Rorschach research. *Journal of Personality Assessment, 75*, 46-81.

Meyer, G. J. (2001). Evidence to correct misperceptions about Rorschach norms. *Clinical Psychology: Science and Practice, 8*, 389-396.

Meyer, G. J., & Archer, R. P. (2001). The hard science of Rorschach research: What do we know and where do we go? *Psychological Assessment, 13*(4), 486-502.

Meyer, G. J., Hilsenroth, M. J., Baxter, D., Exner, J. E., Fowler, J. C., Piers, C. C. et al. (2002). An examination of interrater reliability for scoring the Rorschach Comprehensive System in eight data sets. *Journal of Personality Assessment, 78*, 219-274.

Meyer, G. J., Riethmiller, R. J., Brooks, R. D., Benoit, W. A., & Handler, L. (2000). A replication of Rorschach and MMPI-2 convergent validity. *Journal of Personality Assessment, 74*(2), 175-215.

Meyer, G. J., Viglione, D. J., Erdberg, S. P., Exner, J. E., & Shaffer, T. W. (2004, March 11). *CS scoring differences in the Rorschach Workshop and Fresno non-patient samples.* Paper presented at the Society for Personality Assessment Annual Scientific Exchange, Miami, FL.

Millon, T., Millon, C., & Davis, R. (1994). *Millon Clinical Multiaxial Inventory-III.* Minneapolis: Dicandrien.

Morey, L. C. (1996). *Interpretive guide to the Personality Assessment Inventory.* Psychological Assessment Resources, Inc., Lutz, FL.

Ollendick, D. G., & Otto, B. J. (1984). MMPI characteristics of parents referred for child custody studies. *Journal of Psychology, 117*, 227-232.

Otto, R. K., & Collins, R. P. (1995). Use of the MMPI-2/MMPI-A in child custody evaluations. In Y. S. Ben-Porath, J. R. Graham, G. C. N. Hall, R. D. Hirschman, & M. S. Zaragoza (Eds.), *Forensic applications of the MMPI-2.* Thousand Oaks, CA: Sage Publications.

Peebles-Kleiger, M. J. (2002). Elaboration of some sequence analysis strategies: Examples and guidelines for level of confidence. *Journal of Personality Assessment, 79*(1), 19-38.

Quinnell, F. A., & Bow, J. N. (2001). Psychological tests used in child custody evaluations. *Behavioral Sciences and the Law, 19*, 491-501.

Ritzler, B., Erard, R., & Pettigrew, G. (2002a). Protecting the integrity of Rorschach Expert Witnesses: A Reply to Grove and Barden (1999) re: the admissibility of testimony under Daubert/Kumho analyses. *Psychology, Public Policy, and Law, 5*(1), 201-215.

Ritzler, B., Erard, R., & Pettigrew, G. (2002b). A final reply to Grove and Barden: The relevance of the Rorschach Comprehensive System for expert testimony. *Psychology, Public Policy, and Law, 5*(1), 235-246.

Roseby, V. (1995). Uses of psychological tests in a child-focused approach to child custody evaluations. *Family Law Quarterly, 28*, 97-110.

Rosenthal, R., Hiller, J. B., Bornstein, R. F., Berry, D. T., & Brunell-Neulieb, S. (2001). Meta-analytic methods, the Rorschach, and the MMPI. *Psychological Assessment, 13*, 449-451.

Schneidman, E. S. (2004). Ideas from my undergraduate years: An autobiographical fragment. *Journal of Personality Assessment, 82*(2), 129-137.

Shaffer, T. W., & Erdberg, S. P. (2004, March 11). *Final results of the international non-patient Rorschach project.* Paper presented at Society for Personality Assessment Annual Scientific Exchange, Miami, FL.

Shaffer, T. W., Erdberg, P., & Haroian, J. (1999). Current nonpatient data for the Rorschach, WAIS-R, and MMPI-2. *Journal of Personality Assessment, 73*, 305-316.

Shapiro, J. P., Leifer, M., Marton, M. W., & Kassem, L. (1990). Multimethod assessment in sexually abused girls. *Journal of Personality Assessment, 55*, 234-238.

Siegel, J. C. (1996). Traditional MMPI-2 validity indicators and initial presentation in custody evaluations. *American Journal of Forensic Psychology, 14*, 55-63.

Singer, J. (2001). *The Rorschach and personality characteristics of child custody litigants.* Presented at the Society for Personality Assessment Annual Scientific Exchange, San Antonio, TX.

Stahl, P. M. (1999). *Complex issues in child custody evaluations.* Thousand Oaks, CA: Sage.

Underwager, R., & Wakefield, H. (1993). Misuse of psychological tests in forensic settings: Some horrible examples. *American Journal of Forensic Psychology, 11*(1), 55-75.

Viglione, D. J. (1999). A review of recent research addressing the utility of the Rorschach. *Psychological Assessment, 11*(3), 251-265.

Viglione, D. J. (2002). *Rorschach coding solutions: A reference guide for the Comprehensive System.* San Diego, CA: Author. Available at www.geocities.com/donaldviglione

Viglione, D. J., & Hilsenroth, M. J. (2001). The Rorschach: Facts, fictions, and future. *Psychological Assessment, 13*(4), 452-471.

Weiner, I. B. (1999). What the Rorschach can do for you: Incremental validity in clinical applications. *Assessment, 6*, 327-338.

Weiner, I. B. (2000). Making Rorschach interpretation as good as it can be. *Journal of Personality Assessment, 74*, 164-174.

Weiner, I. B. (2001a). Considerations in collecting Rorschach reference data. *Journal of Personality Assessment, 77*(1), 122-128.

Weiner, I. B. (2001b). Advancing the science of psychological assessment: Rorschach as an exemplar. *Psychological Assessment, 13*(4), 423-432.

Weiner, I. B. (2002). Psychodiagnostic testing in forensic psychology: A commentary. *Journal of Forensic Psychology Practice, 2*(3), 113-119.

Weiner, I. B. (2003). *Principles of Rorschach interpretation* (2nd ed.). Mahway, NJ: Erlbaum.

Weiner, I. B., Exner, J. E., & Sciara, A. (1996). Is the Rorschach welcome in the courtroom? *Journal of Personality Assessment, 67*, 422-424.

Weithorn, L. A., & Grisso, T. (1987). Psychological evaluations in divorce and custody: Problems, principles, and procedures. In L. A. Weithorn (Ed.), *Psychology and child custody determinations* (pp. 157-181). Lincoln: University of Nebraska Press.

Wood, J., Nezworski, M., Garb, H., & Lilienfeld, S. (2001). The misperception of psychopathology: Problems with the norms of the Comprehensive System for the Rorschach. *Clinical Psychology: Science and Practice, 8,* 350-373.

Wood, J. M., Nezworski, M. T., & Stejskal, W. J. (1996). The Comprehensive System for the Rorschach: A critical examination. *Psychological Science, 7,* 3-10.

Wood, J. M., Nezworski, M. T., Stejskal, W. J., & McKinzey, R. K. (2001). Problems of the Comprehensive System for the Rorschach in forensic settings: Recent developments. *Journal of Forensic Psychology Practice, 1*(3), 89-103.

The Rorschach:
Its Use in Child Custody Evaluations

Ginger C. Calloway

SUMMARY. The Rorschach Inkblot Measure is a personality measure uniquely suited for use in child custody evaluations. It allows examiners to directly obtain measures of behavior from subjects and yields descriptions of numerous traits about individuals. When the Comprehensive System is used for scoring and interpreting the Rorschach, administration is conducted in standardized, reliable ways that ultimately yield data about individuals that is normative, reliable, and valid. Recent criticisms of the Rorschach compel examiners to be well versed in understanding the strengths and limitations of this instrument and to be well trained in understanding its uses and misuses. This article seeks to assist examiners in using the Rorschach competently to describe individuals and families in rich and nuanced ways. *[Article copies available for a fee from The Haworth Document Delivery Service: 1-800-HAWORTH. E-mail address: <docdelivery@haworthpress.com> Website: <http://www.HaworthPress.com> © 2005 by The Haworth Press, Inc. All rights reserved.]*

Ginger C. Calloway is a PhD psychologist in Raleigh, NC. Dr. Calloway is in private practice, where she provides various evaluations for the courts and attorneys, including custody, juvenile offender, and personal injury evaluations. She also has a limited clinical practice with children and families. She is a mediator and parent coordinator and has served as a member, Vice-Chair, and Chair of the Ethics Committee for the North Carolina Psychological Association.

Address correspondence to: Ginger C. Calloway, PhD, HSP-P, Licensed Psychologist, 855 Washington Street, Suite 200, Raleigh, NC 27605.

[Haworth co-indexing entry note]: "The Rorschach: Its Use in Child Custody Evaluations." Calloway, Ginger C. Co-published simultaneously in *Journal of Child Custody* (The Haworth Press, Inc.) Vol. 2, No. 1/2, 2005, pp. 143-157; and: *Psychological Testing in Child Custody Evaluations* (ed: James R. Flens, and Leslie Drozd) The Haworth Press, Inc., 2005, pp. 143-157. Single or multiple copies of this article are available for a fee from The Haworth Document Delivery Service [1-800-HAWORTH, 9:00 a.m. - 5:00 p.m. (EST). E-mail address: docdelivery@haworthpress.com].

Available online at http://www.haworthpress.com/web/JCC
© 2005 by The Haworth Press, Inc. All rights reserved.
Digital Object Identifier: 10.1300/J190v02n01_08

KEYWORDS. Rorschach, Comprehensive System, child custody, family description

Child custody evaluations (CCE) are complex and involve several individual evaluations integrated into a final evaluation that describes individuals in the family and the family system. Purposes vary from decision-making about parenting plans and custodial arrangements to assisting parents in settlement. A CCE presents challenges to the evaluator to integrate data about several individuals into a whole that makes sense for the families, the individuals within families, attorneys, and the Court.

Assessment can provide an objective anchor for the integration of data, a base for generating hypotheses, and a framework for understanding the diverse bits of data collected during the CCE. Psychological assessment is uniquely suited to assist the evaluator by virtue of employing measures with psychometric robustness, including reliability, validity, and normative data that allows one to employ neutral, objective analysis and coherent description of individual behavior.

Assessment can be used to educate individual family members about each other and about self. When used this way to educate all in the family system, specific scores on particular tests may be less significant than how various members appear and behave, both in isolation as well as with reference to one another. By educating family members about each other, there is an opportunity for understanding to occur. This understanding of the family can also be used by judges and attorneys.

Evaluators typically select instruments and measures that sample a wide, varied range of behaviors. For example, when assessing children, an evaluator will want to know the cognitive and intellectual strengths and limitations of any child in order to speak to the particular child's likely post-divorce adaptation. This is important in speaking to the child's "best interests," the legal standard by which these evaluations are judged. Cognitive and intellectual abilities allow any child to profit more or less from academic endeavors that can be a source of enhanced self-esteem or conversely an impediment to mastery. Academically successful and intellectually bright children have internal resources that will aid in post-divorce separation. Less successful and less intellectually capable children or children with special needs will require assistance in specific ways to adjust in divorce aftermath. Intellectual measures, then, serve as a beginning point for understanding where a particular child is in regard to his/her ability to adjust after divorce.

Intelligence tests provide a sampling of problem-solving behavior that is informative. They also yield specific intelligence quotient (I.Q.) scores. Because these measures are normed and standardized, they provide more reliable and valid measures of problem-solving behaviors than indirect methods of examining the solitary constructs of intellectual potential or academic achievement. Actually observing an individual solve problems contained in intelligence tests can be instructive and revealing, particularly during the highly stressful time of custody litigation and conduct of a CCE.

An examiner can observe an individual's ability to tolerate frustration, willingness to tackle challenging versus easy tasks, frequency of self-deprecating statements, and degree of self-confidence, for example. Sometimes providing psychoeducational testing for a child can yield information that will speak to the "best interests" of a child's educational needs, as in the case when identifying children with special education needs or those with special learning styles. Personality measures, behavioral rating scales, and behavioral observations, to name a few, are additional sources of data for arriving at an understanding of individuals and the family system that will assist parents and children in the aftermath of divorce.

Descriptions of parents that result from assessment also relate to the "best interests" of the child. A parent who is more narcissistic or "self focused" than another parent may exhibit a lack of parenting skills that fails to consider the child's needs. A parent who is routinely empathic, on the other hand, may exhibit parenting skills that are sensitive to children's needs. Measures of parents' personality traits and styles as well as consideration of their academic, employment, and life successes and failures contribute to an understanding of the "match" between parent and child suggested by American Psychological Association's guidelines for child custody evaluations (APA, 1994).

The Rorschach is particularly suited for use in a CCE for arriving at an understanding of an individual's various internal resources. The Rorschach has been criticized of late (Garb, Wood, Lillenfeld, & Nezworski, 2002; Garb, Wood, Nezworski, Grove, & Stejskal, 2001; Grove & Barden, 1999; Grove, Barden, Garb, & Lillenfeld, 2002; Hunsley & Bailey, 2001; Luther-Starbird, 2004) as lacking with regard to its robustness, particularly under Daubert challenge.

Others (Acklin, McDowell, & Verschell, 2000; Bornstein, 2001; Exner, 2003; Ganellen, 2001; Meyer, 2001; Meyer & Archer, 2001;

Ritzler, Erard, & Pettigrew, 2002a, 2002b; Rosenthal, Hiller, Bornstein, Berry, & Brunell-Neuleib, 2001; Viglione & Hilsenroth, 2001; Weiner, 2001) have refuted complaints about the Rorschach. Many of these authors note that problems with the Rorschach are ones of which the competent practitioner is aware. Others provide evidence that the Rorschach is frequently used by psychologists conducting CCEs (Bow & Quinnell, 2001; Quinnell & Bow, 2001) and that it is respected and accepted in the courtroom (Meloy, 1991; Meloy, Hansen, & Weiner, 1997; Weiner, Exner, & Sciara, 1996).

The child custody evaluator who wants to feel secure in using this instrument can review these various articles, with particular attention to Weiner's (2001) article, articles by Ritzler et al. (2002a, 2002b), and recent surveys about the use of the Rorschach in child custody evaluations (Bow & Quinnell, 2001; Quinnell & Bow, 2001). In addition, evaluators can guard against the kind of problems highlighted by critics of the Rorschach with adherence to standardized administration and careful inquiry, use of specific decision-making strategies for scoring and interpreting, and consulting with other experts when questions arise.

Critical, too, are routine participation in continuing education programs that inform evaluators of changes and improvements to the Comprehensive System (CS) for scoring the Rorschach, that expose the evaluator to other experts and their methods of scoring and interpretation, and that ensure frequent routine updates in knowledge of the empirical bases for interpretation. Participation in continuing education of the type sponsored by the Society for Personality Assessment and Rorschach Workshops informs evaluators of challenges to the Comprehensive System, the vulnerabilities of the Comprehensive System, and the varied means of responding to these challenges and vulnerabilities. Importantly, these programs provide up to date findings regarding research (Exner, 2001b, 2002), exposure to other experts using the Rorschach, and critical examination of assessment batteries.

The Rorschach is a particularly useful instrument for CCEs for several reasons. In a recent article, Medoff (2003) characterized the Rorschach, when scored by the Comprehensive System, as "an objectively scored, performance based, cognitive-perceptual task" (Medoff, 2003, p. 209). First, there is no other single source of data collected in a CCE that samples behavior in the multiple ways the Rorschach does. Behavior is largely sampled objectively on the Rorschach (Medoff, 2003), rather than subjectively. The subject is seated in such a way, for example, that examiner and subject are seated side by side, thus reducing the impact of social cues. Instructions to the subject and procedures for collection of the data are standardized, supporting objectivity.

By using the methods outlined in *A Rorschach Workbook for the Comprehensive System* (Exner, 2001a) and in *The Rorschach: A Comprehensive System: Basic Foundations and Principles of Interpretation* (Exner, 2003), the individual's responses to the inkblots are scored in accordance with established rules. Subjective aspects to Rorschach administration, such as facial gestures, turns of phrase, or gestures, for example, are potentially interesting behaviors that do not enter into the scoring or structural interpretation of the subject's responses. These latter may, however, provide rich data in thinking about the individual comprehensively.

This rigor markedly contrasts with the relative absence of standardization of such information sources as interviewing collateral sources or collecting behavioral observations where standards may vary widely from one examiner to the next. While evaluators can certainly use more structured and standardized methods in collecting interviews from collateral sources or in behavioral observations, there are no or few known psychometric qualities of reliability, validity, and norms inherent to these methods. Such techniques often lack research that demonstrates their reliability and validity. Many kinds of useful behaviors are secured during the conduct of a CCE yet these may lack psychometric qualities, thus increasing their subjectivity and decreasing their objectivity.

Second, the Rorschach, often described as a projective test, is better characterized as performance based when contrasted to self-report tests (Medoff, 2003). The Rorschach is performance based in that it requires the subject to complete a task, and the manner in which the subject does so is then scored or coded into quantitative variables, thus reducing examiner subjectivity. These quantitative variables have been empirically demonstrated to relate to personality characteristics and behaviors.

With self-report measures, the subject is asked to respond directly to specific questions. This can be in oral form during interviews, for example, or in written form with scales, rating forms, and questionnaires. One significant advantage to performance-based measures over self-report is the direct collection of data from the subject, while self-report is indirect and thus subject to conscious distortion or manipulation (Medoff, 2003). Self-report measures likely have greater face validity (they appear to be measuring what they say they are measuring) than the Rorschach. In part because of this, the subject can more easily influence his/her presentation of self.

While performance-based tests are not completely free from influence by the subject, such influence is reduced. Because administration and scoring are standardized, examiner bias is reduced. Interpretation of Rorschach findings involves some degree of inference. In using the CS, however, there are specific rules for interpretation when the examiner uses the *Primer for Rorschach Interpretation* (Exner, 2000) and Exner's most recent revision of Volume I of *The Rorschach: A Comprehensive System* (Exner, 2003) for sequential, empirically based decision-making. Performance-based measures such as intelligence tests and the Rorschach allow for behavioral observations in addition to specific scores. This allows for additional comparison points in data collected during a CCE.

Because the Rorschach is a performance-based measure, even seemingly unproductive, highly defended protocols are informative and can provide additional unexpected data. When an individual refuses to cooperate adequately and gives an insufficient number of responses for scoring, for example, this behavior can be revealing and informative. It follows that the individual can be described as less willing than most individuals to engage in the response process of the Rorschach and was less willing than others to engage with the examiner. This way of responding may indicate difficulties in addressing novel problem-solving situations and further indicates a situational defensiveness.

Speculation then arises that this behavior may characterize the individual in other settings. Does this conform, for example, to what the estranged or former spouse reports or can this finding be explained in some other way? If the individual gives an insufficient number of responses for scoring, is he/she able to shift sufficiently with additional instructions to then produce a sufficient number of responses? The ability or inability to respond with more responses provides additional data with regard to how sensitive, aware, or responsive the individual is to the evaluation setting.

Third, the Rorschach is a cognitive-perceptual task requiring the subject to examine ten inkblots and say what the inkblot might be. When administered and scored by the CS, the Rorschach is a scientifically based, empirically supported measure that has a large body of research and normative data for comparing several different groups and children of varying ages. The empirical bases for the Rorschach have been disputed by some authors mentioned previously, whereas the bulk of authors writing on this subject affirm the solid empirical bases for the Rorschach (Exner, 2002, 2003; Ganellen, 2001; Medoff, 2003; Meyer & Archer, 2001; Ritzler et al., 2002; Weiner, 2001). It has demonstrated high levels of interrater reliability (Exner, 2003; Medoff, 2003; Meyer & Archer, 2001) and high levels of incremental validity in the prediction of criteria for a host of personality disorders as well as for the description of personality function and behavior (Blais et al., 2001, as cited in Medoff, 2003; Medoff, 2003).

Some authors (Grove et al., 2002; Luther-Starbird, 2004) decry the misuses of the Rorschach as a reason not to employ it in parenting evaluations or CCEs. They cite instances in which parents were deprived of visitation and custody based on findings from the Rorschach. This same argument can be made for any measure used unwisely by inexperienced or poorly trained examiners and is not particular to the Rorschach. Competent examiners responsibly consider all the data collected during these evaluations and will not offer a judgment as to terminating parental rights, restricting a parent's time with a child, or opining about personality or mental disorders on the basis of solitary, isolated pieces of data. To throw out the instrument because of incompetent examiners is short sighted and unnecessary. The competent examiner has a responsibility to educate and inform the Court and attorneys about the appropriate or proper use of all assessment instruments, including the Rorschach. Custody evaluators can effectively and competently use the Rorschach in a CCE or parenting evaluation. The remainder of this article will give examples of how the Rorschach may be used.

USING THE RORSCHACH IN CHILD CUSTODY EVALUATIONS

First, the Rorschach can serve as a source of hypotheses that can be evaluated by looking at other data in a CCE. Because the Rorschach yields multiple types of data about numerous traits and allows the examiner to describe individuals in distinctive ways, numerous hypotheses are generated for consideration. In the following scenario, an 11-year-old male child is evaluated as part of a CCE. Father describes mother as "alienating" the child, while mother says that father is overly harsh with the children, particularly this child who is the oldest. The child appears sad and forlorn during the evaluation.

Assessment with the Rorschach reveals the child is positive for the Coping Deficit Index (CDI), an index that identifies those with coping limitations or deficiencies (Exner, 2003, p. 313). This finding suggests this child is more immature than others his age and has poorly developed interpersonal skills. His limitations in social interaction skills include his passivity, ineptness or immaturity, and rigidity. Other findings from the Rorschach suggest the child is experiencing an uncomfortably high level of stress. The child says he does not want increased time with father, which father seeks.

One hypothesis to emerge from Rorschach findings is that this child has aligned himself with mother because her parenting style (a highly organized one) organizes and structures him in ways that reduce his stress and that compensate for his inadequately developed social interaction skills as indicated by his positive finding for CDI. Findings from the Rorschach about the mother's overincorporative style were congruent with her highly organized behavior during the evaluation, by report of others including her children, and also from report of her employers.

Overincorporation on the Rorschach "is an enduring trait-like style that includes the exertion of more effort in scanning activities. Overincorporators apparently want to avoid being careless, and this motivates them to invest more effort than may be necessary to scan the features of a situation. Although somewhat less efficient because of the added effort, overincorporation is often an asset because the thorough approach to scanning usually ensures that all stimulus cues are included in the input" (Exner, 2003, p. 348). In short, overincorporators might be thought of as detail-oriented and/or extremely thorough.

These combined findings suggest this mother does attend to this child in ways that compensate for his limitations in socially adaptive skills. Father, on the other hand, is also positive for CDI and he demonstrates an underincorporative style on the Rorschach. Undercorporation on the Rorschach occurs when "the subject scans hastily and haphazardly, and often may neglect critical bits or cues that exist in a stimulus field. In older children and adults, it can be a significant liability because underincorporation creates a potential for faulty translation of cues that are present, leading to less effective patterns of behavior" (Exner, 2003, p. 347). By comparison to overincorporators, underincorporators may be haphazard and less detail-oriented. This father misses many daily details of his child's life, including paying attention to the child's athletic events and special school events. Discovering that he is also CDI+ on the Rorschach, combined with his "forgetfulness" about the child's activities, suggests he may be less sensitive to the child's limitations and needs than is mother, an important consideration in addressing "best interests."

Findings from the Rorschach are compared to information obtained from other evaluation sources for congruency. From these congruent findings, one develops recommendations appropriate to this child and his family. For this case, recommendations should address ways this child's father can modify his insensitivity and change the level of attention he gives to child-centered matters. Recommendations should address how the mother can assist the child in developing more adaptive interpersonal skills, particularly in ways that allow the child to assume responsibility for organizing his behaviors rather than relying solely on mother.

Recommendations will address the stress overload the child is experiencing and will attempt to modify this to prevent possible depression that could result if untreated or if there were no intervention. Recommendations can include specific activities for the child and father to accomplish together without mother's input, can address transitions, and can address assistance with homework through a tutor rather than continued reliance on mother.

When utilized in this way, the Rorschach adds richness and nuanced understanding to the descriptions of the individuals within the family and their interactions, descriptions that were generated from forming working hypotheses and from integrating information from other sources with Rorschach data. In this case, too, findings from the Rorschach about individual family members explain the family dynamics and explain some reasons this couple may have experienced difficulties in understanding each other pre-divorce and in co-parenting post-divorce. This mother's highly organized manner, for example, was seen by father as overly controlling and intrusive. This father's more relaxed, less organized manner was characterized by this mother as uncaring and insensitive.

The Rorschach allows for description of individuals in uniquely personal ways. Examining two parents' Rorschach protocols further provides information about the interaction between them. For example, a referral question directs the examiner to investigate the question of domestic violence in a family during the marriage. Examiners will interview both parents with structured interviews specific to evaluating domestic violence; will interview children, when possible, to garner their impressions of their parents; might interview family and other collateral sources; and will administer personality and other assessment measures.

The Rorschach will help the examiner to describe the nature of the interaction between the two parents, given their particular constellation of traits and internal resources. If a mother, for example, has a high Affective Ratio while father has a very low Affective Ratio, this finding serves as a beginning point for considering how these parents may have engaged in emotional interchanges that resulted in domestic violence. The Affective Ratio in the CS "relates to a person's interest in experiencing or being around emotional stiumuli" (Exner, 2003, p. 294). How comfortable, in other words, is the individual around emotion and emotional displays? Another variable relating to emotional expression is the FC:CF + C ratio. This variable describes the individual's willingness to make emotional responses and describes how well the individual does or does not control that expression. This ratio is not the only indicator of impulse control on the Rorschach, yet it can contribute to descriptions of impulse control.

While not relying upon these findings alone from the Rorschach, an examiner can use these to explore if a mother may have been more willing initially to engage in emotional exchanges of closeness that a father ineptly tolerated. A father's intolerance of these emotional exchanges of closeness may have ultimately led to some form of domestic violence if his emotional expression was not well controlled or modulated. An understanding of these dynamics may be more completely achieved in terms of the significant differences in this couple's willingness to grapple with their emotions and their ability to control the expression of emotion. Without this kind of complex examination of the dynamics of interpersonal exchanges, the specific avenues for redress in the post-divorce phase are less clear.

The Rorschach can be used as a means to integrate data about individuals in the course of a CCE. By conducting an interpretive search strategy using the *Primer for Rorschach Interpretation* (Exner, 2000), examiners can determine which areas of functioning are of central significance for any individual. In a sequential manner, examiners should then look at all other sources of data gathered during the evaluation for confirming and disconfirming instances of findings from the Rorschach.

Rorschach and MMPI-2 findings, for example, can often be congruent and can just as often be disparate. An individual who elevates on scales L (lie), S (superlative), and K (defensiveness) from the MMPI-2 is describing self as exceedingly morally superior to others and as completely free from the usual failings of other people. To check for other suggestions of this attribute, we could look to the Rorschach for suggestions of narcissism or denial. If we find that denial, for example, is suggested by findings from the Rorschach (Ganellen, 1996), can we also find suggestions of denial from other measures of personality, like the Revised NEO Personality Inventory (Costa & McCrae, 1992), from behavioral observations, and/or from interviews? If we do not find suggestions of denial from findings on the Rorschach and we find suggestions of narcissism instead, then we might seek to determine if narcissism is suggested elsewhere in other data sources. In this kind of analysis, the Rorschach clearly adds incremental value to a battery of tests.

It is critical that examiners consider Rorschach findings in the context of data collected throughout the entire evaluation and that they not place undue weight on any one finding. It may be tempting, for example, to make much of a finding suggesting narcissism for one parent and not the other. To the extent that parents without narcissistic traits may be more attentive to their children's needs and to the extent that this attention is a positive thing, it may seem quite compelling to give such a finding great weight. However, a narcissistic parent may serve as a model for successful achievement for children if the narcissism is based on real world accomplishments. Weiner (2003) suggests there are "nice" narcissists and "nasty" narcissists. Nice narcissists enjoy being the center of attention in social situations and enjoy being entertaining to others. Nasty narcissists are more critical of others and are more often considered arrogant and self-serving by others. The way narcissism is expressed, its function for a particular parent, and how it is experienced by children is critical to consider in light of all data collected during a CCE.

The issue of norms and over diagnosing pathology arose during some discussions about the Rorschach's utility and normative development as well as those about the Rorschach under scrutiny with regard to Daubert standards. While not the subject of this article and because it requires more in-depth examination than possible here, this point bears some attention nonetheless. When the Rorschach is used as intended, employing the CS, personality description and not personality diagnosis results. This is particularly crucial for child custody examiners who evaluate parents and children additionally at risk for being overpathologized by the legal system and those working within it.

For example, with regard to over diagnosing pathology, we discover in the course of conducting a CCE that a Rorschach finding yields a Perceptual Thinking Index (PTI) of three or four. This should not reflexively be interpreted as indicative of a thought disorder. As Exner (2003) notes, "the PTI is *not* used as a primary source for specific diagnostic decisions. Rather, it should be viewed as a continuous scale on which higher values are less preferable than lower values. Its main purpose is to alert interpreters about the likelihood of mediational and ideational difficulties" (pp. 392-393).

Mediational and ideational difficulties are difficulties in accurate perception and interpretation that individuals have of the world. The PTI ascertains how appropriately an individual is able to evaluate his/her world so behaviors are generally appropriate and expectable. The PTI also indicates the nature of an individual's thinking and judgment. Does a parent, for example, have the basic ingredients necessary for conventional reality testing? Do the emotional and thinking patterns lead a parent to see his/her world in more personal, perhaps inaccurate, ways? Is a parent's thinking sufficiently mature and controlled for sound judgment? If an examiner is *alerted* to the possibility of difficulties in accurate perception and interpretation of the world, it follows that a positive PTI finding yields only a working hypothesis and is not a conclusion. A competent examiner will proceed to look for both confirming and disconfirming instances of inaccurate translation and understanding of the world.

Those trained in the interpretation of the Rorschach understand that a more thorough analysis of the individual's thinking processes is considerably more helpful and yields more descriptive information than a single label to guide recommendations or inform families about areas in need of change. As Exner (2003) notes further, "It seems clear that PTI scores of four or five signify considerably more mediational/ideational trouble than scores of zero, one, or two, but that is a concrete differentiation. The true extent of any mediational or ideational problems unfolds only as the clusters of data pertaining to these features are thoroughly reviewed" (p. 393). Experienced examiners who routinely use the Rorschach view it as one more tool, albeit a quite excellent and unique one, in the battery of measures providing data in a CCE. It is the integration of data from divergent data sources that is at issue in a CCE and not a single data point that guides thinking about families, family dynamics, and best interests of children. The richness and depth of data offered by the Rorschach is a unique contribution to an assessment battery.

The value of the Rorschach to child custody evaluations lies in its unique contributions as an objectively scored, performance-based, cognitive-perceptual task. It is uniquely suited to CCEs because it allows for integration and organization of substantial amounts of data with common sense categories of emotion, thinking, coping styles, interpersonal information, data about self-perception, impulse control, and situational stress, all of which may not occur in other solitary measures of personality. When used appropriately and sensibly, the Rorschach is an anchor against which to test hypotheses about information gathered from other sources and generates hypotheses as well. It is a unique source of data against which other sources of data can be compared.

The Rorschach allows for a deeper understanding of individuals. By providing richness and depth to the descriptions of individuals, the Rorschach contributes to understanding among family members about others in the family system, as well as understanding their own personal characteristics that contributed to pre-divorce and to the impasse post-divorce. Individuals within a family system are enabled to understand self and interactions with others more completely, as are professionals and those in the legal system who come in contact with these families. The Rorschach provides a description of parents to each other and about their children that can aid in a more healthy adjustment for the children in the post-divorce period. Not least of all, data obtained from Rorschach administration leads directly to sensible, thoughtful recommendations that address the "best interests" of children.

REFERENCES

Acklin, M. W., McDowell, C. J., & Verschell, M. S. (2000). Interobserver agreement, intraobserver reliability, and the Rorschach Comprehensive System. *Journal of Personality Assessment, 74,* 15-47.

American Psychological Association. (1994). Guidelines for child custody evaluations in divorce proceedings. *American Psychologist, 49, 7,* 677-688.

Bornstein, R. F. (2001). Clinical utility: Reframing the debate. *Journal of Personality Assessment, 77,* 39-47.

Bow, J., & Quinnell, F. (2001). Psychologists' current practices and procedures in child custody evaluations: Five years after American Psychological Association Guidelines. *Professional Psychology: Research and Practice, 32(3),* 261-268.

Costa, P. T., & McCrae, R. R. (1992). *Revised NEO Personality Inventory: Professional manual.* Odessa, FL: Psychological Assessment Resources.

Exner, J. E. (2000). *A primer for Rorschach interpretation.* Asheville, NC: Rorschach Workshops.

Exner, J. E. (2001a). *A Rorschach workbook for the Comprehensive System* (5th ed.). Asheville, NC: Rorschach Workshops.

Exner, J. E. (2001b, September). *A preliminary report on a new set of Rorschach Comprehensive System norms.* Presented at the Annual Meeting of Rorschach Workshops, Incorporated, Asheville, NC.

Exner, J. E. (2002). A new nonpatient sample for the Rorschach Comprehensive System: A progress report. *Journal of Personality Assessment, 78,* 391-404.

Exner, J. E. (2003). *The Rorschach: A Comprehensive System: Basic foundations and principles of interpretation. Vol. I* (4th ed.). New Jersey: Wiley & Sons.

Ganellen, R. J. (1996). *Integrating the Rorschach and MMPI-2 in personality assessment.* Mahwah, NJ: Lawrence Erlbaum Associates, Inc.

Ganellen, R. J. (2001). Weighing evidence for the Rorschach's validity: A response to Wood et al. (1999). *Journal of Personality Assessment, 77,* 1-15.

Garb, H. N., Wood, J. M., Lillenfeld, S. O., & Nezworski, M. T. (2002). Effective use of projective techniques in clinical practice: Let the data help with selection and interpretation. *Professional Psychology: Research and Practice, 33*(5), 454-463.

Garb, H. N., Wood, J. M., Nezworski, M. T., Grove, W. M., & Stejskal, W. J. (2001). Toward a resolution of the Rorschach controversy. *Psychological Assessment, 13*(4), 433-448.

Grove, W., & Barden, C. (1999). Protecting the integrity of the legal system: The admissibility from mental health experts under *Daubert/Kumho* analyses. *Psychology, Public Policy, and Law, 5*(1), 224-242.

Grove, W. M., Barden, R. C., Garb, H. N., & Lillenfeld, S. O. (2002). Failure of Rorschach-Comprehensive-System-based testimony to be admissible under the Daubert-Joiner-Kumho standard. *Psychology, Public Policy and Law, 8*(2), 216-234.

Hunsley, J., & Bailey, J. M. (2001). Whither the Rorschach? An analysis of the evidence. *Psychological Assessment, 13*(4), 472-485.

Luther-Starbird, L. (2004). Rorschach use in parenting evaluations: Recommendations for cross-examining expert witnesses. *Colorado Family Law Newsletter, 33*(7), 97-103.

Medoff, D. (2003). The scientific basis of psychological testing: Considerations following Daubert, Kumho, and Joiner. *Family Court Review, 41*(2), 199-213.

Meloy, R. (1991). Rorschach testimony. *The Journal of Psychiatry and Law, 19,* 221-235.

Meloy, J. R., Hansen, T. L., & Weiner, I. B. (1997). Authority of the Rorschach: Legal citations during the past 50 years. *Journal of Personality Assessment, 69,* 53-62.

Meyer, G. J. (2001). Introduction to the final special section in the special series on the utility of the Rorschach for clinical assessment. *Psychological Assessment, 13*(4), 419-422.

Meyer, G. J., & Archer, R. P. (2001). The hard science of Rorschach research: What do we know and where do we go? *Psychological Assessment, 13*(4), 486-452.

Quinnell, F. A., & Bow, J. N. (2001). Psychological tests used in child custody evaluations. *Behavioral Sciences and the Law, 19,* 491-501.

Ritzler, B., Erard, R., & Pettigrew, G. (2002a). Protecting the integrity of Rorschach expert witnesses: A reply to Grove and Barden (1999) re: the admissibility of testimony under Daubert/Kumho analyses. *Psychology, Public Policy and Law, 8*(2), 201-215.

Ritzler, B., Erard, R., & Pettigrew, G. (2002b). A final reply to Grove and Barden: The relevance of the Comprehensive System for expert testimony. *Psychology, Public Policy and Law, 8*(2), 235-246.

Rosenthal, R., Hiller, J. B., Bornstein, R. F., Berry, T. R., & Brunell-Neuleib, S. (2001). Meta-analytic methods, the Rorschach, and the MMPI. *Psychological Assessment, 13*(4), 449-451.

Viglione, D. J., & Hilsenroth, M. J. (2001). The Rorschach: Facts, fictions, and future. *Psychological Assessment, 13*(4), 452-471.

Weiner, I. B. (2001). Advancing the science of psychological assessment: The Rorschach inkblot method as exemplar. *Psychological Assessment, 13*(4), 423-432.

Weiner, I. B. (2003). *Principles of Rorschach interpretation* (2nd ed.). Mahwah, NJ: Lawrence Erlbaum Associates.

Weiner, I. B., Exner, J. E., & Sciara, A. (1996). Is the Rorschach welcome in the courtroom? *Journal of Personality Assessment, 67,* 422-424.

Clinical Ratings of Parenting Capacity and Rorschach Protocols of Custody-Disputing Parents: An Exploratory Study

Janet R. Johnston
Marjorie G. Walters
Nancy W. Olesen

SUMMARY. In this study, the Rorschach protocols of 98 parents undergoing custody evaluations were correlated with clinical judgments of their alienating co-parenting behavior, parent-child role reversal, lack of warm and involved parenting, and abuse of the child. The results indicate that this personality assessment instrument, scored according to the

Janet R. Johnston, PhD, is Professor, Department of Justice Studies, San Jose State University, whose research and clinical practice has focused on highly conflicted custody-litigating families.

Marjorie G. Walters, PhD, and Nancy W. Olesen, PhD, are clinical psychologists in private practice specializing in child custody evaluations and therapy with divorcing families.

Address correspondence to: Janet R. Johnston, PhD, Justice Studies Department, San Jose State University, One Washington Square, San Jose, CA 95192-0050 (E-mail: johnston@email.sjsu.edu).

This research was made possible by a grant from the Amini Foundation for the Study of Affects. The data, without subject identifiers, were made available from members of the Judith Wallerstein Center for the Family in Transition.

[Haworth co-indexing entry note]: "Clinical Ratings of Parenting Capacity and Rorschach Protocols of Custody-Disputing Parents: An Exploratory Study." Johnston, Janet R., Marjorie G. Walters, and Nancy W. Olesen. Co-published simultaneously in *Journal of Child Custody* (The Haworth Press, Inc.) Vol. 2, No. 1/2, 2005, pp. 159-178; and: *Psychological Testing in Child Custody Evaluations* (ed: James R. Flens, and Leslie Drozd) The Haworth Press, Inc., 2005, pp. 159-178. Single or multiple copies of this article are available for a fee from The Haworth Document Delivery Service [1-800-HAWORTH, 9:00 a.m. - 5:00 p.m. (EST). E-mail address: docdelivery@haworthpress.com].

Comprehensive System, is likely to provide a relatively rich source of data relevant to assessing parenting skills and capacities in custody-disputing families that are convergent with clinical assessments drawn from clinical interviews, parent-child observations, and substantiated histories of child abuse. *[Article copies available for a fee from The Haworth Document Delivery Service: 1-800-HAWORTH. E-mail address: <docdelivery@ haworthpress.com> Website: <http://www.HaworthPress.com> © 2005 by The Haworth Press, Inc. All rights reserved.]*

KEYWORDS. Child custody evaluations, personality testing, parenting capacity, parental alienation, role reversal, child abuse

During the past decade, there have been increasing demands made upon forensic mental health professionals who serve the family court to develop standards and protocols for conducting child custody evaluations in ways that are more scientifically sound and ethically defensible (Gould, 1999a,b; Gould & Stahl, 2000; Greenberg, Martindale, Gould, & Gould-Saltman, 2004; Stahl, 1994). Major professional organizations have begun to clarify the goals and recommended procedures for custody evaluations where assessment of each parent's capacity to parent as it relates to the psychological functioning and developmental needs of their children has central focus (American Academy of Child and Adolescent Psychiatry [AACAP], 1997; American Psychological Association [APA], 1994; Association of Family and Conciliation Courts [AFCC], 1994). To this end, current guidelines for best practices endorse the need for gathering data from a variety of sources using different methods: clinical assessments of parents and children, self-report using structured questionnaires, standardized psychological testing, direct parent-child observations, and review of documents and interviews with collateral sources.

A number of surveys have been conducted of psychologists' practices in custody evaluations before and after the guidelines by APA and AFCC were published (Ackerman & Ackerman, 1997; Bow & Quinnell, 2001; Hagen & Castagna, 2001; Hysjulien, Wood, & Benjamin, 1994; Keilin & Bloom, 1986; LaFortune & Carpenter, 1998; Quinnell & Bow, 2001). Most recently, Bow and Quinnell's (2002) review of this research showed an increasing sophistication and comprehensiveness of custody evaluations performed by psychologists during the past fifteen years, with most current practices and procedures adhering to APA guidelines, especially in the use of diverse and multiple sources of data.

The expectation is that the custody evaluator will be able to integrate this voluminous and complex data in a logical and rational way to provide more informed and balanced expert testimony to courts that must decide on what custody arrangements are in the best interests of children. Interestingly, despite the growing sophistication and comprehensiveness of custody evaluations, little attention has been given to the extent to which different, independent sources of information coincide– also called "convergent validity" (Gould, 2004). Only a few published works have addressed the calculus of weighting and integrating disparate information from different sources (Ackerman & Schoendorf, 1992; Austin, 2000, 2002; Kirkland, 2002).

Virtually all custody evaluators agree that clinical interviews are an essential component of custody evaluations. Furthermore, the majority of psychologists who conduct custody evaluations use some kind of psychological testing of parents (90%) and of children (60%) in their assessment battery (Quinnell & Bow, 2001). Obviously, information gained from psychological testing of family members is only one piece of the equation and interestingly, it appears to carry far less weight than clinical interviews. In their survey, Bow and Quinnell (2001) asked custody evaluators to rank order (or weight) the importance of different types of information. Their data show that clinical interviews and history with parents rank most highly (1.8), and psychological testing of parents rank only moderately (5) on a scale of 1-10. This seems to imply that psychological test results are subject to interpretation and modification within the context of clinical interviews, behavioral observations, and family histories. Of particular interest is the question: To what extent are clinical inferences derived from interviews and observations of parenting capacity compatible with inferences drawn from psychological testing? Data addressing this question may shed light on the ongoing debate about whether there is an overdependence upon and inappropriate use of psychological tests in custody reports (Brodzinsky, 1993; Roseby, 1995).

Amongst adult objective personality tests, the Minnesota Multiphasic Personality Inventory MMPI/MMPI-2 has continued to be the most frequently used in custody evaluations, with the Millon Clinical Multiaxial Inventory II or III (MCMI) gaining in popularity (Quinnell & Bow, 2001). The frequent use of these particular tests has not been without controversy, partly because they do not address parenting capacity directly, but mostly because they are subject to impression management (i.e., "faking good") and other forms of defensive responding such as "self-deception." The use of the Lie (L) and Correction (K) scales to evaluate potential bias when using the MMPI-2 seems not to have settled the controversy (Bagby, Nicholson, Buis, Radovanovic, & Fidler, 1999; Bathurst, Gottfried, & Gottfried, 1997; Posthuma & Harper, 1998; Strong, Green, Hoppe, Johnston, & Olesen, 1999).

Although there is an increasing usage of parenting inventories like the Child Behavior Checklist (CBCL), the Parenting Stress Index (PSI), and the Parent-Child Relationship Inventory (PCRI), all of these self-report tests are also subject to bias by parents who may confuse their own symptoms of emotional distress with their children's and who may have strong motivation to perceive themselves and their children in ways that would benefit their custody quest. Other tests specifically designed for assessing parent-child relationships in custody evaluations (Bricklin, 1989, 1990; Bricklin & Elliott, 1991) have declined in usage, possibly because of strong criticisms as to their lack of established psychometric properties (e.g., Otto, Edens, & Barcus, 2000), especially in light of the new legal standards for admissibility of expert testimony following U.S. Supreme Court decisions *re Daubert, Kumho,* and *Joiner* (Medoff, 2003).

Over more than a decade, the Rorschach Ink Blot Test has remained a steady favorite instrument for about 45% of custody evaluators and is the most popular amongst the projective tests used for their adult clients (Quinnell & Bow, 2001). When scored by the Exner Comprehensive System (Exner, 1991), the scientific basis of the Rorschach has been generally well established (Meyer, 2000; Meyer et al., 2001) though not without challenge (Wood, Nezworski, Stejskal, Garvan, & West, 2001). Furthermore, the Rorschach's use in legal testimony has been upheld in the large majority of cases (Medoff, 2003; Meloy, Hansen, & Weiner, 1997).

Amongst the purported benefits of the Rorschach is the belief that the test is harder to "fake good" compared to more objective personality tests and self-report parenting scales. Although there is some research to support this contention (Grossman, Wasyliw, Benn, & Gyoerkoe, 2002), it has been suggested that attempts at simulation on the Rorschach may result in just the opposite kinds of bias (i.e., in less than favorable protocols and more elevated rates of pathology on some variables when approval seekers attempt to "show their stuff" with long, elaborate responses; Exner, 1991, p. 429; Viglione, 1996). Custody evaluators who favor the Rorschach also believe that it yields data that are qualitatively different than self-report data such as capacity for empathy and ability to cope with stress and conflict that are the hallmarks of warm, nurturing parenting. However to date there are only a few studies that report Rorschach protocols of parents undergoing custody disputes so that normative data on this population are scant (Exner, 1991; Valente-Torre, Cavani, & Brusca, 1987). Moreover, the Rorschach's relevance to parenting capacity has only been inferentially argued rather than directly examined (Medoff, 2003; Meyer et al., 2001). It is one goal of our research to begin to correct these deficiencies.

In an earlier study, some of our research team examined the Rorschach protocols of 87 divorcing couples ($N = 174$ adults) that were undergoing a child custody evaluation (Walters, Olesen, & Lee, 2004). The aggregate data were compared to that of two current non-patient samples (Exner, 2002 and Shaffer, Erdberg, & Haroian, 1999). It was found that the custody-disputing sample was significantly different from both non-patient samples in a number of domains, but especially in their lack of resilience to separation and loss. Specifically, custody disputants were significantly more depressed (DEPI > 4), more harshly self-critical (SumV > 0), more likely to produce percepts that were devalued or spoiled (MOR > 2), and used more intellectualizing defenses (Intellect > 5). They also tended to be deficient in organized coping skills (AdjD < -1 and D < 0) and were more likely to have a rigid, authoritarian coping style (PER > 0). Although there was little evidence that they were more narcissistically vulnerable than both non-patient samples, custody disputants were significantly more emotionally needy (T > 1) and had more difficulty processing information logically and accurately (WSum6, ALOG > 0).

A second goal of our research is to examine the personality correlates of custody-disputing parents whose parenting behavior is likely to lead to a child becoming alienated from or rejecting of one of the parents after divorce, a problem that is commonly referred to as Parental Alienation (PA) or Parental Alienation Syndrome (PAS).[1] Alienated children are defined as those who freely and persistently express unreasonable negative feelings and beliefs (such as anger, hatred, rejection, and/or fear) toward a parent, disproportionate to their actual experience of that parent (Kelly & Johnston, 2001, p. 251). According to PAS theory, the behavior of the aligned parents of such children is seen as most culpable in influencing the child's rejection of a parent (Gardner, 1998; Warshak, 2003). However, in three previous studies (involving $N = 215$, $N = 125$, and $N = 74$ families), it was found that problematic parenting behaviors of *both* parents, as well as vulnerabilities within the child, contribute to the problem of child alienation (Johnston, 2003; Johnston, Gans Walters, & Olesen, 2004, in press). Specifically, alienating behavior by an aligned parent (mother or father) who is in role-reversal with the child, together with critical incidents of child abuse and/or lack of warm, involved parenting by a marginalized rejected parent (father or mother), jointly explain why some psychologically vulnerable children form a pathological alliance with one parent against the other. The interesting question is whether personality tests, specifically the Rorschach, can validate clinical judgments of these kinds of parenting behaviors in custody-disputing parents.

The specific purpose of the current study is to examine the relationship of clinical ratings of four domains of parenting with selected variables on the Rorschach test in a sample of parents undergoing custody evaluation. It was hypothesized that clinical ratings of (a) alienating co-parenting, (b) parent-child role reversal, (c) lack of warm and involved parenting, and (d) child abuse would be directly related to Rorschach indicators of problems in object relatedness, information processing, coping, and affective functioning.

EMPIRICAL STUDY

Sample and Methods

The sample of parents for this study was drawn from an archival database of custody evaluation records describing parent-child relationships in separating and divorced families. These data were collected over a decade from 1988 through 1998 within several San Francisco Bay Area counties. All subjects were referred by family court order or parties' stipulation to private clinical psychologists for custody evaluations that were paid for by the litigants.

From a total sample of 87 families in the data bank, only those with children under 13 years were selected for this study. We also excluded cases if Rorschach data were not available, family reports were missing from the files, or insufficient data were available to make the clinical ratings. The final sample consisted of 98 parents from 49 families. On average, mothers were 38 years ($SD = 6.7$) and fathers were 42 years ($SD = 7.1$). The average number of children in each family was 1.5 ($SD = 0.7$) and the modal family size was an only child.

In terms of actual residential arrangements, 46% of children were in their mother's custody, 10% were in father's custody, 42% were in joint custody, and 2% were living with another relative. On the average, children saw their fathers 12.7 days per month ($SD = 8.6$).

The majority was Caucasian (90%). Average length of marriage was 6.4 years ($SD = 4.1$). Length of separation for the total sample varied widely ($M = 42$ months, $SD = 32$). On the 7-point Hollingshead and Redlich (1958) occupational index, fathers' mean rating was 2.9 ($SD = 1.8$) indicating a relatively high socioeconomic status and for mothers it was 4.6 ($SD = 2.2$) indicating moderate status.

Procedure

The data gathering consisted of extensive interviews with each family member that included developmental histories of the children and their relationships with each parent; a brief history of each parent's family of origin; a history of the courtship, marriage and separation; observations of the interactions between parents and children; information from collateral professionals and others close to the family, and reviews of written documentation provided by attorneys and parents. Special attention was given to the content and the history of the parental disputes with one another, especially the allegations of abuse each party made about the other that precipitated the referral.

A full battery of psychological tests was administered to all parents, and with children when indicated. The raw data and results of these tests were kept in separate files and were not available for the clinical ratings of parenting behaviors. Custody evaluations typically required 30-50 hours of data collection for each family, following which a full written report, documenting all observational data, together with a clinical summary was prepared and made available to the court.

Using the materials described above (with the exclusion of the standardized psychological tests), two experienced clinicians, working independently, completed clinical ratings of each family utilizing rating scales and a coding manual prepared for the purpose of extracting data for multiple, different studies. They coded significant events in the lives of each parent (especially childhood loss and trauma), the history of the courtship, marriage, and separation; the nature of the ex-spousal relationship; allegations and substantiations of domestic violence including child abuse; parenting behaviors; and the child's attitudes and behavior toward each parent. A total of three clinical psychologists and three clinical social workers were engaged in the task, with one of these rating all cases in the data samples. Where discrepancies of two or more points on the scales arose on any item, and where there were differences in facts reported on a "yes/no" measure, the two raters conferred and attempted to reduce their differences. These discussions helped to produce further elaboration of the coding manual, reducing subsequent discrepancies. It was estimated that this involved less than 8% of the data points. Inter-rater reliabilities for each item on all clinical ratings were calculated using intra-class correlations (ICCs). Any item with missing data on > 15% of the total sample or with ICC < .50 was dropped.

Factor analyses were then conducted on the remaining items within each conceptual category. Principal-component analysis with varimax rotation was utilized. Factors with eigenvalues > 1 were retained, and within each factor, items that loaded > .40 were retained. Items loading together on a factor were evaluated for internal consistency using Cronbach's Alpha. The remaining items for each factor were combined with equal weighting to produce the score for each scale since they were all measured on six-point Likert scales (from none to very high).

The Rorschach was administered and scored by experienced licensed clinical psychologists (who were the custody evaluators) using the standard instructions of the Comprehensive System. Inter-rater reliability was obtained by taking a sub-sample of 30 protocols that were re-scored by the researchers. Inter-rater reliabilities were in the high range according to standards set by Meyer et al. (2002).

Measures of Clinical Ratings of Parenting

Alienating Co-Parent (AlienatM/F) (α = .93; ICC = .76). This factor was made up of 10 items that measure the extent to which the parent sabotages the child's relationship with the other parent by using the child to send negative messages, expressing anger if the child shows positive feelings toward the other parent, and modeling hostile, negative behavior toward the other parent. This factor was negatively correlated with *Supportive Co-Parent (M/FSupport)* r = −.75 and −.66, a second clinical rating measuring the extent to which each parent supports and encourages the child's relationship with the other parent.

Role Reversal with Parent (RolRevM/F) (α = .84; ICC = .77). This factor was made up of seven items that measure the extent of boundary problems, role reversal, or psychological intrusiveness between each parent and child. Items include ones like "[parent has] difficulty distinguishing child's feelings from own," "child comfort's parent; parent's parent," "child is confidante to parent's adult interests and concerns." It is important to note that *RolRevM/F* and *AlienatM/F* are highly correlated (*r* = .63 and .57) indicating that, as measured, these two concepts overlap.

Warm-Involved Parent (WarmInvM/F) (α = .91; ICC = .69). This factor was made up of 12 items, measuring positive parenting capacities. Examples of these items include "parent is able to show love," "parent is involved in child's daily activities," "parent shows confidence in self as parent," "parent (does not have) difficulty listening to what child communicates or requests." This factor was negatively correlated with a second factor measuring each parent's behaviors with the child, namely *Negative-Angry Parent (Neg-AngryM/F) r* = −.60 and −.53.

Substantiated Child Abuse by each parent *(ChAbuseM/F)* (ICC = .71) included child neglect, physical/verbal, and sexual abuse. It was coded as a dummy variable (scored Yes = 1, No = 0). Note that *WarmInvM/F* and *ChAbuseM/F* were inversely correlated at a moderate level (*r* = −.48 and −.36).

Child abuse was coded as substantiated if there was any corroborating evidence cited to back up a parent's allegations of abuse that had not been dismissed as entirely unfounded, such as child protective service reports, partial or complete self-admissions, eyewitness reports considering the credibility of witnesses (as discussed by Austin, 2000), expert testimony, medical records, police reports, arrests, plea-bargains, and criminal convictions. Child abuse identified by persons other than a parent was also included. Inter-rater reliabilities for the data on allegations and substantiations were subject to an additional check by comparing a subset of a related data set (*n* = 41) with ratings that had been completed a decade previously (Johnston, Lee, Olesen, & Walters, 2005).

Measures of Psychological Functioning of Parents

The following Rorschach variables were hypothesized to be related to parenting behaviors (*AlienatM/F, RolRevM/F, lack of WarmInvM/F,* and *ChAbuseM/F*).

In the area of internalized object relatedness they were lack of good human perception (Goodhrv); poor human perception (Poorhrv); no human interest (H = 0); lacking in capacity for empathy (Mqo = 0), humans seen in parts (H < nonPureH); absence of cooperative action (COP = 0); narcissism or self-preoccupation (Fr + rf > 0, Pairs#); and extent of self-involvement and interpersonal neediness (SumT = 0, SumT > 1).

With respect to information processing, the variables were low perceptual accuracy (X + % < .5); few popular responses (POP < 4); use of faulty logic (ALOG > 0); and cognitive slippage (Wsum6 > 6, SmLvl2SpSc > 0).

With regards to coping, we looked for the presence of a coping deficit (CDI > 3); lack of organized coping (AdjD < 0); a rigid, authoritarian coping style (PER > 0); a passive stance (Mp > Ma, p > a + 1), and a tendency to oversimplify (Lambda > .99). Eb coping styles were examined without any hypothesis as to direction of effects (Ambitent, Introversive, and Extratensive).[2]

In the domain of affective functioning, the variables chosen were clinical depression (DEPI > 4), harsh self-criticism (SumV > 0); diffuse anxiety (Y > 0); percepts that were spoiled or devalued (MOR > 2); intellectualization (Intellect > 5); low self-esteem (EgoC < .33); painful confusion (ColShdBld > 0); avoidance of affect (Afr < .40); relative emotional control (CF + C > FC + 1; CF + C > CF + 2); emotional outbursts (C > 0); inhibition of painful affect (SumC' > 0); and internalized anger (Space > 2).

Other possible measures of these concepts were precluded because of distribution problems in the data that were found when checking to ensure variables were fairly normally distributed or dummy variables with at least 10% variance. The data analysis for this study involved testing our hypotheses by examining the correlations between the clinical measures of parenting behaviors (*AlienatM/F, RolRevM/F, WarmInvM/F*, and *ChAbuseM/F*) with the relevant measures of parent's psychological functioning derived from Rorschach variables. Bivariate correlations were deemed appropriate for this exploratory analysis where we made no distinction between independent and dependent variables. One-tailed tests were used where direction of effects were hypothesized and in this small exploratory study, results with significance levels of *p* < .10 were reported. In examining the results, greatest emphasis was given to comparison of composite scores (the indexes) and then we looked at the individual components within these scores.

FINDINGS

The findings are shown in Table 1. *Alienating Co-parenting* behavior by fathers was directly correlated with their narcissism (Fr + rF > 0), self-preoccupation (Pairs), cognitive slippage (Wsum6 > 6), and rigid

TABLE 1. Correlation of Rorschach Variables with Parenting Behaviors

Psychological Issue	Rorschach Variable	Fathers (N = 49)				Mothers (N = 49)			
		Alienates	RoleRev	WarmInv	ChAbuse	Alienates	RoleRev	WarmInv	ChAbuse
Human Representation and Relatedness									
Good human perception	Goodhrv	.17	-.04	.06	-.11	-.12	-.26*	.31*	-.21+
Poor human perception	Poorhrv	.12	.25*	.05	.01	.09	.14	.04	.15
No human interest	H = 0	-.11	.14	.07	.15	.02	.19+	-.10	-.00
Lacks empathy	Mqo = 0	-.18	.05	.11	.02	-.07	.09	-.21+	-.15
Humans seen in parts	H < NonPureH	-.05	.14	-.01	-.05	.02	.24*	-.10	-.05
No cooperative action	COP = 0	-.23+	-.05	-.08	-.01	.03	.20+	-.08	.21+
Narcissism	Fr + rF > 0	.20+	.07	.10	-.10	.00	-.10	.08	.06
Self-preoccupation	Pairs	.19+	.20+	.09	-.25*	-.02	.06	.13	-.12
Lacks closeness	SumT = 0	.10	.00	-.01	.07	.22+	.20+	-.18	.40**
Needs closeness	SumT > 1	.18	-.06	-.15	-.11	-.26*	-.34**	.07	-.19+
Information Processing									
Low perceptual accuracy	X + % < .5	-.02	-.02	-.06	.03	-.08	-.02	-.03	.03
Few popular responses	Pop < 4	-.06	.02	-.22+	.30*	.03	-.01	.02	.05
Use of faulty logic	ALOG > 0	.17	-.03	-.04	.04	.17	.15	-.36**	.33**
Cognitive slippage	Wsum6 > 6	.22+	.18	-.27*	-.06	.26*	.28*	-.26*	.23+
Severe cognitive slippage	Smlvl2SpSc > 0	.17	.31*	-.20+	.08	-.04	.00	-.14	.10
Coping Resources									
Coping deficit	CDI > 3	-.31*	-.06	.13	.03	.18	.28*	-.40**	.21+
Lack organized coping	AdjD < 0	-.04	-.04	.16	-.05	-.09	.10	.14	-.29*
Rigid, authoritarian coping	PER > 0	.24*	.11	-.15	.19+	.11	.12	-.21+	.22+

TABLE 1 (continued)

Psychological Issue	Rorschach Variable	Fathers ($N = 49$)				Mothers ($N = 49$)			
		Alienates	RoleRev	WarmInv	ChAbuse	Alienates	RoleRev	WarmInv	ChAbuse
Coping Resources									
Passive stance fantasy	Mp > Ma	−.01	.08	−.17	−.03	.20+	.17	−.34**	.32**
Passive stance behavioral	p > a + 1	−.10	−.14	.16	.05	−.16	−.12	.12	.00
Oversimplifies	Lambda > .99	−.01	.13	.05	−.17	.04	.09	−.06	.05
Vascillating coping style	Ambitent	−.08	−.04	.08	−.32*	.06	−.02	−.23*	.11
Introversive coping	Introversive	−.04	−.01	.18	−.08	.05	−.01	.24*	−.10
Extratensive coping	Extratensive	.04	.06	−.28*	.27*	−.11	.03	.01	−.03
Affective Functioning									
Clinical depression	DEPI > 4	.08	−.03	−.27*	.25*	−.14	.12	−.06	.03
Harsh, self-critical	SumV > 0	.20+	.18	−.07	.05	−.02	.02	.10	−.23*
Diffuse anxiety	Y > 0	.12	.10	−.24*	.16	.04	.04	−.42***	.40**
Devaluation of percepts	MOR > 2	.22+	.35**	−.19+	.04	−.28*	−.09	−.10	.02
Intellectualization	Intellect > 5	.16	.13	−.29*	.40**	.09	−.09	−.11	.07
Low self-esteem	EgoC < .33	−.19+	.06	−.14	.15	−.19+	−.11	.13	−.07
Avoidance of affect	Afr < .40	.13	.27*	−.26*	.20+	−.08	−.14	.07	.04
Painful confusing affect	ColShdBld > 0	.21+	.07	−.01	−.01	−.03	−.06	−.13	.19+
Emotion express > control	CF + C > FC + 1	.16	−.03	−.25*	.27*	−.10	−.17	.00	.15
	CF + C > FC + 2	.12	−.00	−.23+	.28*	−.12	−.19+	−.14	.08
Emotional outbursts	C > 0	.04	.08	−.20+	.37**	−.06	.05	−.28*	.27*
Inhibition of painful affect	SumC' > 0	.12	.10	−.10	.29*	.09	.29*	.01	.01
Internalized anger	Space > 2	.08	.19+	−.10	−.03	−.10	−.15	.21+	−.23*

+$p < .10$; *$p < .05$; **$p < .01$; ***$p < .001$ (1-tailed tests)

authoritarian style (PER > 0). In terms of affective functioning, alienating fathers were likely to be harshly self-critical (SumV > 0), produce more devalued or spoiled percepts (MOR > 2), and experience more painful confusing feelings (ColShdBld > 0). Contrary to predictions, alienating fathers were unlikely to have a coping deficit (CDI > 3), were unlikely to perceive no cooperative action (COP = 0), and were less likely to have low self-esteem (EgoC < .33) compared to non-alienating fathers in custody disputes. *Alienating Co-parenting* behavior by mothers was inversely correlated with her need for interpersonal closeness (SumT), and were directly correlated with cognitive slippage (Wsum6 > 6) and a passive stance in fantasy (Mp > Ma). Interestingly, alienating mothers were less likely to produce devalued or spoiled percepts (MOR > 2) and to have low self-esteem (EgoC < .33) compared to non-alienating mothers in these custody-disputing families.

Fathers who were in *Role Reversal* with their children were significantly more likely to have poor human perception (Poorhrv), to be self-preoccupied (Pairs), and to have severe cognitive slippage (Smlvl2SpSc > 0). Affectively, they were more likely to produce devalued or spoiled percepts (MOR > 2), avoid affect (Afr < .40), and experience internalized anger (Space > 0) compared to fathers who were not in role reversal with their children. Mothers who were in *Role Reversal* with their children were likely to lack good human representation (Goodhrv), perceive humans in parts (H < NonPureH), fail to perceive cooperative action (COP = 0), and were more likely to have problems with interpersonal closeness (SumT). *Role Reversing* mothers were also likely to have a coping deficit (CDI > 3) and cognitive slippage (Wsum6 > 6). Their painful affect was more likely to be inhibited (SumC' > 0). Contrary to expectations, they were more emotionally controlled (CF + C > FC + 2) than mothers who were not in role reversal with their children.

Warm-Involved parenting was correlated with a number of the Rorschach variables in expected ways, especially in the realm of affective functioning. *Warm-Involved* fathers were significantly less likely to be clinically depressed (DEPI > 4) and less likely to produce devalued or spoiled percepts (MOR > 2); they had less diffuse anxiety (Y > 0), less avoidance of affect (Afr < .40), and less use of intellectualizing defenses (Intellect > 5); and they were less likely to emote spontaneously (CF + C > FC + 1, CF + C > FC + 2) and have emotional outbursts (C > 0). They were also less likely to have few popular responses (Pop < 4) and cognitive slippage (Wsum6 > 6, SmLvl2SpSc > 0). Their problem-solving style was less likely to be an Extratensive one compared to fathers lacking in warm involvement with their children.

Warm-Involved mothers were less likely to be diffusely anxious (Y > 0) and to have emotional outbursts (C > 0). Unexpectedly they tended to have more internalized anger (Space > 2) compared to custody-disputing mothers lacking in warm involvement with their child. However, most noteworthy, *Warm-Involved* mothers were significantly more likely to have good human perception (Goodhrv) and less likely to lack empathy (Mqo = 0). They were also unlikely to use faulty logic (ALOG > 0) and have cognitive slippage (Wsum6 > 6). Furthermore, *Warm-Involved* mothers were less likely to have a coping deficit (CDI > 3), a rigid, authoritarian coping style (PER > 0), and a passive stance in fantasy (Mp > Ma). Their preferred coping style was more likely to be Introversive and less likely to be an Ambient one compared to mothers lacking in warm involvement with their children in these custody-disputing families.

Substantiated Child Abuse by both parents was significantly correlated with a number of Rorschach indicators, especially of poor affective functioning. *Child Abuse* by fathers was related to their clinical depression (DEPI > 4), use of intellectualizing defenses (Intellect > 5), avoidance of affect (Afr < .40), and several indicators of difficulty modulating emotions (CF + C > FC + 1; CF + C > FC + 2: C > 0; SumC' > 0). In addition, their abuse was directly correlated with their rigid authoritarian coping style (PER > 0) and a preference for an Extratensive rather than an Ambient problem-solving style. Contrary to our hypothesis, fathers' *Child Abuse* was inversely correlated with self-preoccupation (Pairs) and with a lack of popular responses (Pop < 4) compared to non-abusing fathers.

Substantiated Child Abuse by mothers was related to absence of harsh self-criticism (SumV > 0) and lack of internalized anger (Space > 2). It was directly related to their diffuse anxiety (Y > 0), painful confusing feelings (ColShdBld > 0), and emotional outbursts (C > 0). Most noteworthy, child-abusing mothers were also likely to lack good human perception (Goodhrv), did not perceive cooperative action (COP = 0), and lacked a need for interpersonal closeness (SumT). They were more likely to use faulty logic (ALOG > 0) and to have cognitive slippage (Wsum6 > 6). Interestingly, although they were less likely to lack an organized coping style (AdjD < 0), they were more likely to have a coping deficit (CDI > 3). They also tended to have a rigid authoritarian style (PER > 0) and a passive stance in fantasy (Mp > Ma) compared to non-abusing mothers in these custody-disputing families.

DISCUSSION AND CONCLUSIONS

In this study, the Rorschach protocols of 98 custody-disputing parents were correlated with clinical judgments of their co-parenting and parenting capacities in numerous ways that were consistent with our hypotheses. Despite some slight variation in the pattern of findings between the genders, clinical judgments of mothers' and fathers' parenting behaviors were equally likely to be validated by similar domains of Rorschach variables.

Of particular usefulness in the Rorschach is the domain of affective functioning for validating problems in basic parenting capacities. Lack of warm, involved parenting and substantiated child abuse (as judged by clinicians) appear to be consistently related to a number of Rorschach measures of the parents' clinical depression, anxiety, difficulty modulating affect, and excessive use of intellectualizing defenses. These kinds of basic poor parenting behaviors are also associated with Rorschach measures of a coping deficit (for mothers) and a rigid authoritarian coping style (for both parents). In addition, it is important to note that Rorschach indicators of poor human relatedness (indicating lack of capacity for interested, empathic relations with others), and difficulties processing information logically, are found to be features of parents who have been abusive and/or lack warm involvement with their child. These findings on the personality correlates of parenting in custody-disputing families are all consistent with and relevant to a large empirical literature on the link between traits/disorders in parents and adjustment problems in children, and on the importance of parenting that models good ego control as well as being warm, empathic, involved, and authoritative with children (Sroufe, Duggal, Weinfield, & Carlson, 2000; Teti & Candelaria, 2002; Waxler, Duggal, & Gruber, 2002).

The Rorschach domains of object relatedness and information processing, however, appear to be more closely associated with alienating co-parenting behavior and role reversal between parent and child, although here the findings are less numerous. Narcissistic vulnerabilities that are manifested in poor human representation (indicating less capacity for interested, empathic relations with others), self-preoccupation, and an absence of need for closeness with others, tend to be features of parenting problems like alienating behavior and role-reversal. In addition, alienating and role-reversing parents tend to reason loosely or illogically. Problems in quality and expression of affect are less prominent features, although alienating and role-reversing fathers seem to have some difficulties in this domain while mothers tend to have deficits in coping. These preliminary findings support clinical observations that alienating and role-reversal by parents are manifestations of narcissistic injury and disordered thinking (possibly including paranoid thinking) wherein they do not really care about their child's feelings and ideas but are more centered on their own. The findings are less supportive of an alternative clinical hypothesis that alienating and role reversal are functions of parents' emotional neediness and use of the child to stave off depression (Johnston & Campbell, 1988; Kelly & Johnston, 2001; Wallerstein & Kelly, 1980). These overall findings are consistent with and relevant to a growing empirical literature on the adverse effects on children of a parent's psychological control (also called intrusive parenting) and parent-child boundary problems (also called role reversal; Barber & Harmon, 2002; Chase, 1999; Nelson & Crick, 2002; Sroufe et al., 2000).

Although these are suggestive patterns from this study, it would be premature and a gross overgeneralization to conclude that the Rorschach can differentially predict lack of warm-involved and abusive parenting as distinct from alienating and role-reversing parenting behaviors. We found that each of these different problems or deficits in parenting were correlated with one another and were significantly correlated with multiple domains of personality functioning on the Rorschach. Almost all of these were in expected directions, although there were a few counterintuitive findings. Further, more in-depth research is needed to confirm these findings and to explore their meaning.

Other limitations of the research should be kept in mind in interpreting and using the findings. This is an exploratory study of a relatively small number of primarily White, upper-income parents who were undergoing court-ordered custody evaluations conducted by private clinical psychologists. The sample was not chosen randomly and it is not known how it resembles the broader population of families in this context. The research was a correlational study and as such it cannot determine causal direction of effects. Many of the significant correlations were relatively modest in size or only marginally significant, and the majority was not significant. Further, the results described here are aggregate or common patterns and cannot be applied to any specific parent. As cogently explained by Meyer et al. (2001), a well conducted, multi-method, psychological assessment of both parents and children may reach different conclusions than the ones reported in this study and are likely to be more valid for that family situation. The Rorschach test provides no "silver bullet" for diagnosis and no single variable is conclusive evidence about personality or parenting functioning. Rather, the patterning and interaction among the variables is the hallmark of a responsible interpretive strategy using this assessment tool.

In conclusion, despite these caveats, this study provides some evidence that the Rorschach Inkblot test, scored according to the Comprehensive System, is likely to provide a relatively rich source of data relevant to assessing parenting skills and capacities in custody-disputing families. It appears to be especially valuable because it is more resistant to "faking good" compared to more objective personality tests and self-report parenting scales. Moreover, this research study shows that the data drawn from Rorschach testing are remarkably convergent with clinical assessments drawn from clinical interviews, parent-child observations, and substantiated histories of child abuse.

NOTES

1. Although the terms PA and PAS are fairly commonly used, the authors do not endorse the validity of this syndrome as formulated by Gardner (1998). Rather this research is part of a series of studies that have reformulated the problem as the "alienated child" (Kelly & Johnston, 2001) and examined its multiple antecedents (Johnston, 2003).

2. Extratensive refers to a preferred style of problem-solving that involves more affective and interactive engagement with others. In contrast, an Introversive style is one where the subject turns inward to problem solve with affect more peripheral. Ambitent describes those who lack a preferred problem-solving style.

REFERENCES

Ackerman, M. J., & Ackerman, M. C. (1997). Custody evaluation practices: A survey of experienced professionals (revisited). *Professional Psychology: Research & Practice, 28*, 137-145.

Ackerman, M., & Schoendorf, K. (1992). *ASPECT: Ackerman-Schoendorf scales for parent evaluation of custody–Manual.* Los Angeles: Western Psychological Services.

American Academy of Child and Adolescent Psychiatry. (1997). Practice parameters for child custody evaluations. *Journal of the American Academy of Child & Adolescent Psychiatry, 36*, 57S-68S.

American Psychological Association. (1994). Guidelines for child custody evaluations in divorce proceedings. *American Psychologist, 49*, 677-680.

Association of Family and Conciliation Courts. (1994). Model standards of practice for child custody evaluation. *Family and Conciliation Courts Review, 32*, 504-513.

Austin, W. G. (2000). Assessing the credibility in allegations of marital violence in the high conflict child custody case. *Family and Conciliation Courts Review, 38*, 186-201.

Austin, W. G. (2002). Guidelines for utilizing collateral sources of information in child custody evaluations. *Family Court Review, 40,* 177-184.

Bagby, R. M., Nicholson, R. A., Buis, T., Radovanovic, H., & Fidler, B. J. (1999). Defensive responding on the MMPI-2 in family custody and access evaluations. *Psychological Assessment, 11,* 24-28.

Barber, B. K., & Harmon, E. L. (2002). Violating the self: Parental psychological control of children and adolescents. In B. K. Barber (Ed.), *Intrusive parenting* (pp. 15-52). Washington, DC: American Psychological Association.

Bathurst, K., Gottfried, A. W., & Gottfried, A. E. (1997). Normative data for the MMPI-2 in child custody litigation. *Psychological Assessment, 9,* 205-211.

Bow, J. N., & Quinnell, F. A. (2001). Psychologists' current practices and procedures in child custody evaluations: Five years after American Psychological Guidelines. *Professional Psychology: Research & Practice, 32,* 261-268.

Bow, J. N., & Quinnell, F. A. (2002). A critical review of child custody evaluation reports. *Family Court Review, 40,* 164-176.

Bricklin, B. (1989). *Perception of relationships test manual.* Furlong, PA: Village Publishing.

Bricklin, B. (1990). *Bricklin perceptual scales manual.* Furlong, PA: Village Publishing.

Bricklin, B., & Elliott, G. (1991). *Parent perception of child profile manual.* Furlong, PA: Village Publishing.

Brodzinsky, D. M. (1993). On the use and misuse of psychological tests in child custody evaluations. *Professional Psychology: Research and Practice, 24,* 213-219.

Chase, N. D. (1999). Parentification: An overview of theory, research, and societal issues. In N. D. Chase (Ed.), *Burdened children* (pp. 3-33). Thousand Oaks, CA, Sage.

Exner, Jr., J. E. (1991). *The Rorschach: A comprehensive system. Volume 2: Interpretation* (2nd ed.). New York: John Wiley & Sons.

Exner, Jr., J. E. (2002). A new nonpatient sample for the Rorschach Comprehensive System: A progress report. *Journal of Personality Assessment, 78,* 391-404.

Gardner, R. A. (1998). *The parental alienation syndrome* (2nd ed.). Creskill, NJ: Creative Therapeutics.

Gould, J. W. (1999a). Scientifically crafted child custody evaluations. Part one: A model for interdisciplinary collaboration in the development of psycholegal questions guiding court-ordered child custody evaluations. *Family and Conciliation Courts Review, 37,* 64-73.

Gould, J. W. (1999b). Scientifically crafted child custody evaluations. Part two: A paradigm for forensic evaluation of child custody determination. *Family and Conciliation Courts Review, 37,* 159-178.

Gould, J. W. (2004). Evaluating the probative value of child custody evaluations: A guide for forensic mental health professionals. *Journal of Child Custody, 1,* 77-96.

Gould, J. W., & Stahl, P. M. (2000). The art and science of child custody evaluations: Integrating clinical and forensic mental health models. *Family and Conciliation Courts Review, 38,* 392-414.

Greenberg, L. R., Martindale, D. A., Gould, J. W., & Gould-Saltman, D. J. (2004). Ethical issues in child custody and dependency cases: Enduring principles and emerging challenges. *Journal of Child Custody, 1,* 7-30.

Grossman, L. S., Wasyliw, O. E., Benn, A. F., & Gyoerkoe, K. L. (2002). Can sex offenders who minimize on the MMPI conceal psychopathology on the Rorschach? *Journal of Personality Assessment, 78,* 484-501.

Hagen, M. A., & Castagna, N. (2001). The real numbers: Psychological testing in custody evaluations. *Professional Psychology: Research and Practice, 32,* 269-271.

Hollingshead, A. B., & Redlich, F. C. (1958). *Social class and mental illness: A community study.* New York: Wiley.

Hysjulien, C., Wood, B., & Benjamin, G. A. H. (1994). Child custody evaluations: A review of methods used in litigation and alternative dispute resolution. *Family and Conciliation Courts Review, 32,* 466-489.

Johnston, J. R. (2003). Parental alignments and rejection: An empirical study of alienation in children of divorce. *Journal of the American Academy of Psychiatry & Law, 31,* 158-70.

Johnston, J. R., & Campbell, L. E. G. (1988). *Impasses of divorce: The dynamics and resolution of family conflict.* New York: Free Press.

Johnston, J. R., Gans Walters, M., & Olesen, N. W. (2004, June). *The psychological functioning of alienated children in custody disputing families: An exploratory study.* Paper presented at the Vulnerable Child Symposium, American Psychoanalytic Association Meetings, San Francisco, CA.

Johnston, J. R., Lee, S., Olesen, N. W., & Walters, M. G. (2005). Allegations and substantiations of abuse in custody disputing families. *Family Court Review.*

Johnston, J. R., Walters, M., & Olesen, N. W. (in press). Is it alienating parenting, role reversal or child abuse? An empirical study of children's rejection of a parent in child custody disputes. *Journal of Emotional Abuse.*

Keilin, W. G., & Bloom, L. J. (1986). Child custody evaluation practices: A survey of Experienced professionals. *Professional Psychology: Research and Practice, 17,* 338-346.

Kelly, J. B., & Johnston, J. R. (2001). The alienated child: A reformulation of parental alienation syndrome. *Family Court Review, 39,* 249-266.

Kirkland, K. (2002). The epistemology of child custody evaluations: The value of Austin's convergent multimodal approach. *Family Court Review, 40,* 185-189.

LaFortune, K. A., & Carpenter, B. N. (1998). Custody evaluations: A survey of mental health professionals. *Behavioral Sciences and the Law, 16,* 207-224.

Medoff, D. (2003). The scientific basis of psychological testing: Considerations following *Daubert, Kumho,* and *Joiner. Family Court Review, 41,* 199-213.

Meloy, J. R., Hansen, T. L., & Weiner, I. B. (1997). Authority of the Rorschach: Legal citations during the past 50 years. *Journal of Personality Assessment, 69,* 53-62.

Meyer, G. (2000). On the science of Rorschach research. *Journal of Personality Assessment, 75,* 46-81.

Meyer, G. J., Finn, S. E., Eyde, L. D., Kay, G. G., Moreland, K. L., Dies, R. R. et al. (2001). Psychological testing and psychological assessment: A review of evidence and issues. *American Psychologist, 56,* 128-165.

Meyer, G. J., Hilsenroth, M. J., Baxter, D., Exner, Jr., J. E., Christopher Fowler, J., Piers, C. C. et al. (2002). An examination of interrater reliability for scoring the Rorschach Comprehensive System in eight data sets. *Journal of Personality Assessment, 78,* 219-274.

Nelson, D. A., & Crick, N. R. (2002). Parental psychological control: Implications for childhood physical and relational aggression. In B. K. Barber (Ed.), *Intrusive parenting* (pp. 161-190). Washington, DC: American Psychological Association.

Otto, R. K., Edens, J. F., & Barcus, E. H. (2000). The use of psychological testing in child custody evaluations. *Family and Conciliation Courts Review, 38,* 312-340.

Posthuma, A. B., & Harper, J. F. (1998). Comparison of MMPI-2 responses of child custody and personal injury litigants. *Professional Psychology: Research and Practice, 29,* 437-443.

Quinnell, F. A., & Bow, J. N. (2001). Psychological tests used in child custody evaluations. *Behavioral Sciences and the Law, 19,* 491-501.

Roseby, V. (1995). Uses of psychological testing in a child-focused approach to child custody evaluations. *Family Law Quarterly, 29,* 97-110.

Schaffer, T. W., Erdberg, P., & Haroian, J. (1999). Current nonpatient data for the Rorschach, WAIS-R, and MMPI-2. *Journal of Personality Assessment, 73,* 305-316.

Sroufe, L. A., Duggal, S., Weinfield, N., & Carlson, E. (2000). Relationships, development, and psychopathology. In A. J. Sameroff, M. Lewis, & S. Miller (Eds.), *Handbook of developmental psychopathology* (2nd ed., pp. 75-91). New York: Kluwer Academic/Plenum.

Stahl, P. M. (1994). *Conducting child custody evaluations: A comprehensive guide.* Thousand Oaks, CA: Sage.

Strong, D. R., Greene, R. L., Hoppe, C., Johnston, T., & Olesen, N. (1999). Taxometric analysis of impression management and self-deception on the MMPI-2 in child-custody litigants. *Journal of Personality Assessment, 73,* 1-18.

Teti, D. M., & Candelaria, M. A. (2002). Parenting competence. In M. H. Borstein (Ed.), *Handbook of parenting* (Vol. 4, pp. 149-180). Mahwah, NJ: Lawrence Erlbaum Associates.

Valente-Torre, L., Cavani, P., & Brusca, C. (1987). Separation or divorce: Analyse de l'agressivite de patients qui se disputent la charge des enfants [English translation]. *Psychologie Medicale, 19,* 511-513.

Viglione, Jr., D. J. (1996). Data and issues to consider in reconciling self-report and the Rorschach. *Journal of Personality Assessment, 67,* 579-587.

Wallerstein, J. S., & Kelly, K. B. (1980). *Surviving the breakup: How children and parents cope with divorce.* New York: Basic Books.

Walters, M. G., Olesen, N. W., & Lee, M. S. (2004). *What can the Rorschachs of child custody disputants tell us?* Unpublished Technical Report, available from the authors.

Warshak, R. A. (2003). Bringing sense to parental alienation: A look at the dispute and the evidence. *Family Law Quarterly, 37,* 273-301.

Waxler, Z. W., Duggal, S., & Gruber, R. (2002). Parenting and psychopathology. In M. H. Borstein (Ed.), *Handbook of parenting* (Vol. 4, pp. 295-327). Mahwah, NJ: Lawrence Erlbaum Associates.

Wood, J. M., Nezworksi, M. T., Stejskal, W. J., Garven, S., & West, S. G. (2001). Advancing scientific discourse in controversy surrounding the Comprehensive System for the Rorschach: A rejoinder to Meyer (2000). *Journal of Personality Assessment, 76,* 369-378.

POINT-COUNTERPOINT:
THE USE AND PROBATIVE VALUE
OF THE ASPECT

The Ackerman-Schoendorf Scales
for Parent Evaluation of Custody (ASPECT):
A Review of Research and Update

Marc J. Ackerman

Marc J. Ackerman, PhD, is a clinical and forensic psychologist and expert on child custody. He maintains a counseling and consulting practice in Milwaukee, WI, where he has worked with thousands of divorcing families. He is the author of six books for psychologists and lawyers on the subject of child custody and speaks frequently on the topic.

Address correspondence to: Marc Ackerman, PhD, 5900 North Port Washington Road, Suite 150, Milwaukee, WI 53217 (E-mail: mjackerman@aol.com).

The author would like to acknowledge the support and help of Dr. Randy Otto and Dr. Jay Flens in preparing this article.

[Haworth co-indexing entry note]: "The Ackerman-Schoendorf Scales for Parent Evaluation of Custody (ASPECT): A Review of Research and Update." Ackerman, Marc J. Co-published simultaneously in *Journal of Child Custody* (The Haworth Press, Inc.) Vol. 2, No. 1/2, 2005, pp. 179-193; and: *Psychological Testing in Child Custody Evaluations* (ed: James R. Flens, and Leslie Drozd) The Haworth Press, Inc., 2005, pp. 179-193. Single or multiple copies of this article are available for a fee from The Haworth Document Delivery Service [1-800-HAWORTH, 9:00 a.m. - 5:00 p.m. (EST). E-mail address: docdelivery@haworthpress.com].

SUMMARY. The Ackerman-Schoendorf Scales for Parent Evaluation of Custody (ASPECT) was first published in 1992, with the ASPECT-SF developed and published in 2001. Since that time, there have been outcome studies, validity studies, and challenges to the psychometric properties of the ASPECT by various authors. This article addresses the validity studies undertaken since the 1992 publication and responds to the various criticisms leveled against the ASPECT. Discussion includes the use of the original ASPECT and the Short Form in its original format and as a structured interview for child custody evaluations. *[Article copies available for a fee from The Haworth Document Delivery Service: 1-800-HAWORTH. E-mail address: <docdelivery@haworthpress.com> Website: <http://www.HaworthPress.com> © 2005 by The Haworth Press, Inc. All rights reserved.]*

KEYWORDS. Divorce, custody, ASPECT

HISTORY AND DEVELOPMENT

The ASPECT is an instrument that utilizes a battery of information that is designed specifically to provide information for child custody evaluations. It attempts to identify those characteristics that are reported in psychological literature as being determinative of fitness for custody (Barnard & Jenson, 1984; Beaber, 1982; Belsky, Robbins, & Gamble, 1984; Berkman, 1984; Camara & Resnick, 1989; Chasen & Gruenbaum, 1981; Emery, 1988; Exner, 1974; Gardner, 1982; Goldstein, Freud, & Solnit, 1973; Guidubaldi, Cleminshaw, Perry, Nastasi, & Adams, 1984; Hetherington, 1979; Hetherington, Cox, & Cox, 1978; Johnston, Kline, & Tschann, 1989; Karras & Berry, 1985; Keilin & Bloom, 1986; Klopfer & Kelley, 1942; Lowery, 1984; McDermott, Wem-Shing, Char, & Fukunaga, 1978; Rae-Grant & Award, 1977; Wallerstein, 1983; Wolfe, 1985), and was developed in the late 1980s and published in 1992 by Western Psychological Services. The ASPECT was developed by the authors out of frustration generating from questions asked in court during an examination and cross-examination about recommendations that psychologists were making regarding custody and placement of children. Judges and attorneys typically asked questions about how psychologists were able to determine which parent would make a better placement or custodial parent. The authors reviewed the psychological literature at that time and found 63 different variables identified as being related to parenting ability and fitness for parental custody or placement. After a pilot study with 25 couples, this number was reduced to 56 variables, which were utilized in formulating the ASPECT that was eventually published, as seven of the variables were found to be non-discriminators. Some of the 56 items were empirically based and some were rationally based. The manual explains each of these items in greater detail.

The initial stage of using the ASPECT involves each parent completing a Parent Questionnaire, which is composed of questions regarding preferred custody arrangements, living and child-care arrangements, the children's development and education, the relationship between the parent and the children, and the relationship between the parents. Questions are also included about information derived from collateral sources, about the parent's background, mental health history, substance abuse concerns, and legal history. The original ASPECT placed a heavy emphasis on testing. Each parent was administered an intelligence test, the MMPI-2, the Rorschach, Projective Questions, and achievement testing. In addition, each parent was observed with the children. Children completed an intelligence test, the CAT/TAT, and projective drawings. After all data are gathered from the parents, children, and collateral sources and reviewed; the examiner then rates each parent on a total of 56 items. Twelve of the items are described as "critical items" as they represent significant indicators of parenting deficits. The 56 items are equally weighted based on a rational approach, and are combined to form a Parental Custody Index (PCI) for each parent.

ASPECT SUBSCALES

The ASPECT has three subscales that form the combined PCI. The Observational Scale (9 items) assesses the self-presentation and appearance of the parent. The Social Scale (28 items) addresses the parent's social conduct and interaction with others, including children, the other parent, and the community. The Cognitive-Emotional Scale (19 items) reflects the psychological health and emotional maturity of the parents. Data derived from psychological testing are primarily considered on items found on the Cognitive-Emotional Scale. At the time of the development of the ASPECT, the items were divided into the three scales based on face validity. It was hoped at the time that there would be subscale analyses of each of these areas. However, the research never supported the use of looking at the subscales exclusively. As a result, the total PCI is the only measure that should be used for interpretation.

PRINCIPLES OF USE

The ASPECT is intended for use with parents who are disputing custody of one or more of their children. It employs a self-report format and should not be utilized with individuals who are unable or unwilling to cooperate in responding to the Parent Questionnaire. This would include parents who choose to stop after part of the Parent Questionnaire has been completed, or those who are unable to read the questionnaire or unable to understand the questions when read to them. Evaluators must be cautious when examining subjects who have had prior exposure to the questions on the Parent Questionnaire, in that they may have been educated on how to respond to the items by their previous experience with the instrument. Because of its standardization, the ASPECT should not be used in cases involving placement with non-parent relatives, or cases involving same-sex couples, couples who are cohabiting but not married, or grandparents. Furthermore, the ASPECT should not be used with parents who only have children under two years of age since 10% of the items are not applicable.

STANDARDIZATION SAMPLE

The standardization sample consisted of 200 parents and their children. The mean age of the parents was 34.4 years while the mean number of children per family was 2.3. The distribution of occupations among the participants approximated those statistical breakdowns of individuals working in the United States at the time of standardization. Two major differences were noted between the standardization sample and the United States norms. While 20% of those in the United States had less than a high school diploma, only 6% of this sample did. Furthermore, 96.9% of the participants were Caucasian. This skewed number is representative of the fact that non-Caucasians are overrepresented in the lower socioeconomic groups, who tend to not have access to or are unable to afford custody evaluations.

VALIDITY AND RELIABILITY

The ASPECT is considered to be content and face valid because the questions used in the Parent Questionnaire are derived from the literature on custody-related issues. This is supported by Ackerman and

Ackerman (1997), where participants identified items on the ASPECT as being important issues in custody determination. The questions on the Parent Questionnaire were derived from the 56 variables that the literature demonstrated were related to parenting or custody as indicted earlier in this article. The gender study as well as the intercorrelaction matrix give evidence of construct validity. The gender study was performed in an effort to ensure that the ASPECT was measuring parenting and not mothering and fathering. There was not a significant difference between the mean scores of mothers on the PCI and fathers on the PCI. Any difference between mothers and fathers was found on the Social Scale, where mothers had a significantly higher mean score than fathers. However, on the overall PCI there was no significant difference. The original research performed by Western Psychological Services indicated that the PCI summary score had an adequate internal consistency reliability of .76 (Cronbach alpha). The overall interrater reliability on the PCI was .96, with a standard error of measurement of 4.90. The interrater reliability coefficients on the Observational, Social, and Cognitive-Emotional Scales were .92, .94, and .94, respectively.

Some gender differences were noted utilizing a chi square analysis of each item. Mothers were found to be significantly better at identifying age-appropriate developmental milestones ($p < .05$), having an awareness of the child's relevant school information ($p < .05$), more actively participating in the child's education, and providing sex education ($p < .05$), oral hygiene training ($p < .01$) and general hygiene training ($p < .01$). On the other hand, fathers had a significantly higher arrest record ($p < .01$) and significantly higher incidents of being charged with sexual abuse and physical abuse ($p < .01$). This information is also useful for child custody evaluations outside the use of the ASPECT.

Predictive validity was originally assessed by comparing the outcome of a child custody case with the PCI score after the case had been competed. Criticism has been leveled against using judge's orders as a basis for predictive validity, and will be discussed later in this article. Since that time, other research has been performed to address these issues. These studies were all performed post-publication of the original ASPECT, but are included in the most recent revision of the manual. Because of the nature of the new studies, the criterion contamination concern was not an issue as was the case with the "judge's orders" study.

In a sample of 200 parents, Ackerman and Ackerman (1992) subdivided ASPECT scores into a number of categories post judgment. They included: all parents; all placement parents; all non-placement parents;

all placement fathers; all placement mothers; all non-placement fathers; and all non-placement mothers. The overall mean on the ASPECT was 78.1, which was not significantly different from the standardization sample. All placement parents had a significantly higher mean of 81.8 compared to all non-placement parents of 74.3 ($p < .01$). The highest mean was found among all placement mothers of 83.1, while the lowest mean was found in all non-placement fathers of 73.6 ($p < .01$). These means were all calculated with the ASPECT after each case was concluded. This study was performed almost simultaneously with the publication of the ASPECT. Since it was a new instrument, the study was designed to demonstrate that the PCI could adequately discriminate between placement and non-placement parents, placement and non-placement mothers, and placement and non-placement fathers.

Hubbard (1996) compared the ASPECT results with the then newly developed Parent-Child Relationship Inventory (PCRI) ($N = 60$). The PCRI assesses parents' attitudes toward parenting and toward their children. At the time, it was used with about the same frequency as the ASPECT by psychologists conducting child custody evaluations (Ackerman & Ackerman, 1997). When correlating mothers' scores on the PCRI and ASPECT and fathers' scores on the PCRI and PCI on the ASPECT, the results were very low. The correlations for mothers' generally ran in the .2 to .3 range, while the correlations for fathers were around 0. This clearly demonstrates that the PCRI and PCI are measuring different variables. Since the PCRI and PCI are measuring different variables, it may be advantageous to administer both instruments when performing a child custody evaluation since neither of these tests are designed to stand alone in the custody or placement decision-making. As is true of any battery of tests, the utilization of more than one instrument adds to the overall validity of the recommendations being made.

Beyer (1996) examined the relationship between the parents' PCI scores and their children's satisfaction living in each parent's home using the Life Satisfaction Post Divorce (LSPD) Questionnaire. All of the subjects in this study were post-judgment and not currently involved in any custody-related litigation. An average of three years after the divorce, 67% of the children who found life with their fathers to be more satisfying had fathers with higher PCI scores then their mothers at the time of the divorce, while 73% of the children who considered living with their mothers to be more satisfying than living with their fathers had mothers with higher PCI scores than their fathers at the time of the administration. Although this study had a relatively low sample size ($N =$

22), its implication for predictive validity is strong. Replications with a larger total sample would be desirable.

Schoendorf (2001) performed a study investigating the relationship between the PCI of the Ackerman-Schoendorf Scales for Parent Evaluation of Custody-Short Form (ASPECT-SF) and various scales of the Minnesota Multiphasic Personality Inventory-Second Edition (MMPI-2). The sample size of this study was 100 pairs of divorced parents who were no longer involved in a custody dispute, but had been previously. Since six scores from the MMPI-2 are utilized to determine the PCI on the ASPECT, the ASPECT-SF was used for this study as it does not rely on psychological testing. Schoendorf found that a significant inverse correlation existed between the PCI of the ASPECT-SF and Scales 4, 6, and 9; Content Scales ASP, FAM, and WRK; and the MAC-R. The only significant positive correlation existed between the Responsibility Scale and the PCI of the ASPECT-SF. When looking at the Clinical Scales, Content Scales, Subscales, and Supplementary Scales, there was no best single predictor of a lower PCI-SF score on the MMPI-2.

Caldwell and Ackerman are currently working on a project comparing the ASPECT scores with the interpretation program that Alex Caldwell has developed for the use of the MMPI-2 in custody cases.

ASPECT-SHORT FORM (ASPECT-SF)

In 2000, the ASPECT-SF was developed for two reasons. In the ten years since the ASPECT had been developed, there appeared to be less emphasis placed on psychological testing in making custody and/or placement recommendations. Secondly, the ASPECT-SF can be used by all mental health professionals since no testing is required. The ASPECT-SF consists of the 41 ASPECT items that are not tied to test results. ASPECT-SF scores are highly correlated with ASPECT scores ($r = .93$). The logical question that evolves from these data is: why would one give the full ASPECT when the PCI-SF correlates .93 with the PCI (Ackerman & Schoendorf, 2000, p. 1)?

INTERPRETATION

The ASPECT has a mean of approximately 78 and a standard deviation of 10. This mean and standard deviation has held up over a half dozen different research projects cited above. Since the standard deviation is 10, it is suggested that when the PCI scores are within 10 points of one another, the parents are relatively equal in their parenting capacity. As a result, joint custody with substantially equal placement with both parents is recommended. When the PCIs are more than 20 points apart, it suggests that the parent with the higher PCI is substantially more fit to parent and primary placement with the possibility of sole custody should be explored for the parent with the higher score. The authors decided that when there is more than one child and the scores are different for specific items, the ASPECT items would be scored in the majority direction. When the scores are between 10 and 20 points apart, more careful scrutiny should be given to the collateral information to help determine whether this difference is more representative of a joint custody substantially equal placement schedule or a primary sole custody type of a situation. As is true of all tests that are administered in child custody evaluations, there is no one instrument that should "rule the day." A combination of all factors must be considered. One of the values of the ASPECT is that it summarizes these variables in helping make the custody and placement decisions.

USAGE

Between 1992 and 2004, 2,300 ASPECT kits were sold by Western Psychological Services (Louis Warren, personal communication, April 23, 2004). Of course, purchase of the ASPECT does not necessarily mean its use. Ackerman and Ackerman (1997) reported that 11.4% of the psychologists they surveyed who conducted child custody evaluations indicated use of the ASPECT. Those psychologists who employed the measure reported using it in the large majority (90%) of the of the custody evaluations they performed. Quinnell and Bow (2001) report about the use of custody batteries in child custody evaluations. They indicate that 16% of those surveyed used the ASPECT 74% of the time. Although this still represents a relatively small percentage of psychologists, it is approximately a 50% increase in usage as reported in the Ackerman and Ackerman study (1997). The authors also indicate that it is the most "commonly used battery" (p. 498) even with this limited usage. The ASPECT was used twice as frequently as any other custody battery approach. Twenty percent of 156 family law judges throughout the country who were surveyed by Ackerman and Steffen (2001) reported familiarity with the ASPECT, while 38% of the 15 family law attorneys surveyed by Ackerman and Kelley-Poulos (2001) reported familiarity with the measure. In general, the attorneys were about as familiar with the ASPECT as any other specialized test developed for the purpose of performing child custody evaluations.

CRITICISM

When the ASPECT was originally developed, it was reviewed in the *Twelfth Mental Measurements Yearbook* (Conoley & Impara, 1995) and in other literature. Brodzinski (1993) reviewed a number of instruments that have been used for custody evaluations. He states, "Two interesting and more quantitative approaches to the assessment of custody and visitation disputes have been developed by Bricklin (1984) and Ackerman and Schoendorf (1992)" (p. 21) and concludes:

> Despite the limitations of these alternative assessment procedures, they represent a valuable addition to the field of child custody evaluations. Most important, they shift the focus from a more traditional clinical assessment to one in which the evaluator is focusing more on a functional analysis of the parties' competencies within specific childcare roles. As such, these instruments are likely to provide information that is particularly relevant to the issues before the court. (p. 218)

Wellman (1994) wrote a critique of the ASPECT indicating that "the terms making up the ASPECT relate closely to the current literature on appropriate criteria for custody decisions. Further the measure uses criteria from many sources (intellectual, personality, and academic achievement tests, interviews, and observations) creating a comprehensive database" (p. 18).

Otto, Buffington-Vollum, and Edens (2003) and Otto, Edens, and Barcus (2000) provide thoughtful critiques of the ASPECT. Otto et al. (2000) report three primary concerns. The basic concern that is identified throughout the literature is with regards to basic psychometric properties (Arditti, 1995; Melton, 1995; Wellman, 1994). In addition, concerns are generated that some of the items have "no clear relation to custody outcomes," that some "key factors" relevant to final custody decision are not incorporated into the assessment process, and that the PCI "encourages clinicians to offer ultimate issue opinions" (p. 331).

Otto et al. (2003) point out another common criticism with regards to using judge's decisions as a criterion for predictive validity. They state, "moreover, although the PCI results apparently were not presented to the judges, it is unclear exactly what (if any) mental health information they were provided about the parents and whether or not this had any impact on their custody determinations" (p. 267).

Joyce Arditti (1995) reviewed the ASPECT stating, "The ASPECT represents an important effort to quantify elements associated with parental effectiveness, as well as provide a sophisticated interpretation of test results. Its major shortcomings are its lack of internal validity and cumbersome administration, given the battery of tests deemed necessary." (p. 23)

Melton (1995) states,

> In short, the ASPECT was ill-conceived: An instrument that results in a score showing the parent who should be preferred in a custody decision necessarily results in over-reaching by experts who use it. Even if the idea had merit, though, the psychometric properties of the ASPECT remain essentially unknown, and the item selection and scoring procedures appear to pull for often irrelevant conclusions. (p. 23)

Melton et al. (1997) raise several concerns about the ASPECT addressed later in the Otto et al. (2000, 2003) works. Melton et al. raise concerns about psychometric properties, item selection, averaging scores, and ignoring some factors (p. 503). While accurate, item-related concerns reflect less than five of the 56 items on the ASPECT. Psychometrically, these few items could be eliminated without affecting the overall reliability of the PCI. Although some of the psychometric concerns that Melton et al. raise may have merit, it does not seem prudent to "throw out the baby with the bath water" because a few items may not be as reflective of parental capacity as once thought.

It is not surprising that Melton takes this position. In previous publications, Melton has indicated that he does not believe that psychologists should be testifying to the ultimate issue in custody cases. Because the ASPECT is specifically designed to help the psychologist answer the ultimate issue for the court, it would be surprising if Melton supported use of the instrument. Furthermore, Arditti's (1995) comments are well taken. However, the authors of the ASPECT do not apologize for a "cumbersome administration given the battery of tests deemed necessary" (Ackerman & Kane, 1998, p. 548). It is felt that one of the strengths of the ASPECT is its broad-based database that requires information from a wide battery of instruments. The best interest of the child criterion requires that the assessments be comprehensive.

Otto et al. (2000, 2003) raise some of the issues that Arditti (1995), Wellman (1994), and Melton (1995) had previously raised in their writings. They also address new issues. It must be remembered that there are 56 items on the ASPECT that were judged to be relevant to custody decision-making in the early 1990s when the instrument was developed. Some of these issues may not be as relevant in 2005 as they were in 1990. However, as the manual points out, seven of the 56 items can be eliminated without affecting the overall PCI. Therefore, if several items are not as relevant today as they were fifteen years ago or are deemed not to be related to parental competencies as suggested by Melton et al. (1997) and Otto et al. the overall PCI is not affected until the research or criticism reach the level of demonstrating that more than seven items are not relevant.

Otto et al. (2003) correctly point out that third party interviews are not incorporated into the assessment process on the PCI. However, they state that other "key factors" are not incorporated. They do not identify factors other than third party interviews that are not included. Lastly, they address the issue of psychologists offering ultimate issue opinions. Ackerman, Ackerman, Steffen, and Kelley-Poulos (2004) indicate that approximately 70 to 75% of family law judges, family law attorneys, and psychologists support psychologists testifying to the ultimate issue. Those not supporting psychologists testifying to the ultimate issue are espousing a minority opinion not representing the standard of practice within the profession.

CURRENT USAGE

Daubert v. Merrell Dow Pharmaceuticals (1993) changed the landscape of expert testimony, which had relied on the Frye Standard for 70 years. A number of states have officially adopted the Daubert standard by law, while others have encouraged its usage and still others have not adopted the Daubert standard. However, as forensic psychologists it is this author's position that the Daubert standard should be followed whether the practioner's state has adopted it by law or not. Heilbrun (1992) established criteria for the use of tests in forensic settings. When taken together, the ASPECT meets the Daubert standard and the Heilbrun criteria with the exception of a measure of response style. As suggested by Heilbrun, it is commercially available, it has a manual, has been reviewed in the *Mental Measurements Yearbook* (Conoley & Impara, 1995), is found in the literature, has standard administration, has a formula, has high correlation coefficients, is developed for usage in the setting within which it is used, and has a standard error of measurement. As a result, the ASPECT has met the Daubert standard and has been accepted in many states where the Daubert standard is used by law as reported by psychologists who use the instrument.

The ASPECT was developed in the late 1980s. It is now more than fifteen years later and the items that were selected for usage in the ASPECT are still purported by the literature today to be those variables that should be addressed when making recommendations for parental fitness, parental capacity, and placement-related questions. It has clearly been recognized that the ASPECT is test laden and can be cumbersome in its usage. However, the ASPECT-SF alleviates this concern and can be used by all mental health professionals involved in child custody and placement decisions without the need for psychological testing. It has also been reported to the author that there are a number of mental health professionals who find the Parent Questionnaire of the ASPECT to be useful as a comprehensive structured interview of parents in child custody cases. Since child custody evaluations are about decision-making and since the more information gathered in our decision-making process the better the decision will be, the ASPECT provides three different levels of information gathering that can be useful to child custody evaluators and those performing child custody studies.

Questions contributing to the PCI of the ASPECT rely on other tests that have been solidly validated in the past. It is useful way of organizing data as a supplemental instrument. It is not a "silver bullet." Psychologists should feel comfortable using it with the understanding of what it is, what its strengths are, and what its shortcomings are. There is enough data to support its use, and the authors still believe that it is a strong supplement to the entire child custody evaluation process.

REFERENCES

Ackerman, M. J., & Ackerman, M. C. (1997). Child custody evaluation practices: A survey of experienced professionals (revisited). *Professional Psychology Research and Practice, 28,* 137-145.

Ackerman, M. J., & Ackerman, S. D. (1992). Comparison of different subgroups on the MMPI of parents involved in custody litigations. Unpublished manuscript in M. J.

Ackerman (1995), *Clinicians guide to child custody evaluations.* New York: John Wiley & Sons.

Ackerman, M. J., Ackerman, M. C., Steffen, L., & Kelly-Poulos, S. (2004). Psychologists practices compared to the expectations of family law judges and attorneys in child custody cases. *Journal of Child Custody, 1*(1), 41-60.

Ackerman, M. J., & Kane, A. W. (1998). *Psychological experts in divorce actions* (3rd ed.). New York: Aspen Law & Business.

Ackerman, M. J., & Kelley-Poulos, S. (2001). *Child custody evaluation practices: A survey of family law attorneys.* Unpublished doctoral dissertation, Wisconsin School of Professional Psychology, Milwaukee, WI.

Ackerman M. J., & Schoendorf, S. (2000). *The Ackerman-Schoendorf Scales for Parent Evaluation of Custody-Short Form.* Los Angeles: Western Psychological Services.

Ackerman, M. J., & Steffen, L. J. (2001). Family law judge's expectations of psychologists performing child custody evaluations. *American Journal of Family Law, 15*, 12-16.

Arditti, J. A. (1995). Ackerman-Schoendorf Scales for Parent Evaluation of Custody. In J. C. Conoley & J. C. Impara (Eds.), *The twelfth mental measurements yearbook* (pp. 20-22). Lincoln, NE: Buros Institute of Mental Measurements.

Barnard, C. P., & Jenson, G. (1984). Child custody evaluations: A rational process for an emotion-laden event. *The American Journal of Family Therapy, 12*(2), 61-67.

Beaber, R. J. (1982). Custody quagmire: Some psychological dilemmas. *Journal of Psychiatry and Law, 10*, 309-326.

Belsky, J., Robbins, J., & Gamble, W. (1984). The determinants of parental competence: Toward a theory. In M. Lewis (Ed.), *Beyond the dyad* (pp. 251-275). New York: Plenum Press.

Berkman, C. F. (1984). Psychodynamic and family issues in post-divorce child custody litigation. *Journal of the American Academy of Child Psychiatry, 23*, 708-712.

Beyer, P. (1996). *The development and preliminary validation of the Life Satisfaction in Children Scale: Post divorce.* Unpublished doctoral dissertation, Wisconsin School of Professional Psychology, Milwaukee, WI.

Brodzinski, D. (1993). The use and misuse of psychological testing in child custody evaluation. *Professional Psychology: Research and Practice, 24*, 213-218.

Camara, K. A., & Resnick, G. (1989). Styles of conflict resolution and cooperation between divorced parents: Effects on child behavior and adjustment. *American Journal of Orthopsychiatry, 59*, 560-575.

Chasen, R., & Gruenbaum, H. (1981). A model for evaluation in custody disputes. *The American Journal of Family Therapy, 9*(3), 43-47.

Conoley, C., & Impara, J. C. (Eds.) (1995). *The twelfth mental measurements yearbook.* Lincoln, NE: Burros Institute.

Daubert v. Merrell Dow Pharmaceuticals, Inc., 509 U.S. 579 (1993).

Emery, R. E. (1988). *Marriage, divorce and children's adjustment.* Newberry Park, CA: Sage.

Exner, J. E. (1974). *The Rorschach: A comprehensive system* (Vol. 1). New York: John Wiley & Sons.

Gardner, R. A. (1982). *Family evaluation in child custody litigation.* Cresskill, NJ: Creative Therapeutics.

Goldstein, J., Freud, A., & Solnit, A. J. (1973). *Beyond the best interests of the child.* New York: Free Press.

Guidubaldi, J., Cleminshaw, H., Perry, J., Nastasi, B., & Adams, B. (1984, August). *Longitudinal effects of divorce on children: A report from the NASP-KSU nationwide study*. Paper presented at the meeting of the American Psychological Association, Toronto, Canada.

Heilbrun, K. (1992). The role of psychological testing in forensic assessment. *Law & Human Behavior, 16,* 257-272.

Hetherington, E. M. (1979). Divorce: A child's perspective. *American Psychologist, 34,* 851-858.

Hetherington, E. M., Cox, M., & Cox, R. (1978). The aftermath of divorce. In J. Stevens & M. Matthews (Eds.), *Mother-child, father-child relations* (pp. 149-176). Washington, DC: National Association for the Education of Young Children.

Hubbard, G. (1996). *Validity study of the parent-child relationship inventory for determining child custody*. Unpublished doctoral dissertation, Wisconsin School of Professional Psychology, Milwaukee, WI.

Johnston, J. R., Kline, M., & Tschann, J. M. (1989). Ongoing postdivorce conflict: Effects on children of joint custody and frequent access. *American Journal of Orthopsychiatry, 59,* 576-592.

Karras, D., & Berry, K. (1985). Custody evaluations: A critical review. *Professional Psychology: Research and Practice, 16,* 76-85.

Keilin, W. G., & Bloom, L. J. (1986). Child custody evaluation practices: A survey of experienced professionals. *Professional Psychology: Research and Practice, 17,* 338-346.

Klopfer, B., & Kelley, D. M. (1942). *The Rorschach technique*. Yonkers, NY: World Books.

Lowery, C. R. (1984). Parents and divorce: Identifying the support network for decisions about custody. *The American Journal of Family Therapy, 12*(3), 26-32.

McDermott, J. F., Wem-Shing, T., Char, W. I., & Fukunaga, M. A. (1978). *Child custody decisions making*. New York: American Academy of Child Psychiatry.

Melton, G. B. (1995). Ackerman-Schoendorf Scales for Parent Evaluation of Custody. In J. C. Conoley & J. C. Impara (Eds.), *The twelfth mental measurement yearbook* (pp. 22-23). Lincoln, NE: Buros Institute of Mental Measurement.

Melton, G. B., Petrila, J., Poythress, N. G., & Slobogin, C. (1997). *Psychology evaluations for the courts* (2nd ed.). New York: Guilford Press.

Otto, R. K., Buffington-Vollum, J. K., & Edens, J. F. (2003). Child custody evaluation. In A. M. Goldstein (Volume Ed.), & I. B. Weiner (Series Ed.), *Handbook of psychology: Volume II, forensic psychology* (pp. 179-208). New York: John Wiley & Sons.

Otto, R. K., Edens, J. F., & Barcus, E. H. (2000). The use of psychological testing in child custody evaluations. *Family and Conciliation Courts Review, 38,* 312-340.

Quinnell, F. A., & Bow, J. N. (2001). Psychological tests used in child custody evaluations. *Behavioral Sciences and the Law, 19,* 491-501.

Rae-Grant, Q., & Award, G. (1977). The effects of marital breakdown. In P. D. Steinhauer & Q. Rae-Grant (Eds.), *Psychological problems of the child in the family* (pp. 565-591). New York: Basic Books.

Schoendorf, S. (2001). *A correlation study of parental custody index (PCI) of the Ackerman-Schoendorf Scales for Parental Evaluation of Custody-Short Form (ASPECT-*

SF) and selected scales from the Minnesota Multiphasic Personality Inventory-2 (MMPI-2). Unpublished doctoral dissertation, Wisconsin School of Professional Psychology, Milwaukee, WI.

Wallerstein, J. S. (1983). Children of divorce: The psychological tasks of the child. *American Journal of Orthopsychiatry, 53*, 230-243.

Wellman, M. (1994). Ackerman-Schoendorf Scales for Parent Evaluation of Custody. In D. Keyser & R. Sweetwater (Eds.), *Test critiques* (Vol. 10, pp. 13-19). Austin, TX: PRO-ED.

Wolfe, D. A. (1985). Child-abusive parents: An empirical review and analysis. *Psychological Bulletin, 97*, 462-482.

Review
of "The Ackerman-Schoendorf Scales
for Parent Evaluation of Custody"
(ASPECT)

Mary Connell

The editors for this volume invited me to review and write a commentary on Ackerman's (this volume) contribution, "The Ackerman-Schoendorf Scales for Parent Evaluation of Custody (ASPECT)." I gladly undertook to do so, having long been concerned about the poor psychometric properties of the instrument. Custody evaluators are always in search of reliable and relevant techniques for assessment in this most difficult forensic practice area, and as such are at risk to be attracted to the ASPECT's ostensible relevance to custody evaluation. Reading Ackerman's article, in which he reviewed the genesis of the

Mary Connell is a forensic psychologist in private practice, Fort Worth, TX. Areas of primary interest are evaluations in family dissolution matters and capital sentence mitigation. She also engages in some focused assessment of standard of care and related issues in tort litigation cases, and in fitness for duty evaluation. She is President of the American Academy of Forensic Psychology. She provides training, through the American Academy of Forensic Psychology Intensive Forensic Practice Workshops, in child custody evaluation, ethics in forensic evaluation, and evaluation in child protection matters. She serves on the APA Board of Professional Affairs Committee on Professional Practice and Standards.

Address correspondence to: Mary Connell, EdD, ABPP, 100 East 15th Street, Suite 635, Fort Worth, TX 76102-6566.

[Haworth co-indexing entry note]: "Review of "The Ackerman-Schoendorf Scales for Parent Evaluation of Custody" (ASPECT)." Connell, Mary. Co-published simultaneously in *Journal of Child Custody* (The Haworth Press, Inc.) Vol. 2, No. 1/2, 2005, pp. 195-209; and: *Psychological Testing in Child Custody Evaluations* (ed: James R. Flens, and Leslie Drozd) The Haworth Press, Inc., 2005, pp. 195-209. Single or multiple copies of this article are available for a fee from The Haworth Document Delivery Service [1-800-HAWORTH, 9:00 a.m. - 5:00 p.m. (EST). E-mail address: docdelivery@haworthpress.com].

Digital Object Identifier: 10.1300/J190v02n01_11
195

ASPECT (Ackerman & Schoendorf, 1992), responded to some of the published reviews, and reported research developments, I was troubled to find that he seemed to give short shrift to critiques of the instrument. Ackerman reported some changes that were made to address the criticisms (e.g., elimination of testing in a new edition, the Ackerman-Schoendorf Scales for Parent Evaluation of Custody-Short Form [ASPECT-SF, 2000]), described two doctoral dissertations that examined concurrent validity, and then went on to report increasing use of the ASPECT by evaluators, apparently as evidence of its merit. He made some errors in logic, as will be briefly discussed below, in assessing its Daubert-worthiness. Given that others (Heinze & Grisso, 1996; Melton, 1995; Otto, 1997; Otto & Butcher, 1995; Otto & Edens, 2003) have thoroughly described the ASPECT's psychometric shortcomings (principally, its inherent lack of reliability, the focus upon factors derived on the basis of techniques not established to be reliable measures of parenting capacity or fitness, and the misdirected efforts at establishing predictive validity), they will not be revisited at length here. I agree with these reviews on every count, and believe these critiques alone support a conclusion that the ASPECT should be laid to rest.

The two essential shortcomings of the ASPECT that have been identified in critiques involved its ill-conceived structure and its tendency to move the user too close to offering unsubstantiated opinion on the central issue to be determined by the trier of fact. With regard to these two global areas of criticism, I will offer a few comments. My primary focus, however, will be on the shifting emphasis in the field, from "winner take all" custody determinations (such as the ASPECT may tend to lead the evaluator to make), to the more reasonable "shared parenting" focus gaining recognition across the country. It is in this arena that I believe the ASPECT falls so far short as to be utterly obsolete. This, then, is my ode to the ASPECT and the concept of sole custody.

THE PSYCHOMETRIC INADEQUACY OF THE ASPECT

Foremost, the ASPECT relies on data such as intelligence scores and TAT and Rorschach protocols for adults; and projective and cognitive test results for children, not established to contribute meaningfully to the assessment of parenting. The MMPI-2 and a parenting questionnaire, more defensibly, are also included in the data set. From this data set, a Parental Custody Index (PCI) is derived, to provide a summary index of parenting effectiveness to assist the evaluator in making a recommendation for custodial disposition (Ackerman, this volume).

The domains presumed to be reflective of effective parenting, however, were derived by non-standard procedures, and traditional efforts to establish content validity were bypassed in favor of more expedient methods (Otto & Edens, 2003). From those early conceptual problems onward, the ASPECT was a flawed piece of work and its use in custody evaluations could not be supported, particularly as the focus for admissibility of expert testimony was refined with *Daubert v. Merrell Dow Pharmaceutical, Inc.* (1993) and its progeny.

Reviews of the ASPECT have consistently identified fundamental shortcomings (Arditti, 1995; Brodzinski, 1993; Heinze & Grisso, 1996; Melton, 1995; Melton, Petrila, Poythress, & Slobogin, 1997; Otto, 1997; Otto & Butcher, 1995; Otto & Edens, 2003). No independent studies of reliability or validity of the instrument have been published in peer-reviewed journals, and the instrument has been rated poorly by reviewers in the *Twelfth Mental Measurements Yearbook* (Conoley & Impara, 1995). Arditti (1995) noted that its standardization demographic ($n = 200$) was predominantly white and relatively homogeneous, and that the ASPECT therefore may not be sensitive to cultural variations in parenting practices. Also, she noted the absence of important information concerning each parent's history of experience and involvement in parenting the children. Her summary comments, however, did recognize the ASPECT as an important effort toward quantifying elements associated with parental effectiveness, with a sophisticated interpretation.

Melton (1995) noted the absence of internal validity and the cumbersome administration of the ASPECT. He highlighted the authors' incorrect reference to "construct validity" in their study of the ultimate dispositional decisions in 118 cases in the normative sample of 200, in which a recommendation was made and information was available. The sample was highly unrepresentative, Melton noted, in that nearly half of the cases resulted in father custody. Melton further observed that the 75% claimed hit rate was surprisingly low, given that the ASPECT results were likely used in making the custody recommendations. The editors of the *Twelfth Mental Measurements Yearbook* (Conoley & Impara, 1995) noted, however, that the hit rate was reported erroneously in the manual and that the correct figure was 91% rather than 75%.

Otto (1997) also criticized the use of outcomes of the cases as validity criteria, and noted (Otto & Butcher, 1995) that at the time of that writing, little peer-reviewed published research was available to satisfy questions of validity. Otto (1997) further criticized the inclusion, within the ASPECT, of instruments not demonstrated to be relevant to parenting ability.

According to Otto (1997), use of Parent Custody Index (PCI) was indefensible; he noted, as had others (Arditti, 1995; Melton, 1995), that the PCI was established by examining the correlation of outcome on cases with performance on the ASPECT. It would be reasonable to assume that outcome was often affected by the evaluation results, a circular process that fails to establish predictive validity (Arditti, 1995; Melton, 1995; Otto, 1997). Further, there was no independent corroboration for the effectiveness of the WAIS or the Rorschach, for example, in predicting parenting skill (Otto, 1997).

Heinze and Grisso (1996) found strengths and weaknesses in the ASPECT. They noted that it provided an extensive and varied overview of parents, and of their familiarity with the child and the child's activities. It provided a standardized approach to quantifying and integrating the various parts of an evaluation. However, they criticized the absence of an established link between the resultant scores and quality of parenting. More normative reliability and validity data must be amassed, they suggested, before the instrument fulfilled the promise of being a practical, objective, and standardized approach to child custody evaluation. It was cautioned that the graphic representation of the results might tend to encourage users to misinterpret the data as suggestive that one parent was preferred over the other for purposes of custody determination (Heinze & Grisso, 1996).

Ackerman's continuing assertion (this volume) that the PCI of the ASPECT relies on " . . . other tests that have been solidly validated in the past" (p. 190) reflects an apparent failure to appreciate both the notion of psychometric validity and the potential irrelevance of the instruments upon which the ASPECT relies. Otto and Edens (2003) noted that:

> Many of the components of the PCI may in fact have some indirect connection to parenting capacity (e.g., psychopathology as identified by select MMPI-2 scores, which may limit a parent's ability to parent in some cases). But the burden is on the developers to demonstrate this connection, particularly given the very concrete manner in which several of these indices are employed (e.g., MMPI-2

MacAndrews Alcoholism scale > 65T). Moreover, the bifurcation and summation of these diverse dimensional measures (even if reliable and valid themselves) into a single numerical indicator needs to be justified by data suggesting that such methods are actually measuring some homogeneous construct of "parenting." (pp. 266-227)

Otto and Edens concluded, after reviewing the instrument, "In practice, however, the lack of information about the validity of the instrument leaves unanswered whether the methods used and the ways in which the information has been combined produce PCI scores that actually reflect the true degree of congruence between the parent and the child(ren)" (p. 268).

That the ASPECT continues to lack the necessary psychometric strength to merit inclusion in a forensic assessment is clear. Ackerman (this volume) reported insufficient improvements, no peer-reviewed studies, and no other data to support reconsideration of the volume. Its conceptual and design problems cannot be corrected simply by eliminating substantial parts. Ackerman said, "Although some of the psychometric concerns that Melton et al. [sic] raise may have merit, it does not seem prudent to 'throw out the baby with the bath water,' because few items may not be as reflective of parental capacity as once thought" (p. 188). I disagree. I think these structural problems are so fundamental that it is, indeed, necessary and prudent to discard the effort as an irremediable one.

THE ULTIMATE ISSUE PROBLEM

The ASPECT was, by design, intended to contribute to a determination of which parent should be granted the primary parenting role in a family facing dissolution (Ackerman & Schoendorf, 1992). Ackerman said the authors conceived and developed it, " . . . out of frustration generating from questions asked in court during an examination and cross-examination about recommendations that psychologists were making regarding custody and placement of children. Judges and attorneys typically asked questions about how psychologists were able to determine which parent would make a better placement or custodial parent" (p. 180). By devolving to a single score (the Parental Custody Index, or PCI), the data amassed in the evaluation could presumably lead the evaluator to a recommendation for the court on who should get custody, or if the parents were roughly equal in parenting ability, as reflected in this single score, then the evaluator would consider recommending joint custody (Ackerman & Schoendorf, 1992; Ackerman, this volume).

Melton (1995) expressed concern that this PCI numeric identification of the better parent would indeed lead the examiner to address, without substantial base, the ultimate opinion. Ackerman answered challenges to this question of the appropriateness of "ultimate issue" testimony with a rather sweeping dismissal, as if there are simply two camps or sets of thinking on this issue. Ackerman described the ASPECT "as a technique specifically designed to help the psychologist answer the ultimate issue for the court," adding that, as such, " . . . it would be surprising if Melton supported use of the instrument" (p. 188). He acknowledged that Otto and Edens (2003) echoed Melton's concern, but added that his own research reflected strong support among family law judges, attorneys, and psychologists for forensic examiners to testify to the ultimate issue, concluding that "Those not supporting psychologists testifying to the ultimate issue are espousing a minority opinion not representing the standard of practice within the profession" (p. 189).

Standard of practice for forensic psychology is, of course, not established by judges and attorneys, however valuable their opinions may be to psychology, and is not established by simple majority. It is established by the ethical standards, professional guidelines, and honored treatises that inform professional training and practice. In fact, there is a substantial voice, within the learned forensic community, for withholding such opinion testimony. Heilbrun (2001), Heilbrun, Marczyk, and DeMatteo (2002), Grisso (2003), Melton et al. (1997), Otto, Buffington-Vollum, and Edens (2002), and Shuman and Sales (1999) have held that it is not just a question of whether or not we go to the ultimate issue *per se*, even though that issue may embrace moral, political, or values issues not within the specialized expertise of the evaluator to address, but if and when we do, the data upon which we rely to develop our opinions must be both reliable and relevant.

The admonitions of Melton and colleagues (1997) against offering opinion in areas that have traditionally been the province of the fact finder, and about which we lack expertise to offer opinion, are more weighty than the descriptor, "a minority opinion," suggests. Heilbrun (2001) identified as an emerging principle in the field of forensic psychology, though indeed one continuing to generate considerable debate, to withhold opinion on the ultimate legal question. Grisso (2003) also noted the moral or legal considerations required in making the final judgment and the tendency of clinicians to continue to fail to adequately describe the limitations of their data in addressing the ultimate issue, and concluded that it remains inadvisable to go to the ultimate issue in most circumstances. These important voices cannot be so easily dismissed as representing only a different opinion from that held by practitioners who argue that situational demands compel them to develop and express opinions on the issues to be decided by the court.

Data derived from tools customarily used in psychological evaluation may contribute little to an opinion on the ultimate issue. That is, we may have a well founded opinion that a parent has or lacks certain parenting skills, might benefit from intervention to ameliorate some tendency, or might even suffer from a mental health problem potentially rendering the parent unfit; however, to link that opinion to a recommendation that may embrace issues far beyond parenting skill, such as the relative merits of one- and two-parent households, the importance of religious affiliation in a home environment, or the relative value of cleanliness and order versus spontaneity and relaxation, would be to go beyond the data. To opine that a child will be best served by alternating homes every three or seven days, or having a primary home and a "visitation" relationship with the other parent, contrasted to having roughly equal involvement, is not something we can presently do with an acceptable degree of *psychological* certainty. We can make educated guesses, applying the data we have derived to the standard by which "best interest" is determined in our jurisdiction, and attempt to make some reasonable recommendations to guide the court in allocating time and responsibility to each parent. Circumspection is recommended, however, until our research and assessment techniques solidly lead us to determinations of these matters. Considering the extraordinary weight given to our opinions in courts, the far-ranging impact the judicial outcome may have on those we evaluate, and the fact that most of our tools were not effectively validated for the purpose of deciding custody matters, we must acknowledge to the court the limitations of our data in deriving such opinions.

The Focus of the Assessment: Fitness or Best Interest? More immediately relevant, however, is the overarching issue of whether the ASPECT has potential to contribute meaningfully to the specific question before the court, which may have shifted somewhat during the last few decades. When Ackerman and Schoendorf (1992) introduced the instrument, there prevailed a "winner take all" notion about custody, with the courts tending to establish one parent as the primary caregiver and the other parent as the weekend visitor. Disneyland Dads (Lamb, 1999) were relegated to significantly limited roles in the lives of their children, reflecting the idea that children needed the stability of a primary attachment figure and a primary residence, usually with their mom, and could maintain, through "standard access," sufficiently meaningful contact with a visiting parent, usually their dad.

Our societal patterns have changed markedly in the past twenty years. A shift in our views of parenting and of childhood has led to greater focus on the importance of meeting children's needs, more emphasis on children participating in after-school extracurricular activities, and greater legitimization of parents' roles in the emotional development of their children. Fathers' contribution to that emotional development remains relatively undervalued, compared to mothers', but as fathers are increasingly involved in child care before separation, there is far greater recognition of their important roles following dissolution. We have come to recognize that children do better when they have meaningful time and opportunities for intimate relationships with both parents (e.g., see Bauserman, 2002; Gunnoe & Braver, 2001; Hetherington, Bridges, & Insabella, 1998; Johnson, 1995; Kelly, 2000; Kline, Johnston, & Tschann, 1991; Lamb, 1999; Maccoby, Buchanan, Mnookin, & Dornbusch, 1993; Pruett, 2000; Pruett, Williams, Insabella, & Little, 2003; Whiteside & Becker, 2000). Consequently, we have moved away from the win/lose, "custody as ownership" determination to the idea of shared parenting. Parenting plans typically describe the roles each parent will have in decision-making and in parenting time, with the understanding that children should be able to derive from each parent those benefits that flow from that parent's active involvement in their lives. Both parents, likewise, can expect reasonably unfettered access to their children and the opportunity to participate in the rearing of their children, and the rebuttable presumption of joint parenting as serving the child's best interest has rapidly gained momentum across states (American Law Institute [ALI], 2002).

The assessment of "fitness to parent" missed the mark for *child custody evaluations* in 1992, and it misses it to an even greater degree today. In *child protection* assessments, there may indeed be a question before the court about a parent's fitness or capacity to parent. In custody/access matters at marital dissolution, the question has generally been conceived to be, "What arrangement of residence, parenting time, and decision-making will be in this child's best interest?" The task challenging the court is to determine which parental situation represents the best prospects for ensuring the welfare of the child (Grisso, 2003). This does not mean that one parent, rather than the other, must be determined to offer the best prospects for providing for the child's welfare. Aiming the forensic assessment toward "Who is the better parent?" as the ASPECT did, contributed to a misapprehension of the issue, and, as Melton (1995) noted and others have amplified (Heilbrun, 2001), led to an inclination, on the part of the evaluator, to hold forth on moral or political issues that may be best left to the court to decide. Wherever one stands on the important and thorny question of ultimate issue testimony, that issue is almost never "Is one parent more fit than the other and therefore should that parent have sole custody?"

Ackerman (this volume) said,

> When the PCIs are more than 20 points apart it suggests that the parent with the higher PCI is substantially more fit to parent and primary placement with the possibility of sole custody should be explored for the parent with the higher score. The authors decided that when there is more than one child and the scores are different for specific items, the ASPECT items would be scored in the majority direction. When the scores are between 10 and 20 points apart, more careful scrutiny should be given to the collateral information to help determine whether this difference is more representative of a joint custody substantially equal placement schedule or a primary sole custody type of a situation. (p. 186)

I cannot agree that a decision as critical as the determination to be made by the court about a parent's access to her child should rest on such capricious and arbitrary formulae. The relative "fitness" of the parents is not the issue to be determined by the court. The parents' roles in their child's upbringing, including decision-making, division of time, and allocation of responsibilities, are determined based upon what is in the child's best interest, as defined by statute or case law, or by the court's determination. Termination of a parent's meaningful participation and involvement in the child's life is unwarranted in the vast majority of cases, since utter unfitness or incompetency to parent is rarely extant. When termination of active involvement with the child is warranted, it is because of a parent's abandonment or severe and irremediable abuse or neglect of the child, or other extreme circumstances.

The best interest of the child, the indeterminate standard by which custody/access issues have been decided in most states for the past 30 or more years, has been described by the ALI (2002) to embrace a plan that facilitates parental planning and agreement about the child's custodial arrangements and upbringing; continuity of existing parent-child attachments; meaningful contact between the child and each parent; caretaking relationships by adults who love the child, know how to provide for the child's needs, and place a high priority on doing so; security from exposure to conflict and violence; and expeditious, predictable decision making and avoidance of prolonged uncertainty respecting arrangements for the child's care and control (pp. 95-96). There are jurisdictional differences in how *best interest* is to be determined. Thus far, only a small number of states have adopted or appear to be near to adopting the ALI model, but it may be reasonable to assume there will be a trend toward increasing homogeneity in defining the standard. It may be anticipated that this convergence will, to a significant degree, mirror the substance of the ALI model.

As a backdrop to the ALI's proposed definition of *best interest*, we might consider the thrust of statutory language abounding in various jurisdictions. Michigan's rendering of *best interest* (Child Custody Act of 1970) has served as the standard for many states for the past 34 years. That rendering suggests that the child's best interest involves:

1. the love, affection, and other emotional ties existing between the parties involved and the child;
2. the capacity and disposition of the parties involved to give the child love, affection, and guidance and continuation of the educating and raising of the child in its religion or creed, if any;
3. the capacity and disposition of the parties involved to provide the child with food, clothing, medical care, and other material needs;
4. the length of time the child has lived in a stable, satisfactory environment, and the desirability of maintaining continuity;
5. the permanence as a family unit, of the existing or proposed custodial home or homes;
6. the moral fitness of the parties involved;
7. the mental and physical health of the parties involved;
8. the home, school, and community record of the child;
9. the reasonable preference of the child, if the court deems the child to be of sufficient age to express preference;
10. the willingness and ability of each of the parents to facilitate and encourage a close and continuing parent-child relationship between the child and the other parent;
11. domestic violence, regardless of whether the violence was directed against, or witnessed by the child;

12. any other factor considered by the court to be relevant to a particular child custody dispute.

These issues that the courts strive to consider in making determinations about how to best apportion parenting time and responsibility should not be decided, by the courts or by the evaluators, by a formula that reduces the elements to numeric values and adds them together to see which parent has the highest score. The notion is, on its face, obviously flawed. In a Maryland case, *Taylor v. Taylor* (1986), the court said, "Formula or computer solutions in child custody matters are impossible because of the unique character of each case, and the subjective nature of the evaluations and decisions that must be made" (p. 970). While the indeterminate best interest standard has not been without tremendous resistance and controversy (Goldstein, Freud, & Solnit, 1973; Krauss & Sales, 2000), it has nevertheless prevailed as the standard by which the court must make determinations in matters of family dissolution.

The best interest of the child, as it may be increasingly construed by statute and state law, may be insured by taking careful account of the child's parents' own construction of parenting plans or, in the absence of agreement between divorcing parents, some reflection of how they have heretofore divided the activities and responsibilities of parenting (ALI, 2002). Attention should, of course, be given to changing circumstances that would justify a different allocation of time and responsibility following separation, such as changes wrought with the divorce itself in parents' availability (a "stay at home" parent now having to work outside the home, for example), a demonstrable environment of domestic violence, or other evidence that the same apportionment would not be in the child's best interest. Further, there may be special factors to consider, such as justifiable need, on the part of one parent, for relocation such that former division of responsibility becomes untenable (ALI, 2002).

Parents, under the ALI model and in the practice of many jurisdictions, explicitly identify their own proposed parenting plans. Those preferences can then be considered by the court, with a focus upon the importance of active participation of both parents in the child's development; what is known of the child's wishes, needs, and preferences; the need to establish a means for expeditious decision-making; the critical importance of insuring the child an environment free of conflict and hostility; and, finally, the importance of a just outcome for the adults (ALI, 2002).

Thus, we find that dynamic, individualized, and customized parenting plans are being contemplated and that courts are soliciting parental input in creating such plans. The custody evaluator can contribute to this process by focusing upon the court's task and finding ways to enrich the database at the court's disposal. This may include collecting hard data on how parenting time and responsibility has been allocated in the past, investigating circumstances or allegations that might argue for a deviation from the previous pattern of time apportionment in the family, and when allegations or observations merit it, performing assessment to address safety issues and treatment needs. Principally, however, the task may be to increasingly focus on each parent's expressed preferences, an assessment of the child's capacity and willingness to participate in planning (currently and potentially in the future), and methods by which to resolve differing sentiments and wishes among the parties. The expertise of psychologists may be solicited in specialized areas such as evaluation of sexual abuse or other domestic violence allegations in the context of the marital dissolution, of relocation requests, or of allegations of systematic estrangement or alienation from a parent. Our utility to the courts may continue to grow as research tells us more about the effects of various arrangements on the child, influences of developmental stages in determinations about sharing time with each parent, and other issues relevant to matters before the court. Expressing the limitations of our data is our affirmative obligation, and will help the trier of fact in determining how best to use our input to achieve an enlightened and just outcome.

SUMMARY

With the shift away from custody/visitation to parenting plans that are predicated on the notion of active involvement of both parents, the ASPECT has virtually nothing to offer. It specifically draws the user away from that information that would be useful to the courts, identifying the specific strengths and capacities that each parent has to offer, the deficits and how they might be ameliorated through intervention, and the child's specific needs, talents, abilities, wishes, and concerns that might be addressed by the determination made by the court. Rather, in the reductionistic design of the ASPECT, this rich store of data is pulverized down to a "final score" that treats all of those important issues as relatively equal and numerically additive phenomena leading to the formation of a singular recommendation. Worse, it throws into the mix specific test results that have no established relationship to effective parenting (Melton, 1995; Otto & Edens, 2003).

Ackerman (this volume) seemed to miss the substance of Heilbrun's (1992) criteria for test selection in forensic settings, arguing that the ASPECT met those criteria in that, " . . . [I]t is commercially available, it has a manual, has been reviewed in the *Mental Measurements Yearbook*, is found in the literature, has standard administration, has a formula, has high correlation coefficients, is developed for the setting within which it is used, and has a standard error of measurement" (pp. 189-190). As made explicit by *Daubert* (1993), but familiar to all scientists, one index of the merit of a theory or technique is its survival of a test review or peer review process. Ackerman (this volume) cited as evidence of the ASPECT's *Daubert*-worthiness the fact that it was peer-reviewed, apparently without concern that reviews were devastatingly negative.

It would have been nice if it had been so easy to find an objective measure of parenting fitness, if indeed parenting time was to be apportioned on the basis of parenting fitness, and if it was to be determined in an "all or nothing" way, with the more fit parent (according to Ackerman, the one with a PCI score more than 20 points higher than the other parent) walking away with all of the spoils. Thankfully, we have moved beyond such concrete conceptualizations of post-dissolution family life, and have moved into a more enlightened age, one in which we legitimize the importance of both parents in not just the conception of the child but in carrying through to the completion of the parenting process. Like the notion of winning a custody battle, the ASPECT can finally be laid to rest.

REFERENCES

Ackerman, M. J. (2005). The Ackerman-Schoendorf Scales for Parent Evaluation of Custody (ASPECT): A review of research and update. *Journal of Child Custody*, 2(1/2), 179-193.

Ackerman, M., & Schoendorf, K. (1992). *ASPECT: Ackerman-Schoendorf Scales for Parent Evaluation of Custody-Manual*. Los Angeles, CA: Western Psychological Services.

American Law Institute. (2002). *Principles of the law of family dissolution: Analysis and recommendations*. Newark, NJ: Mathew Bender & Co.

Arditti, J. A. (1995). Ackerman-Schoendorf Scales for Parent Evaluation of Custody. In J. C. Conoley & J. C. Impara (Eds.), *The twelfth mental measurements yearbook* (pp. 20-22). Lincoln, NE: Buros Institute of Mental Measurements.

Bauserman, R. (2002). Child adjustment in joint-custody versus sole-custody arrangements: A meta-analytic review. *Journal of Family Psychology, 16*, 91-102.

Brodzinski, D. (1993). The use and misuse of psychological testing in child custody evaluation. *Professional Psychology: Research and Practice, 24*, 213-218.

Child Custody Act of 1970, Mich. Comp. Laws Ann. § 722.23 (2001).

Conoley, J. C., & Impara, J. C. (Eds.) (1995). *The twelfth mental measurements yearbook.* Lincoln, NE: Buros Institute of Mental Measurements.

Daubert v. Merrell Dow Pharmaceutical, Inc., 509 U.S.579, 113 S. Ct. 2786 (1993).

Goldstein, J., Freud, A., & Solnit, A. J. (1973). *Beyond the best interest of the child.* New York: The Free Press.

Grisso, T. (2003). *Evaluating competencies: Forensic assessments and instruments* (2nd ed.). New York: Plenum.

Gunnoe, M. L., & Braver, S. L. (2001). The effects of joint legal custody on mothers, fathers, and children controlling for factors that predispose a sole maternal versus joint legal award. *Law and Human Behavior, 25*, 25-43.

Heilbrun, K. (1992). The role of psychological testing in forensic assessment. *Law & Human Behavior, 16*, 257-272.

Heilbrun, K. (2001). *Principles of forensic mental health assessment.* New York: Kluwer Academic/Plenum Publishers.

Heilbrun, K., Marczyk, G. R., & DeMatteo, D. (2002). *Child custody.* In K. Heilbrun, G. R. Marczyk, & D. DeMatteo (Eds.), *Forensic mental health assessment: A casebook* (pp. 299-348). New York: Oxford University Press.

Heinze, M. C., & Grisso, T. (1996). Review of instruments assessing parenting competencies used in child custody evaluations. *Behavioral Sciences and the Law, 14*, 293-313.

Hetherington, E. M., Bridges, M., & Insabella, G. M. (1998). What matters? What does not? Five perspectives on the association between marital transitions and children's adjustment. *American Psychologist, 53*, 167-184.

Johnson, J. R. (1995). Research update: Children's adjustment in sole custody compared to joint custody families and principles for custody decision making. *Family and Conciliation Courts Review, 33*, 415-425.

Kelly, J. B. (2000). Children's adjustment in conflicted marriage and divorce: A decade of research. *Journal of the American Academy of Child & Adolescent Psychiatry, 39*, 963-973.

Kline, M., Johnston, J. R., & Tschann, J. M. (1991). The long shadow of marital conflict: A model of children's postdivorce adjustment. *Journal of Marriage and the Family, 53*, 297-309.

Krauss, D. A., & Sales, B. D. (2000). Legal standards, expertise, and experts in the resolution of contested child custody cases. *Psychology, Public Policy, and Law, 6*, 843-879.

Lamb, M. (1999). Noncustodial fathers and their impact on the children of divorce. In R. A. Thompson & P. R. Amato (Eds.), *The postdivorce family: Children, parenting, and society* (pp. 105-125). Thousand Oaks, CA: Sage Publications.

Maccoby, E. E., Buchanan, C. M., Mnookin, R. H., & Dornbusch, S. M. (1993). Postdivorce roles of mothers and fathers in the lives of their children. *Journal of Family Psychology, 7*, 24-38.

Melton, G. (1995). Ackerman-Schoendorf Scales for Parent Evaluation of Custody. In J. C. Conoley & J. C. Impara (Eds.), *The twelfth mental measurements yearbook* (pp. 22-23). Lincoln, NE: Buros Institute of Mental Measurements.

Melton, G., Petrila, J., Poythress, N., & Slobogin, C. (1997). *Psychological evaluations for the courts: A handbook for mental health professionals and lawyers* (2nd ed.). New York: Guilford.

Otto, R. K. (1997). *Child custody evaluations: Law, ethics, & clinical practice.* Tampa, FL: University of South Florida, Florida Mental Health Institute.

Otto, R. K., Buffington-Vollum, J. K., & Edens, J. F. (2003). Child custody evaluation. In A. M. Goldstein (Volume Ed.), & I. B. Weiner (Series Ed.), *Handbook of psychology: Volume II, forensic psychology* (pp. 179-208). New York: John Wiley & Sons.

Otto, R. K. & Butcher, J. N. (1995). Computer-assisted psychological assessment in child custody evaluations. *Family Law Quarterly, 29,* 79-96.

Otto, R. K., & Edens, J. F. (2003). Parenting capacity. In T. Grisso (Ed.), *Evaluating competencies: Forensic assessments and instruments* (2nd ed., pp. 229-307). New York: Kluwer Academic/Plenum.

Pruett, K. D. (2000). *Fatherneed: Why father care is as essential as mother care for your child.* New York: Free Press.

Pruett, M. K., Williams, T. Y., Insabella, G., & Little, T. D. (2003). Family and legal indicators of child adjustment to divorce among families with young children. *Journal of Family Psychology, 17,* 169-180.

Shuman, D. W., & Sales, B. D. (1999). The impact of Daubert and its progeny on the admissibility of behavioral and social science evidence. *Psychology, Public Policy, & Law, 5,* 3-15.

Taylor v. Taylor, 306 Md. 290, 508 A.2d 970 (1986).

Whiteside, M. F., & Becker, B. J. (2000). Parental factors and the young child's postdivorce adjustment: A meta-analysis with implications for parenting arrangements. *Journal of Family Psychology, 14,* 5-26.

Transfusion Maybe, Laid to Rest, No:
A Response to the Mary Connell Review
of the Ackerman-Schoendorf Scales
for Parent Evaluation of Custody (ASPECT)

Marc J. Ackerman

I have read a number of reviews of the ASPECT during the past decade or so. There is relative unanimity about the opinion that the ASPECT has inadequate psychometric properties. I will not even attempt to disagree with this notion since it is based on sound thinking. However, I am taken by the appearance that very few or none of the reviewers of the ASPECT during the past decade have used it in their custody evaluation work. Each of the critiques gives the appearance that the writer obtained knowledge of the ASPECT through review of the manual and not through usage or careful examination of the Parent Questionnaire or the Examiner Questionnaire. Mary Connell's review and critique is no exception.

Marc J. Ackerman, PhD, is a clinical and forensic psychologist and expert on child custody. He maintains a counseling and consulting practice in Milwaukee, WI, where he has worked with thousands of divorcing families. He is the author of six books for psychologists and lawyers on the subject of child custody and speaks frequently on the topic.

Address correspondence to: Marc Ackerman, PhD, 5900 North Port Washington Road, Suite 150, Milwaukee, WI 53217 (E-mail: mjackerman@aol.com).

[Haworth co-indexing entry note]: "Transfusion Maybe, Laid to Rest, No: A Response to the Mary Connell Review of the Ackerman-Schoendorf Scales for Parent Evaluation of Custody (ASPECT)." Ackerman, Marc J. Co-published simultaneously in *Journal of Child Custody* (The Haworth Press, Inc.) Vol. 2, No. 1/2, 2005, pp. 211-214; and: *Psychological Testing in Child Custody Evaluations* (ed: James R. Flens, and Leslie Drozd) The Haworth Press, Inc., 2005, pp. 211-214. Single or multiple copies of this article are available for a fee from The Haworth Document Delivery Service [1-800-HAWORTH, 9:00 a.m. - 5:00 p.m. (EST). E-mail address: docdelivery@haworthpress.com].

Available online at: http://www.haworthpress.com/web/JCC
Digital Object Identifier: 10.1300/J190v02n01_12

Mary Connell's review identifies two essential shortcomings of the ASPECT, stating "its tendency to move the user too close to offering unsubstantiated opinion on the central issue to be determined by the trier of fact" and ". . . the shifting emphasis in the field, from 'winner take all' custody determinations such as the ASPECT may tend to lead the evaluator to make" (p. 196). Hopefully, this response will clearly demonstrate that the opinion rendered as a result of the ASPECT is not "unsubstantiated." Furthermore, there is no implied or direct assertion in the manual or any of the writings that the ASPECT is designed as a "winner takes all" instrument.

Mary Connell goes on to state, "foremost, the ASPECT relies on data, such as intelligence scores, TAT and Rorschach protocols, for adults; and projective and cognitive test results for children" (p. 196). A statement of this nature is based on not adequately understanding what the items on the ASPECT relate to with regards to these specific tests. The examiner questions specifically asked about the Rorschach address whether an underlying thought disorder exists or the individual has difficulty controlling emotions. The literature clearly demonstrates that these are two negative characteristics that can impact an individual's ability to parent adequately. Intelligence and achievement test scores are used for two purposes. It is important for an individual to be able to adequately support his or her children academically. As a result, one of the items on the ASPECT requires achievement test scores at the ninth grade level or higher. Another item addresses whether the parents' I.Q. scores fall within five points of the child's I.Q. scores (generally one standard error of measurement). The questions on the ASPECT regarding the Children's Apperception Test (CAT) allows the examiner to interpret the CAT responses to determine if the child is feeling threatened by the parent or experiencing anger from the parent. The six questions on the ASPECT regarding the MMPI-2 involve the Dominance Scale, the Mac Andrews Alcoholism-Revised Scale (MAC-R), elevations in the Clinical Scales above 65, elevations on the Over-Controlled Hostility Scale and Ego Strength below 40. Substance Abuse concerns, anger concerns, and evidence of psychopathology are further examples of issues that need to be addressed in determining who would make the best placement parent or whether their should be shared placement.

Mary Connell takes issue with my statement that "those not supporting psychologists testifying to the ultimate issue are espousing a minority opinion not representing the standard of practice within the profession" (p. 200). She states, "standard of practice for forensic psychology is, of course, not established by judges and attorneys, however valuable their opinions may be to psychology, and is not established by simple majority" (p. 200). In fact, standard of practice or standard of care is established by simple majority. It represents what a majority of professionals would do in a given situation. Therefore, we still live in a professional community where the standard of practice is that psychologists testify to the ultimate issue.

Mary Connell spends a considerable amount of time throughout her paper addressing the issue of the obsolescence of the notion of selecting sole custody versus joint custody. Joint custody is a legal concept that allows for both parents to participate in the decision-making process regarding religious upbringing, non-emergency medical care, and education. It is desired in most cases, supported by the results of the ASPECT in the vast majority of cases, and supports a relatively equal placement schedule. The ASPECT manual clearly states that when the PCIs of the parents are within 10 points of one another that joint custody with a relatively equal placement schedule is desired. The vast majority of individuals have ASPECT scores within 10 points of one another. These results, then, would support placement schedules that would allow for substantially equal periods of placement for each of the parents. On the other hand, when the PCIs are more than 20 points apart, the ASPECT results can be a valuable piece of information to give the court to demonstrate the divergence in appropriate parenting characteristics. Individuals with scores that are 20 or more points apart tend to be those who are active substance abusers, those who engage in maltreatment, and those who have significant mental health issues.

Mary Connell goes on to state, "Parents, under the ALI model and in the practice of many jurisdictions, explicitly identify their own proposed parenting plans. Those preferences can then be considered by the court, with a focus upon the importance of active participation of both parents in the child's development; what is known of the child's wishes, needs, and preferences; the need to establish a means for expeditious decision-making; the critical importance of insuring the child an environment free of conflict and hostility; and finally, the importance of a just outcome for the adults" (p. 205). I do not disagree with any of the issues that Mary Connell raises in this statement. However, they are all issues that are reflected by questions on the Parent Questionnaire or the Examiner Questionnaire of the ASPECT. Certainly these issues are not only addressed by the ASPECT but can be used in developing the parenting plans. In her summary, Mary Connell states, "with a shift away from custody/visitation to parenting plans that are predicated on the notion of active involvement of both parents, the ASPECT has virtually nothing to offer" (p. 206). When one takes a careful look at the items on the ASPECT questionnaires, it is clear that its utility has transcended the era of the custody/visitation emphasis to the current status of child custody determination by the very nature of questions that were used in the ASPECT originally and are still being asked when establishing parenting plans. Furthermore, recent research (Ackerman & Ackerman, 1997; Ackerman et al., 2004) indicate that the very questions asked on the ASPECT are those that a majority of psychologists, family law attorneys, and family law judges ask when attempting to determine whether shared placement, primary placement, joint custody, or sole custody should be sought in a case. When carefully examining the item content of the ASPECT, it is clearly apparent that it has much to offer in this decision-making process. The ASPECT may need a transfusion, but it does not need to be laid to rest.

REFERENCES

Ackerman, M. J., & Ackerman, M. C. (1997). Child custody evaluation practices: A survey of experienced professionals (revisited). *Professional Psychology Research and Practice, 28*, 137-145.

Ackerman, M. J., Ackerman, M. C., Steffen, L., & Kelley, S. (2004). Psychologists' practices compared to the expectations of family law judges and attorneys in child custody cases. *Journal of Child Custody, 1*, 41-60.

Connell, M. (2005). Review of "The Ackerman-Schoendorf Scales for Parent Evaluation of Custody" (ASPECT). *Journal of Child Custody, 2*(1/2), 195-209.

CONCLUSION

Final Thoughts and Future Directions

James R. Flens

In this volume, we have examined the use of psychological tests in child custody evaluations. The article I wrote focused on factors associated with appropriate test selection. It also addressed the relationship between rules of evidence, standards of admissibility, and test selection.

Jon Gould's article described a model for choosing psychological tests to be used in child custody evaluations. Gould suggested that evaluators choose assessment tools that measure factors relevant to current individual and family functioning. David Martindale discriminated between confirmatory bias and confirmatory distortion in his article on the

James R. Flens, PsyD, has a private practice in Brandon, FL. His practice focuses on family law-related evaluations, including evaluations regarding custody, modification and relocation, work product review, and consultation with both the legal community and custodial evaluation professionals. He is also an instrument-rated pilot and factory-trained bicycle mechanic.

Address correspondence to: James R. Flens, PsyD, 1463 Oakfield Drive, Suite 111, Brandon, FL 33511 (E-mail: jayflens@aol.com).

[Haworth co-indexing entry note]: "Final Thoughts and Future Directions." Flens, James R. Co-published simultaneously in *Journal of Child Custody* (The Haworth Press, Inc.) Vol. 2, No. 1/2, 2005, pp. 215-216; and: *Psychological Testing in Child Custody Evaluations* (ed: James R. Flens, and Leslie Drozd) The Haworth Press, Inc., 2005, pp. 215-216. Single or multiple copies of this article are available for a fee from The Haworth Document Delivery Service [1-800-HAWORTH, 9:00 a.m. - 5:00 p.m. (EST). E-mail address: docdelivery@haworthpress.com].

Available online at http://www.haworthpress.com/web/JCC
Digital Object Identifier: 10.1300/J190v02n01_13

role of bias in the selection and the use of psychological tests in custody evaluations while Dianna Gould-Saltman provided a Family Law attorney's perspective on the use of psychological tests.

Alex Caldwell's article on the use of the MMPI-2 in child custody evaluations provided an important new step in understanding how to examine context-specific responses against conventional MMPI-2 interpretations. Three articles examined the role of the Rorschach in child custody evaluations. Robert Erard and Ginger Calloway identified ways in which data from the Rorschach may assist in child custody and parenting time evaluations. Janet Johnston, Marjorie Walters, and Nancy Olesen provided empirical data examining the use of Rorschach data in predicting parental capacity.

The final area discussed in this volume focused on Ackerman and Schoendorf's ASPECT. Marc Ackerman's first article addressed concerns in the literature expressed by others about the psychometric usefulness of the ASPECT. Mary Connell provided a critique of the theory and psychometric properties of the ASPECT, and Marc then responded to Mary's concerns about the ASPECT.

Where do we go next? Perhaps in future journal issues authors will examine specific tests that may be used to assess relevant factors associated with custodial recommendations. Also, the *Journal of Child Custody* could have a "question-and-answer" section regarding testing and other methodologies. This section might address a question sent to the journal with a response from a guest expert.

The articles in this volume represent a strong base from which to expand our knowledge and understanding. I want to provide a special thank you to the editor of the *Journal of Child Custody*, Leslie Drozd, PhD, who believed in this project and who believed in my ability to get it done.

Index